SEVEN GRAMMARS OF THE DIALECTS AND SUBDIALECTS OF THE BIHĀRĪ LANGUAGE

SEVEN GRAMMARS OF THE DIALECTS AND SUBDIALECTS OF THE BIHÁRÍ LANGUAGE

SPOKEN IN THE PROVINCE OF BIHÁR, IN THE EASTERN PORTION OF THE NORTH-WESTERN PROVINCES, AND IN THE NORTHERN PORTION OF THE CENTRAL PROVINCES

(Volume-1 in Three Parts)

Part-1. Introductory
Part-2. Bhojpúrí Dialect
Part-3. Mágádhí Dialect

George A. Grierson, BC.S.

Publications

KALPAZ PUBLICATIONS
DELHI-110 052

Seven Grammars of the Dialects and Subdialects of the Bihárí Language

ISBN : 81-7835-451-9 (Set)
ISBN : 81-7835-452-7 (Vol.1)

Published in 2005 in India by
Kalpaz Publications,
C-30, Satyawati Nagar,
Delhi-110 052
E-mail : kalpaz@hotmail.com

Laser Typesetting at: Tact Computer Graphics, Delhi
Printed at: Salasar Imaging Systems, Delhi

SEVEN

GRAMMARS

OF THE DIALECTS AND SUBDIALECTS OF THE

BIHÁRÍ LANGUAGE.

SPOKEN IN THE PROVINCE OF BIHÁR, IN THE EASTERN PORTION OF THE NORTH-WESTERN PROVINCES, AND IN THE NORTHERN PORTION OF THE CENTRAL PROVINCES.

PART I.
INTRODUCTORY.

Compiled under orders of the Government of Bengal

By GEORGE A. GRIERSON, B.C.S.,

OFFG. JOINT-MAGISTRATE OF PATNA.

CALCUTTA:

PRINTED AT THE BENGAL SECRETARIAT PRESS.

1883.

कस कस कसमर किना मगहिया ।
का भोजपुरिया की तिरहुतिया ॥

Popular song.

For "what," Kasmar (Sáran) has *kas kas*, and Mágadhí *kiná*; Bhojpúrí has *ká*, and Tirhutí *kí*.

FROM

G. A. GRIERSON, ESQ., C.S.,

Offg. Joint-Magistrate of Patna,

To

THE DIRECTOR OF PUBLIC INSTRUCTION, BENGAL.

Dated Bankipore, the 24th January 1882.

SIR,

I HAVE the honour to forward herewith final proofs of the first or introductory part of the series of Bihárí grammars which I was deputed to compile in the early part of 1881. The remaining seven parts are ready for the printer, and one is already in the press.

It will be advantageous here to recapitulate briefly the grounds on which my proposal for compiling these grammars was originally made. As stated in a letter written to you in February 1881, they were as follows: "Many Bihár officials have complained to me of the impossibility of understanding the *gaoñwárí bolí* of the witnesses who come into their courts, and more than one has suggested to me that I should compile a grammar of it, imagining apparently that the *gaoñwárí bolí* was one uniform language current over the whole of Bihár. This, of course, was not the case; the vernacular of Bihár really consisting of three well-defined dialects, each of which itself varies according to its locality." I then proceeded to give examples showing how the various dialects differed amongst themselves and from High (or classical)

Hindí. These examples it is not necessary to repeat here. I then observed that these dialects differed little in vocabulary; "their main point of difference is grammar, and it is a compendious grammar of the dialect of each district which I wish to compile for the use of officials. No grammar of any of the dialects of Bihár has ever been published except the Bhojpúrí Grammar of Mr. Beames, which is now, I believe, out of print. Professor Hœrnle's Grammar gives rather the forms current round Benares, and my Maithilí Grammar, which is being printed by the Asiatic Society, will not meet the requirements of the Mágadhí and Bhojpúrí-speaking parts of Bihár." This proposal was adopted by Government, and I was deputed for a period of about six weeks on special duty to collect the materials necessary for the work. It would, of course, have been impossible for me to carry it out in the time, had not I already collected a large quantity of information which only required arranging; and, as it was, with the assistance of the officers of the Education Department I was able to complete the heaviest part of the work within the period allotted. Since then I have continually devoted to it all the time I could spare from other duties, and now the grammars are ready for the press. Beyond the cost of printing, Government has been put to no expense whatever in the work, for I have done all the work of arrangement with my own hand, no other method indeed being possible.

The scope of these grammars will be found detailed on page 17 of this part, and I need not repeat it here.

In the historical division of this introduction I have endeavoured to avoid anything like controversy, or any statement of facts which are not now regarded as proved by all schools of philologists, both here and in England, who have taken up the subject. I have purposely avoided all disputed points, as a work compiled for general use is not the fit place to contain any theories which, however well founded, are not yet received by many as conclusively proved.

In conclusion, I wish to thank the various Deputy Inspectors of Schools who have rendered me most intelligent and efficient help. Without their aid it would have been impossible for me to accomplish the task within the time allowed. I wish specially to record the assistance rendered to me by Paṇḍit Śiv Náráyaṇ Trivedí, Deputy Inspector of Schools, Gayá; Munshí Rádhá Lál, Deputy Inspector of Schools, Sháhábád; and Munshí Rám Prakáś Lál, Deputy Inspector of Schools, Sáran.

I have the honour to be,

SIR,

Your most obedient servant,

G. A. GRIERSON,

Offg. Joint-Magistrate.

CONTENTS.

DIVISION I.

Historical.

DIVISION II

Grammatical.

Chapter I.—Alphabet.

Chapter II.—Spelling, &c.

PART I.

GENERAL INTRODUCTION.

DIVISION I.

HISTORICAL.

Introductory.

SECTION 1. The speeches treated of in the accompanying series of Grammars are all various forms of one class of languages, called by some Eastern Gauḍian and by others Eastern Neo-Indo-Aryan. These languages are the Asámí (or Assamese), the Bangálí, the Uṛiyá, and the ones at present treated of. These last are usually called the Eastern Hindí dialects; but that name is liable to objection on the score that it suggests the fact that they are merely dialectic forms of the so-called Hindí language which we meet in the Bágh-o-Bahár and the Prem-Ságar, and which is a modified form of the Braj Bháshá or dialect of the Doáb. This is not the fact; for though, doubtless, Hindí and the dialects herein treated of may ultimately be traced up to a common parentage, this point of departure is so extremely distant, and the stems of these languages have developed and branched off so luxuriantly in different directions, that they have nothing in common but their roots.

Meaning of the word 'dialect.'

SECTION 2. Besides this, there is this other grave objection against the use of the term 'dialect,' that this term, as popularly (though not scientifically) accepted, necessarily presupposes the existence of some one closely connected form of speech to which the dialects can be referred as a standard. Thus there are Yorkshire and Somersetshire dialects of literary English, and Provençal and Norman dialects of literary French. But there is no standard language of which, say, Tirhutí or Bhagalpúrí can be called dialects, for there is no standard of the so-called Eastern Hindí language. If, therefore, we use the word 'dialect' at all, it must be with the distinct understanding that it is not used in its popularly accepted sense, but in the sense of speech used by the people of a certain limited tract of country, and that all idea of reference to another standard speech must be rigorously excluded. With this *proviso* there is no objection to the use of the word; and in this sense it will be used when referring to the languages herein treated of.

Nomenclature.

SECTION 3. The term 'Eastern Hindí' being manifestly objectionable as a name descriptive of this group of dialects, it remains to find a better. The term 'Bihárí' exactly supplies the need. Bihárí means the language of Bihár; and though it will subsequently be seen that the so-called Eastern Hindí dialects are spoken as far south as Jabalpúr and as far west as Banáras, in the absence of a better name this cannot be called a serious objection. The name Bihárí is therefore proposed on the following grounds:—

(1) It is a local name, like the names of other languages, as Bangálí, Panjábí, &c.

(2) The extension of the name to cover all the dialects of Eastern Hindústán has a parallel in the case of Maráṭhí, which has been extended to cover the Dakhaní dialect of Berár, while it means literally only the dialect of the Maráṭhá country.

(3) There is a historical propriety in the name, as the word Bihár is derived from the Buddhist *viháras* or monasteries, once so thickly spread over that region; and Bihárí in its most ancient form was the language of the early Jains and Buddhists.

And (4) Bihárí has a prescriptive right to the dignity of assuming a general character, for the only one of all the dialects of Eastern Hindústán which possesses any literature is Maithilí, a dialect of North Bihár.

For reasons which will be seen further on, the group of dialects at the head of which stands Braj Bháshá, and which are referred to literary (or

High) Hindí as a standard, can then be called the 'Hindí group of dialects.'

The Eastern Neo-Indo-Aryan or Gauḍian languages.

SECTION 4. I have already stated that the Bihárí group of dialects, together with Uṛiyá, Bangálí, and Assamese, form together a class of languages called by some the Eastern Gauḍian languages, and by others the Eastern Neo-Indo-Aryan languages. Both these names have their objections. The latter is far too long for ordinary use, and there are also objections to the former term. Gauḍian means the language of the people of Gauḍa; and the term Gauḍa represents two countries, both Bangál, of which the capital was the famous city of Gauṛ in Máldá, and the Eastern part of Audh, which is the ancient Gauḍa of Sanskrit literature. Either of these is a comparatively small tract, and rather insignificant to give a name to all the Neo-Aryan languages of India, from Maráṭhí to Asámí; but it is a convenient word, and may be adopted for want of a better, and as such has been accepted by many modern scholars. I shall, therefore, when referring to these languages, generally use the word Gauḍian, reserving at the same time the right to call them also Neo-Indo-Aryan when I wish to be scientifically accurate.

Western, Northern, and Southern Neo-Indo-Aryan or Gauḍian languages.

SECTION 5. In the same way we find a *Western* Neo-Indo-Aryan or Gauḍian class of languages, including the Hindí dialects (with High Hindí as a standard), Panjábí, Gujarátí, and Sindhí; a *Northern* Neo-Indo-Aryan or Gauḍian class of languages, including Naipálí, Gaṛhwálí, and Kumaoní; and a *Southern* Neo-Indo-Aryan or Gauḍian language, Maráṭhí, forming a class by itself.

It will now be advantageous to trace the connection between these four classes of languages:—

(1) The Eastern Neo-Indo-Aryan or Eastern Gauḍian.
(2) The Western Neo-Indo-Aryan or Western Gauḍian.
(3) The Northern Neo-Indo-Aryan or Northern Gauḍian.
(4) The Southern Neo-Indo-Aryan or Southern Gauḍian.

It will be seen that they include amongst them all the modern Aryan languages of India. Other languages are Draviḍian, such as Tamil; or

Kolarian, such as Saontálí; or Tibeto-Burman, such as the languages of the Gáros; or Khásí, like those of inhabitants of the Khasi and Jaintia hills.

Their origin.

SECTION 6. It is well known that the earliest documents which we possess of the Aryan languages of India are the older hymns of the Ṛig Veda. These, however, can hardly be taken as representing the actual form of the language spoken by the people at the time at which they were written. They must be taken as representing the literary form of that language, as distinct from the spoken form: just as at the present day there are literary and colloquial forms of English. The language of the Ṛig Veda became, however, a sacred language, and was jealously conserved, and forced into a peculiar development of its own, by its guardians the Bráhmaṇs. It finally became stereotyped by the labours of the great grammarian Páṇini and his followers about the middle of the fourth century (B.C.). As fixed by them it became known as the *Saṅs-kṛita* (Sanskrit) or pure language, as distinct from the *Prákṛita* or vulgar language of every-day speech. It thus appears that Sanskrit cannot be called the origin of the vernaculars of India. On the contrary, it and they had a common origin, and they grew up side by side. Each has, no doubt, greatly influenced the other in the matter of vocabulary,* but neither can be said to be derived from the other.

It is therefore the Prákrit languages of ancient India to which we must look for the origin of the modern Aryan vernaculars. These languages developed in the mouths of the people from the original vernacular of the time of the Ṛig Veda. They also received a certain amount of literary cultivation, and we find them also acquiring the twofold character of combining two languages, a literary and a colloquial, at a time usually stated as about the commencement of the Christian era.

* Sanskrit contains many words which show an unmistakeable Prákṛit origin, *e.g.* गेह *geha*, 'a house,' beside the equally classical गृह *griha*; and the modern languages have largely supplemented their vocabularies by substituting Sanskrit words for other words which the continual attrition of thousands of years had worn away into almost unpronounceable masses of vowels. *E.g.*, when it was found inconvenient to use such words as निओओ *n-i-o-o*, the vernaculars borrowed in comparatively modern times the Sanskrit word नियोग *niyoga*, and used *it*.

The two great Prákrit languages.

SECTION 7. At this time there were two Prákrit languages current over Northern India,—one called Sauraseni, and covering the greater part of the tract of country now occupied by the Western Gauḍian languages; and the other called Mágadhí, and covering the tract now occupied by the greater part of the Eastern Gauḍian languages. These two met, and to a certain extent overlapped west of the province of Audh, in the country round Alláhábád and the Maráṭhá country, and the mixed language there spoken was called Ardha Mágadhí or 'half Mágadhí.'

The annexed map attempts to show roughly the distribution of these languages in Northern India. It is based partly on rock inscriptions and partly on the map in Hœrnle's edition of the Prákṛita Lakshaṇa. It does not pretend to be accurate.

These two languages both received the honors of literature. Sauraseni in several of its dialects is used in the Sanskrit plays, and Mágadhí is also used in the same plays to a lesser extent. They can hardly be called two distinct languages,—that is, as different as French and Italian are from each other. Each has, however, its own literature and its own set of native grammarians; and it is a most erroneous idea to consider that either of them was a phase of, or a dialect derived from, the other. Indeed circumstances appear to point out that Mágadhí is incomparably the older of the two, and that

Their history.

SECTION 8. "Some time in the remote past it must have reached up to the extreme western frontiers, and have been the only language of North India; but in course of time it gradually receded more and more towards the south and east before the advancing tide of the Sauraseni tongue, leaving here and there in the deserted territories traces of its former presence. What the eastern and southern frontiers of Mágadhí may have been in those early times, when it reached to the far west of India, it is impossible to say. Very probably as it receded before the Sauraseni it may have conquered fresh territories in the south and east, which had not been before occupied by any Aryan tongue. The head-quarters of the Sauraseni tongue, whence it gradually spread towards the north-east and east, appear to have been in Western Rájputáná . . . . . .

"From these indications it would appear that the Mágadhí tongue is the older of the two; that is, that its occupation of North India preceded the development and extension of the Saurasení. Perhaps this may be taken to point to the fact that two great immigrations of people of the Aryan stock into India took place at different periods, both speaking essentially the same language, though in two different varieties."*

Their final location.

SECTION 9. As time went on, the Saurasení continued its eastern progress, displacing the western portions of the Ardha Mágadhí, which was also encroached upon from the east by Mágadhí, which in its turn apparently found a vent not only in the east, but in the south-west. Mágadhí seems to have been forced through the narrow neck of territory between Alláhábád and Jabalpúr, and thence to have spread down the valley of the Narmadá over the Maráṭhá country, which had formerly been occupied by Ardha Mágadhí and by a debased dialect of Saurasení. At the same time it failed to conquer this southern tract entirely; the language of this southern tract became itself a kind of Ardha Mágadhí, having traces of the old Saurasení influence, which were almost over-powered by Mágadhí. The Saurasení in the south was in fact almost, but not entirely, suppressed, and the language of the south became a strongly Mágadhized (*sit venia verbo*) Ardha Mágadhí. The accompanying map, based on that in Hœrnle's Comparative Grammar, will show the new state of affairs, and serve as a basis of comparison with the preceding map. These maps, it must be distinctly remembered, only pretend to be rough exemplifications by means of definite lines of our present knowledge regarding a state of affairs essentially indefinite; for languages are not separated by straight lines, but insensibly merge into each other.

The traces of this exchange exist to the present day, for while the Eastern and Western Gauḍian languages show plainly and clearly their direct descent from their Prákrit ancestors, it is not so with the Northern and Southern. The Southern Gauḍian language, although undoubtedly of

* Hœrnle's Comparative Grammar, pp. xxxi and xxxii.

Mágadhí stock, still bears traces of the old Sauraseni influence; and similarly the Northern Gaudian languages, which were similarly conquered from Ardha Mágadhí by Sauraseni, though undoubtedly of Sauraseni stock, still bear traces of the old Mágadhí influence.*

Their modern representatives.

SECTION 10. It is this Mágadhí-derived Eastern Gaudian language which in process of time still further subdivided itself into the Bihárí group of dialects, Uriyá, Bangálí, and, at a later period, Asámí; and in the same way the Sauraseni-derived Western Gaudian language subdivided itself into the Híndí group of dialects, Panjábí, Sindhí, and, at a later period, Gujarátí.

Hence it appears that while the Bihárí and the Hindí groups of dialects are widely distinct languages, each has its congeners of similar origin: that is to say, Bangálí is much more nearly related to, and much more like, the Bihárí dialects than they are to the Hindí dialects; and *vice versâ*, Panjábí is much more nearly related to and like the Hindí dialects than they are to the Bihárí. It therefore follows as a necessary logical sequence that if Bangálí or Panjábí are to be considered as languages independent of the Bihárí and Hindí groups of dialects respectively, much more must these Bihárí and Hindí groups of dialects be considered as languages independent among themselves and of each other.

Hence I shall for the future no longer designate them in these pages as groups of dialects, but shall call them the Bihárí language and the Hindí language respectively.

The accompanying table shows the mutual relationship of the various Neo-Indo-Aryan or Gaudian vernaculars.

Comparison of Bihárí and Hindí languages.

SECTION 11. I now proceed to point out the main points of differences which exist between the Bihárí and Hindí languages. Before doing so, however, it will be necessary to clear our ground by explaining the meaning of certain technical terms which have to be used.

---

* Thus the Southern Gaudian language Maráṭhí possesses a long form for nouns in *ayá* and an active case in *ne*, both of which forms point to a Sauraseni origin; and again Naipálí agrees with Eastern Gaudian languages in the active construction of the past tense of transitive verbs.

TATSAMA AND TADBHAVA.

Preliminary definitions.

SECTION 12. Omitting words of entirely foreign origin which have been adopted into the Gaudian languages, such as the English word *ṭikaṭ*, 'a ticket,' or the Arabic word *zulm*, 'oppression,' their vocabularies are entirely of Aryan origin. This Aryan portion of the vocabulary has again been subdivided by native scholars into two classes, called respectively *tatsama* and *tadbhava*.

Tadbhava words are those which have descended into modern vernaculars from Prákrit sources, while *tatsama* words are those which have been borrowed in later times direct from the Sanskrit, to supply real or fancied deficiencies in the vocabulary. Thus the word *ráy*, 'a king,' has come down to the modern Gaudian languages through the Prákrit, and is therefore a *tadbhavá*; but *rájá*, 'a king,' has been borrowed direct from the Sanskriṭ in later times, and is therefore a *tatsama*. Similarly *bhái*, 'a brother,' *khet*, 'a field,' *dahin*, 'right,' are *tadbhavas*; while *bhrátá*, 'a brother,' *kshetra*, 'a field,' and *dakshiṇ* (corrupted to *dakhin*), 'right,' are *tatsamas*.

A similar division of words of Latin origin may be made in the English language; for example, *honour* is a *tadbhava* word derived from Latin through the French 'honneur,' while *honor* is a *tatsama* word borrowed directly from the Latin by our American cousins.

WEAK FORMS, STRONG FORMS, LONG FORMS, AND REDUNDANT FORMS.

These are technical terms for the four forms every substantive in the Gaudian languages is liable to take. In practice every noun does not take all these four forms—generally only three of them; and it can be only learnt by practice which of the first two of these forms is used in the case of any particular noun; but theoretically all nouns, and in reality some nouns do take both. All nouns can optionally take the last two forms, viz. the long and the redundant.

The weak form is the shortest form of the noun, generally ending in a short vowel or silent consonant. Thus Bihárí *ghoṛ*, 'a horse,' *loh*, 'iron,' or *miṭh*, 'sweet.'

The strong forms are simply the weak forms strengthened by the lengthening of the final vowel. Thus *ghoṛá*, 'a horse,' *lohá*, 'iron,' or *miṭhá*, 'sweet,' all of which are common to all Gauḍian languages of India. Weak and strong forms are collectively called *short forms.*

The long forms are formed by adding a suffix, such as *yá* or *wá*, to the weak form of any noun. Thus *ghŏṛ'wá*, 'a horse;' *lŏh'wá*, 'iron;' or *miṭh'wá*, 'sweet,' all of which are the Bihárí long forms of the above words. Other examples in Bihárí are—

Short forms.	Long forms.
Málí, 'a gardener'	*Maliyá.*
Ghar, 'a house'...	*Ghar'wá.*
Pothí, 'a book'...	*Pŏthiá.*
Ā̃sú, 'a tear'	*Ā̃suwá.*

The redundant forms are formed by reduplicating the final suffix of the long form. These forms are principally used by the vulgar. Examples are—

Long forms.	Redundant forms.
Maliyá	*Maliyawá.*
Ghar'wá	*Gharauwá.*
Pŏthiyá	*Pŏthiyawá.*
Asuwá	*Asuwawá.*

We now proceed to consider the difference between the Bihárí and Hindí languages, comparing the former with its congener Bangálí.*

Pronunciation.

SECTION 13. *First*, as regards pronunciation. Bihárí has a tendency to dentalise lingual semi-vowels: thus B.† has often *r* and *rh* where H. has *ṛ* and *ṛh.* Thus the verb meaning 'to fall' in B. is frequently pronounced *parab*, but in H. it is always *paṛ'ná.* Again it often has *r* or *n* where H. has *l.* Thus B. *phar*, 'fruit,' but H. *phal;* B. *gárí*, 'abuse,' but H. *gálí;* B. *nangoṭ*, 'a waist-cloth,' but

* Much of the following will be found in Hœrnle's Gauḍian Grammar, p. ix.

† Throughout the following sections I have used the contractions B. for Bihárí, H. for Hindí, and H. H. for High or literary Hindí. Unless specially stated, I have taken Bhojpúrí as spoken in Arrah and Chhaprá as the typical Bihárí dialect, and Braj Bháshá as the typical Hindí dialect. I have in Sections 14–16 specially selected as examples words common to all or nearly all the Gauḍian languages. The examples must, hence, not be taken as invalidating what I shall subsequently say regarding vocabulary in Section 17.

H. *langoṭi*. The same tendency is observable in Bangálí, where *l* is even written *n*. The vulgar in Bangál pronounce *Lakshmí* as if it were *nakkhi*; and the Bangálí for a waist-cloth is *nĕng'ṭi*.

(2) While H. sometimes omits medial *h*, B. inserts an euphonic *h*. Thus B. *dihalas*, 'he gave,' but H. *diá* or *diyá*.

(3) While B. and Bangálí never tolerate an initial *y* or *w* except in interjections, H. not only tolerates them, but sometimes adds them euphonically. Thus B. *e me*, 'in this;' *o me*, 'in that:' but H. *yá mē*, *wá mē*.

(4) B. and Bangálí have the short vowels *ĕ*, *ăi*, *ŏ*, and *ău*, which are unknown to H. Thus B. *bĕṭiyá*, 'a daughter;' *bŏláwat*, 'calling:' and Bangálí *ĕk*, 'one;' *bĕkti* (*byakti*), 'a person;' and *gŏm*, 'wheat:' but H. *biṭiyá*, *buláwat*, &c.

(5) B. generally prefers to retain the hiatus *aï* and *aü*, while H. always contracts them to *ai* and *au*. Thus B. *baïsaï*, 'he sits,' but H. *baiṭhe*; B. *aür*, 'and;' H. *aur*.

Derivation.

SECTION 14. *Second*, as to derivation. (1) The strong form of masculine nouns of the *a* base has in B. a final *á*, as *ghoṛá*, 'a horse;' *bhalá*, 'good;' and the short form of pronouns a final *e*, as *je*, 'who.' But in H. these forms end in *au* or *o*, as *ghoṛau*,* 'a horse;' *bhalau*,* *bhalo*, 'good;' *jau* or *jo*, 'who.'

(2) The singular possessive (or genitive) case of the personal pronouns has in B. a medial *o*, but in H. *e* or *á*: thus B. *mor*, 'my,' but H. *merau* or *márau*.* Compare the Bangálí *mor*.

(3) B. prefers the weak form ending in a silent consonant of masculine nouns with an *a* base, but H. the strong forms in *au* or *o*. Thus B. *baṛ*, 'great,' H. *baṛau* (High Hindí *baṛá*); B. *mor*, 'my,' H. *merau*; B. *det*, 'giving,' H. (Máṛwáṛí) *deto*; B. *paṛhal*, 'read,' H. *paṛhyau* (High Hindí *paṛhá*). Compare the Bangálí *bŏṛŏ*.

(4) B. prefers the long form of substantives in *'wá* or *au*, but H. that in *ayá* or *ai*: thus B. *Ram'wá* or *Ramau*, 'Ram,' but H. *Ramayá* or *Ramai*.

---

* The forms *ghoṛá* and *bhalá*, &c., which we meet in Úrdú and High Hindí, are not real Hindi forms, but are borrowed from Panjábí.

(5) While H. uses, as a rule, only the short form of pronouns, B. has generally also a long form in *n*: thus B. *se* or *taun*, 'he,' but H. only *so*.

(6) While H. declines its nouns entirely with the aid of postpositions, B. has in some dialects true inflections for the instrumental and locative cases singular. Thus in Maithilí we have *ghoṛē* (Sanskrit *ghoṭakena*), 'by a horse,' and *ghoṛe* (Sanskrit *ghoṭake*), 'in a horse;' so also in Bangálí we have *bálake*, 'in a boy,' while in H. we only have *ghoṛe se*, *ghoṛe mē*,* and *bálak mē*.

SECTION 15. *Third*, as to inflection. This is the most important point to be noticed. The conjugation especially of verbs in Bihárí is radically different from that in Hindí, while it closely approximates to that in Bangálí.

Inflection.

a.—Declension.

(1) B. does not possess the active case in *ne*, which we meet in Hindí: thus B. *ú kaïlas* 'he did,' but H. *wá ne kiyau*, High Hindí *us ne kiyá*.

(2) The oblique form singular of strong masculine nouns in *á* has in B. a final *á*, but in H. a final *e*: thus B. *ghoṛá kĕ*, 'of a horse,' but H. *ghoṛe kau*, High Hindí *ghoṛe ká*.

(3) Nouns ending in a silent consonant have in some B. dialects an oblique form in *a* or *ĕ*; but in H. in such nouns the oblique form is always the same as the direct form. Thus (Mágadhí) *gharĕ sē*, 'from a house,' abl. sing. of *ghar*, 'a house,' but H. always *ghar se*. This explains the oblique form of the verbal noun ending in *ĕ*, formed from an obsolete direct form ending in a silent consonant, which corresponds to the High Hindí form of the verbal noun (miscalled the past participle) in desiderative sentences: thus (Bhojpúrí) *ú bolĕ ke cháhalá*, 'he wishes to speak,' equivalent to the High Hindí *wah bolá cháh'tá hai*.

(4) The B. verbal noun in *l* makes its oblique form end in *á*: thus *máral*, 'the killing;' *már'lá me*, 'in the killing.' This form does not occur in H.

---

* It is fair to add that in some of the more vulgar forms of the Hindí dialects a locative in *e* is found. It is, however, quite unknown as a literary form.

(5) In B. the instrumental and locative cases singular can be used in a true inflected form, as explained under the 6th clause of the second head.

(6) In B. the postpositions denoting cases differ considerably from those in Hindí.

(7) In H. the genitive postpositions are *kau* (H. H. *ká*), *ke*, and *kí*, and their use depends upon two factors—(1) whether the governing noun is in the direct or oblique form, and (2) whether it is masculine or feminine: thus H. H. *uská ghoṛá*, *uske ghoṛe par*, *uskí ghoṛí*. In B. this is not the fact. There are generally two sets of genitival postpositions,—(*a*) one which never changes, as *okar ghoṛá*, *okar ghoṛá par*, *okar ghoṛí*; and (*b*) a set which changes according as the governing noun is in the direct or oblique case, but not changing for gender, as (Bhojpúrí) *ŏk'rĕ ghoṛá*, *ŏk'rĕ ghoṛí*, *ŏk'rá ghoṛá par*, *ŏk'rá ghoṛí par*.

In some dialects there are genitive postpositions which change according to the gender of the governing noun, but then they are not affected by its being direct or oblique. Thus (Mágadhí) *ŏk'rá ghoṛá*, *ŏk'rá ghoṛá par*, *ŏk'rí ghoṛí*, *ŏk'rí ghoṛí par*.

With reference to the above genitival affixes, it should be noticed that Bangálí agrees with B. in their use. Thus we have *uhár ghoṛá*, *uhár ghoṛáy*, *uhár ghoṛí*, and *uhár ghoṛíte*.

b.—Conjugation.

(1) In some dialects of B. the present indicative is formed by adding *lá* to the ancient (Sanskrit) present: *e.g. dekhilá*, 'I see.' This tense does not exist in Hindí.

(2) The periphrastic present is formed in H. by adding the verb substantive to the present participle. In some B. dialects it is formed by adding the verb substantive to the inflected verbal noun: thus B. (Mágadhí) *ham dekhĕ hi*, 'I see' (*quasi* 'I am on seeing,' *vulgo* 'I'm a-seeing'), but H. *maĩ dekh'tá hũ*. Compare the colloquial Bangálí *dĕkh'chhi* (*i.e. dekhĕ hi*) beside the literary *dekhitechhi* (*dekhait hí*).

(3) The past tense in B. is formed by means of the suffix *al*; in H. by means of the suffix *yau* or *yo* (H. H. *á*). Thus B. *rahal*, 'he remained;' H. *rahyau*; H. H. *rahá*. Compare the Bangálí *róhilŏ*.

(4) The perfect and pluperfect tenses are in Hindí formed by adding the auxiliary verb to the past participle. The auxiliary is then alone conjugated: thus High Hindí *mãi girá hū̃*, 'I have fallen;' *tú girá hai*, 'thou hast fallen;' *wah girá hai*, 'he has fallen.' Besides forming its perfect and pluperfect in this way, Bihárí also forms them by adding the third person singular of the auxiliary verb to the preterite, which last, and not the auxiliary, is then conjugated : thus (Mágadhí) *ham gir'lū̃ haï*, 'I have fallen;' *tõ gir'lē haï*, 'thou hast fallen;' *ú giral haï*, 'he has fallen.'

(5) In the periphrastic tenses of transitive verbs in B., the perfect participle is used in its oblique, and not in its direct form. This is not the case in H.: thus, *ham dĕkh'lĕ báṭi*, 'I have seen.'

(6) The future tense is made in B., like Bangálí, by the affix *ab*, but in H. by the suffixes *ih* or *as*. This does not apply to High Hindí, which forms its future in another and third way: thus B. *karab*, Bangálí *kŏribŏ*, 'I shall do,' but H. *karihãũ*, or *karasū̃*, and High Hindí *karū̃gá*.

(7) Bihárí has five distinct tenses which are formed directly from the root or participles, and which are not periphrastic, viz. the present, preterite, and future indicative, and the present and preterite conjunctive. High Hindí has only one such tense,—the present conjunctive; for the present imperative is only a variety of that tense, and the future indicative is formed from it also by the simple addition of the syllable *gá*.

(8) Finally on this point, with the exception of one or two forms in the present conjunctive, Bihárí has not a single verbal form of any description which bears even a resemblance to the verbal forms of Hindí; Bangálí, on the contrary, throughout its whole series of verbal forms shows a close relation to those of Bihárí.

(9) The present participle in B. ends in *ait*, but in H. H. in *tá*: thus B. *dekhait*, 'seeing;' but H. H. *dekh'tá*.

(10) Hindí has three forms of the verbal noun, viz. one in *ab* (*chalabãũ*), one in *n* (*chalanãũ*, High Hindí *chal'ná*), and one in *í*, with its oblique form in *á* (*chalí*, *chalá*). Bihárí also has one in *ab* (*chalab*), but it has not the two others, having instead one in *al* (*chalal*) and one in the form of the root (*chal*), having its oblique form in *ĕ* (*chalĕ*). The verbal nouns in *b* and *l* also occur in Bangálí in the oblique form, as *chŏlibár*, 'of going,' and

chŏlile (loc. sing.) 'on going,' which last is usually called the 'conjunctive participle,' and is translated 'having gone.'

(11) In Bihárí the causal verb is (except in Purníyá) formed by adding *áw* to the simple verb, while in High Hindí it is formed by adding *á* (*áy*). Thus B. *karáwal*, 'to cause to do,' but H. H. *karáná*.

SECTION 16. *Fourth*, as regards construction. There is one great difference, that in the case of the past tense of transitive verbs B. possesses a regular active construction with a proper active past tense, whereas H. uses a passive construction with the help of the active case (in *ne*) of the subject.

Construction.

SECTION 17. *Fifth*, as regards vocabulary. Some of the commonest and most important vocables are altogether different. Thus the auxiliary verb is in one dialect of B. 3 sing. pres. *báṭaï*, 'he is;' preterite *rahal*, 'he was:' but in H., pres. *hai* (or *chhai*), past *tho* (H. H. *thá*). Compare the Bangálí *bŏṭe*, 'he is.'

Vocabulary.

Again the prohibitive particle is in B. *jin*, *jani*, or *mati*, and in H. only *mat*: again the causative postposition is in B. *bade*, *khátir*, *lágí*, or *lel*, 'for the sake of,' but in H. *liye*.

SECTION 18. It thus appears that all the Eastern Gauḍian languages (taking Bihárí and Bangálí as samples) differ from the Western Gauḍian languages (taking Braj Bháshá and High Hindí as samples) in nearly identical points, and while closely connected amongst themselves are as distinct as possible in pronunciation, derivation, inflection, construction, and vocabulary from the latter.

Final results of the above.

SECTION 19. I now proceed to exhibit the geographical distribution of the Bihárí language. The accompanying map* will illustrate my remarks. Its *language* boundaries are as follows:—It is bounded on the north by Naipálí; on the east by Santhálí and Bangálí; on the south by the hill dialects of Chutiá Nágpúr and Central India, and by Maráṭhí; on the west it is bordered by the Hindí language. Between the Hindí and Bihárí languages there is a triangular-shaped tract, corresponding to the ancient Ardha-Mágadhí occupied by Baiswárí and Baghelkhaṇḍí, which belong partly

Geographical distribution.—Language boundaries.

* See map facing the title-page.

to the Eastern and partly to the Western language, being in fact a kind of debatable ground.

Political boundaries.

SECTION 20. Its *political* boundaries are as follows. The tract of country in which the Bihárí is spoken is bounded on the north by the lower ranges of the Himálaya Mountains; on the east by the district of Dinájpúr and by the Saontál Pergunnahs; on the south by the hills of Chutiá Nágpúr and Central India; and on the west by a line passing nearly north and south a little to the west of Lakhnau down to the junction of the river Ken with the Jamuná. Thence the western boundary follows the course of the river Ken to about the latitude of Jabalpúr, where it meets the southern boundary. It thus includes the Nepál Tarai, the provinces of Bihár and Audh, the eastern half of the North-Western Provinces, and the northern half of the Central Provinces. The dialects, however, of Audh (Baiswárí) and of Baghelkhaṇḍ, or the district between the river Ken and Rewá, are not pure Bihárí, but are largely mixed with Hindí. In the north of the tract, in fact, pure Bihárí is not spoken further west than Alláhábád. The languages, therefore, treated of in this Grammar do not include Baiswárí and Baghelkhaṇḍí. These Grammars, moreover, do not nominally refer to Nepál, nor to the Eastern districts of the North-Western Provinces, such as Gorakhpúr, Mirzápúr, and Jaunpúr, but the dialects of these tracts will probably be found to differ little from those of the Northern and Western districts of Bihár.

Dialects of Bihárí.

SECTION 21. Bihárí has three dialects, viz. Bhojpúrí, Maithilí, and Mágadhí. It is difficult to fix upon any exact limits for the tracts occupied by them, as they everywhere insensibly merge into each other. The following remarks must therefore be considered as only approximate, and as illustrating the map facing the title-page.

Bhojpúrí.

SECTION 22. Bhojpúrí is the extreme western of the three dialects. It takes its name from Bhojpúr, once a famous town, but now a small village near Baksar (Buxar), and a few miles south of the Ganges. Of the three dialects, it covers much the largest extent of country, running north and south from the Himálaya Mountains down to Jabalpúr in the Central Provinces. In Bihár it occupies the whole of the districts of Sháhábád, Sáran, and Champáran, and the north-west corner of Muzaffarpúr. In this tract it has few local peculiarities, and is a homogeneous and flexible language, but possesses no literature.

SECTION 23. Maithilí. Maithilí was originally the language of the ancient Mithilá, the kingdom of Janaka, the father of Sítá, which was bounded on the west by the river Gaṇḍak, on the north by the Himálaya mountains, on the east by the Kosí, and on the south by the Ganges. It has, however, in later times been encroached upon by Bhojpúrí on the west, and in revenge has itself crossed the Ganges and occupied North Patna and so much of the Munger and Bhágalpúr districts as lie to the south of that river. It has also crossed the Kosí and occupied Purníyá. Its conquest, however, has not been complete, for in Purníyá and South Bhágalpúr it is much mixed with Bangálí, and parts of Munger still retain the old Mágadhí speech. Maithilí is spoken in its greatest purity in the northern half of the Darbhangá district, and in the Supaul subdivision of North Bhágalpúr. As there spoken, it retains many characteristics which show that it is the least developed of the Bihárí dialects—that is to say, that it still retains many old forms which have been lost by the two other more advanced dialects.* Hence it is a dialect which attracts the attention of the philologist, as offering a key to many grammatical puzzles which would otherwise remain unsolved. In the rest of the tract occupied by Maithilí the dialect is in a much more developed state, so that we are justified in stating that Maithilí contains two subdialects,—a northern and a southern.

The northern subdialect will not be illustrated in these Grammars, as a separate Grammar of it is being now published by the Asiatic Society of Bengal with Government aid. In order, however, to make the series complete, the selections given with the other Grammars will also be given for northern Maithilí, and will be found at the end of this introduction.

SECTION 24. Mágadhí. Mágadhí is the dialect of the old kingdom of Magadha, whose capital was in ancient times Rája-Gṛiha or Rájgír, and subsequently Bihár in the subdivision of that name in the Patna district. It is spoken throughout the south of the

* *E.g.*, the Maithilí instrumental in *ĕ* and the locative in *e*; and, in verbs, the 1st person plural in *ahū*, and 2nd plural in *húnhi*.

Patna district, the whole of Gayá, and the north of Chutiá Nágpúr. It is also spoken in the south-west of the Munger district. It has no subdialects and no literature.

Bihárí literature.

SECTION 25. Bihárí has not a large literature. As already remarked, Bhojpúrí and Mágadhí have none at all. Maithílí, however, has one famous poet in Bidyápati Ṭhákúr, who lived at the end of the fourteenth and beginning of the fifteenth centuries. Many of his songs have survived, and they are now being published by the Asiatic Society of Bengal.

The Rámáyan of Tulsí Dás is usually said to have been written in Bihárí. It is rather written in an archaic form of the Baiswárí of Audh, and hence contains a large number of Hindí forms. Apart from its intrinsic merit, however, it will well repay study as an introduction to the Bihárí language: and hence it has most rightly been adopted by the Educational Department of Bengal as a text-book for vernacular schools.

General plan of these Grammars.

SECTION 26. The following series of Grammars has been so arranged that the Grammar of each dialect or subdialect shall be so far as is possible uniform with the others. The series consists of seven Grammars, arranged as follows:—

(1) No. 1 refers to the Bhojpúrí dialect of Sháhábád, Sáran, Champáran, and North Muzaffarpúr.

(2) No. 2 refers to the Mágadhí dialect of Gayá and South Patna.

(3) No. 3 refers to the South-Maithilí dialect mixed with Bhojpúrí of Central and South Muzaffarpúr.

(4) No. 4 refers to the South-Maithilí dialect of South Darbhangá, North Munger, and the Madhepúrá subdivision of Bhágalpúr.

(5) No. 5 refers to the South-Maithilí dialect affected by Mágadhí of South Munger.

(6) No. 6 refers to the Maithilí-Bangálí of South Bhágalpúr.

(7) No. 7 refers to the Maithilí-Bangálí of Central and Western Purníyá. In Eastern Purníyá a dialect of Bangálí is spoken which is not represented in these Grammars.

In this introduction I shall give so much of Bihárí Grammar as refers to all the dialects alike, and this will not be repeated in the separate Grammars.

DIVISION II.

GRAMMATICAL.

CHAPTER I.

ALPHABET.

Character.

SECTION 27. The characters used in writing Bihárí are three—the Deva Nágarí, the Kaithí, and the Maithilí. The two first are sufficiently well known, and need not be described here; the last is closely connected with the Bangálí character, and is used only in Northern Mithilá. It is fully described in my Maithilí Grammar published by the Asiatic Society, and the description need not be repeated.

Throughout this series of Grammars, a modification of the Deva Nágarí alphabet will be used, as adopted in most of the modern languages. The Deva Nágarí alphabet is as follows:—

VOWELS.

अ *a*, आ *á*, इ *i*, ई *í*, उ *u*, ऊ *ú*, ए *e*,
ऐ *ai*, ओ *o*, औ *au*.

CONSONANTS.

क *ka*,	ख *kha*,	ग *ga*,	घ *gha*,	ङ *ṅa*.
च *cha*,	छ *chha*,	ज *ja*,	झ *jha*,	ञ *ńa*.
ट *ṭa*,	ठ *ṭha*,	ड *ḍa*,	ढ *ḍha*,	ण *ṇa*.
		ड़ *ṛa*,	ढ़ *ṛha*.	
त *ta*,	थ *tha*,	द *da*,	ध *dha*,	न *na*.
प *pa*,	फ *pha*,	ब *ba*,	भ *bha*,	म *ma*.
य *ya*,	र *ra*,	ल *la*,	व *wa*.	
श *śa*,	ष *sha*,	स *sa*,	ह *ha*.	

In addition to the above there is the sign ं, called *anuswár*, which is (properly) only used in Hindí as a *compendium scripturæ* instead of any of the nasals when immediately preceding any consonant of its own class.

Anunásik.

SECTION 28. There is also the sign ँ, called *anunásik*, which gives a nasal sound to a vowel, something like the nasal sound in the French word *bon*. In transliteration this will be represented by a circumflex placed over a vowel or diphthong. Thus में *mẽ*, कैं *kaĩ*. When *anunásik* is placed over a long vowel, if that vowel is for any reason shortened, *anunásik* remains unchanged. Thus when the long *í* in भींजल *bhĩjal*, 'to be wet,' is shortened, the *anunásik* remains unaltered, as in भिँजावल *bhĩjáwal*, 'to moisten.' So also when the long *á* in हाँस *hã́s*, 'a goose,' is shortened, *anunásik* is not changed, as in the word हँस॰वा *hãs'wá*, 'a goose.' When, however, *anuswár* is placed over a short vowel, and that vowel for any cause becomes lengthened, *anuswár* becomes *anunásik*. Thus when the अ *a* in the word बंधल *bandhal*, 'to be tied,' becomes lengthened, the *anuswár* becomes *anunásik*, as in बाँधल *bã́dhal*, 'to tie.'

The neutral vowel.

SECTION 29. There is one vowel, called the neutral vowel, which has no representative in the Deva Nágarí alphabet. It is the shortest possible vocal utterance, and is pronounced like the *o* in the word *Brighton* (*Bright'n*), or the obscure vowel sound in the final syllables of *amiable*, *centre*. This neutral vowel sound I shall represent by a *dot* ॰ placed after the consonant to which it refers, and in transliteration by an apostrophe: thus घर॰वा *ghar'wá*, 'a house.' This neutral vowel can never commence a word, and hence it has no initial form.

Final sonant *a*.

SECTION 30. Generally, when a word ends in a consonant, that consonant is silent,—that is to say, the inherent *a* in it is not pronounced. Thus घर is pronounced *ghar*, and not *ghara*. When the inherent *a* in a final consonant is pronounced, which not unfrequently occurs in Bihárí, this will be denoted by a small circle ऽ placed after the final consonant. Thus देख *dekh*, but देखऽ *dekha*.

Short diphthongs.

SECTION 31. Besides the above signs, however, there are four vowels which are peculiar to Bihárí, and which have no equivalent in Hindí. They are *ĕ*, *ŏ*, *ăi*, and *ău*.

ĕ is pronounced like *e* in the English word *met*.

ŏ has no equivalent in English, and is pronounced like the *o* in *note* shortened.

aĭ has no equivalent in English, and is pronounced like the *i* in *mite* shortened.

aŭ has no equivalent in English, and is pronounced like the *ow* in *owl* shortened.*

The following signs have been added to the Deva Nágarí alphabet to express these sounds :—

	Initial.	Non-initial.
ĕ	ऎ	ॆ
ŏ	ऒ	ॊ
aĭ	ऐ	ै
aŭ	औ	ौ

The complete series of Bihárí vowels.

SECTION 32. The following table therefore shows the complete series of Bihárí vowels as used in these Grammars :—

	Neutral ('),	*a*,	*á*,	*i*,	*í*,	*u*,	*ú*,	*ĕ*,	*e*,	*ŏ*,	*o*.
Initial . .	*wanting*,	अ,	आ,	इ,	ई,	उ,	ऊ,	ऎ,	ए,	ऒ,	ओ.
Non-initial .	॰,	. .	ा,	ि,	ी,	ु,	ू,	ॆ,	े,	ॊ,	ो.

	aĭ,	*ai*,	*aŭ*,	*au*.
Initial	ऐ,	ऐ,	औ,	औ.
Non-initial	ै,	ै,	ौ,	ौ.

The manner of writing the non-initial vowels is as follows :—

क॰ *k'*, क *ka*,† का *ká*, कि *ki*, की *kí*, कु *ku*, कू *kú*, कॆ *kĕ*, के *ke*, कॊ *kŏ*, को *ko*, कै *kaĭ*, कै *kai*, कौ *kaŭ*, कौ *kau*.

When nasalized, the vowels are written as follows :—

कँ *kã*, काँ *kā́*, किँ *kĩ*, कीँ *kī́*, कुँ *kũ*, कूँ *kū́*, कॆँ *kĕ̃*, केँ *kẽ*, कॊँ *kŏ̃*, कोँ *kõ*, कैँ *kaĭ̃*, कैँ *kaĩ*, कौँ *kaŭ̃*, कौँ *kaũ*.

The consonants.

SECTION 33. The remaining letters call for no remark.

* The representation of Bihárí vowel sounds by examples of English words is convenient, but not absolutely accurate. No Bihárí vowel sound has an absolutely exact equivalent in English.

† Except at the end of a word, when it is written कऽ.

CHAPTER II.

SPELLING AND PRONUNCIATION.

Concurrent vowels. Euphonic *y* and *w*.

SECTION 34. When इ *i* is followed by अ *a* or आ *á*, the letter य *ya* may always be inserted to avoid a hiatus. Thus we have मलिआ *maliá* or मलिया *maliyá*, 'a gardener.'

Similarly when उ *u* is followed by अ *a* or आ *á*, the letter व *wa* may be inserted. Thus आँसुआ *ãsuá* or आँसुवा *ãsuwá*, 'a tear.'

These inserted letters I shall call euphonic य *ya* and euphonic व *wa* respectively. I shall generally insert them throughout this series of Grammars, except when in special cases it is not customary to do so. As a rule euphonic य *ya* is inserted, and euphonic व *wa* omitted.

Contraction.

SECTION 35. When अ *a* is followed immediately by इ *i* (or in Northern Maithilí by इ *i* or ए *ĕ*), the two letters may optionally be contracted into ऐ *ai*. Thus हइ *haï* or है *hai*. Similarly when अ *a* is followed immediately by उ *u* (or in Northern Maithilí by उ *u* or ओ *ŏ*), the two may be contracted into औ *au*. Thus हउ *haü* or हौ *hau*.

The custom in the above respect somewhat varies. Everywhere both forms can be used, but in some districts it is more usual to adopt the open, and in others the contracted form. In this series of Grammars, I shall in each Grammar give the form most current in the tract to which the Grammar refers.

Shortening of antepenultimate vowel.

SECTION 36. The following rules are most important, and must be thoroughly mastered before the declensional and conjugational paradigms can be understood. The whole declensional and conjugational paradigms depend upon them; and as the reader will not be likely to have met anything like them in his reading in High Hindí, his special attention must be directed to them. They were first pointed out by Dr. Hœrnle in his Gauḍian Grammar, and by the present Author in his Maithilí Grammar. As reference will be made to the counting of syllables, it must first be understood that a final silent consonant does *not* count as a syllable. Thus घर *ghar*, 'a house,' is one syllable; देखब *dekhab*, 'I shall see,' is a word of two syllables, viz. दे *de*, खब *khab*; while देखबऽ *dekhaba*, 'you will see,' is a word of three syllables, viz. दे *dĕ*, ख *kha*, बऽ *ba*, as the final consonant बऽ *ba* is not silent.

We now come to the first rule.

1. Whenever the vowel आ *á* finds itself in a word in a position further from the end than the last syllable but one, it is shortened to अ *a*. *Example*: नाऊ *náú*, 'a barber.' Here आ *á* is in the last syllable but one, and is not shortened; but in the long form of the word, नउआ *naüwá*, it is shortened, as it is now three syllables from the end. So also माली *máli* becomes in its long form मलिया *maliyá*; and the √ पाव *páw*, 'obtain,' whose infinitive is पावल *páwal*, becomes in the 2nd plur. pret. ind. पउल० *paüla*, and not पाउल० *páüla*.

2. Similarly any other vowel or diphthong is in the last syllable but two of a word shortened, *provided a consonant which is not euphonic* य *ya or* व *wa* (see Section 34) *follows it*. Thus the ए *e* in the √ देख *dekh*, 'see,' is shortened in देखलूँ *dĕkh'lú*, 'I saw,' because it is in the last syllable but two, and is followed by the consonant ख *kha*; but the √ चू *chú*, 'drip,' becomes in the 1st sing. pret. ind. चूअलूँ *chúalú* or चूवलूँ *chúw'lú*, 'I dripped,' and not चुअलूँ *chualú* or चुवलूँ *chuw'lú*, for ऊ *ú* remains long although it is in the last syllable but two, as it is followed by the vowel अ *a* or by the euphonic letter व *wa*.

3. The third rule is that any vowel whatever is shortened when it is more than three syllables from the end of a word, *whether it is followed by a consonant or not*. Hence while ऊ *ú* by the second rule remains long in चूइतूँ *chúitú*, the 1st sing. pret. conj. of √ चू *chú*, it is shortened in the second person plural, viz. चुइतहू *chuit'hú*, where it is in the fourth syllable from the end.

Similarly we have the 1st plur. pres. conj. of the √ हो *ho*, 'become,' होइअइ *hŏiaï*, with the ओ *o* shortened to ओ *ŏ*; but when the final two syllables अइ *aï* become contracted according to Section 35 to ऐ *ai*, the ओ *o* is only in the third syllable from the end, and is not shortened. Hence we get होइऐ *hoïai*, and not होइऐ *hŏïai*.

4. In connection with this last example, note that a vowel which is shortened by any of the foregoing rules may be liable to be lengthened again if the number of syllables following it is lessened by contraction. Hence, while we have देखइत *dĕkhaït*, when अ *a* and इ *i* are contracted to ऐ *ai*, the ए *ĕ* is lengthened to ए *e*, as it is then only in the last syllable but one, viz. देखैत *dekhait*. Of course, if after the contraction the number of syllables following the vowel is still sufficient to render it short, the vowel remains short. Thus,

take the 1st plur. pret. conj. (Mágadhí) of √ देख *dekh*. One of its forms is देखइतिअउ *děkhaïtiaü*, a word of six syllables. Here by Section 35 खइ *khaï* is liable to be contracted to खै *khai* and अउ *aü* to औ *au*, so that we may also write देखैतिऔ *děkhaĭtiau*. Here ए *ĕ* is still more than three syllables from the end, and hence remains short. Note also in the above that ऐ *ai* is shortened to ऐ *aĭ*, as it is more than two syllables from the end, and is followed by a consonant which is not euphonic य *ya* or व *wa*.

Exceptions—1. There is one important exception to the above rules. The long vowel contained in a causal root is never shortened. Thus the causal of मरल *maral*, 'to die,' is मारल *máral*, 'to kill,' and the oblique form of its verbal noun is मारऽला *már'lá*, and not मरऽला *mar'lá*.

2. Note also that in Northern Maithilí the above rules only apply to the declension of nouns, pronouns, &c. They do not apply to verbs, for which a series of special rules will be found in the Grammar.

3. In the Bhojpúrí present indicative the vowel must be one syllable further back in the word before it can be shortened. Thus देखीला *dekhílá*, and not देखीला *dĕkhílá*.

Section 37. When य *ya* and व *wa* are followed by the neutral vowel, thus यऽ *y'* and वऽ *w'*, they become what is called silent.

Silent *y* and *w*.

When this occurs in the middle of a word, यऽ *y'* and वऽ *w'* are changed to इ *i* and उ *u* (or in Northern Maithilí to ए *ĕ* and ओ *ŏ*) respectively.

This इ *i* or उ *u* (or ए *ĕ* or ओ *ŏ*) combines optionally with a preceding अ *a* to ऐ *ai* or औ *au*, respectively (see Section 35). Thus गयल + अस *gayal* + *as* becomes गयऽलस *gay'las*, which becomes गइलस *gaïlas* or गैलस *gailas*, 'thou wentest.' Similarly in North Maithilí पावल + अहुँ *páwal* + *ahũ* becomes पवऽलहुँ *paw'lahũ* (see Section 36. 1), which becomes पओलहुँ *paŏlahũ* or पौलहुँ *paulahũ*.

CHAPTER III.

NOUNS.

Section 38. Every noun (including adjectives) has at least three forms,—a short, a long, and a redundant. The nature of these forms has already been explained (see Section 12), and need not be repeated here. The method of forming them will be seen

Nominal forms.

from the paradigms of declension. The short form may be either weak, as घर *ghar*, 'a house,' or strong, as घोड़ा *ghoṛá*, 'a horse.' The weak is the simplest form of a noun, formed without the addition of any suffix.

Generally speaking, the strong varieties may be formed by lengthening the final vowel of the weak. That is to say, weak forms generally end in a silent consonant or in a short vowel, but strong forms in a long vowel. Few nouns have both a weak and a strong form. They generally have either one or the other. There are, however, a few nouns which appear in both: thus—

Weak form.	Strong form.
घोड़ *ghoṛ* (Maithilí).	घोड़ा *ghoṛá*, 'a horse.'
लोह *loh*.	लोहा *lohá*, 'iron.'
घर *ghar*.	घरा *ghará*, 'a house' (Mágadhí).

But always बात *bát*, 'a word;' रात *rát* or राति *ráti*, 'night' (weak forms); and माली *málí*, 'a gardener;' पोथी *pothí*, 'a book;' नाउ *náú*, 'a barber;' and बहू *bahú*, 'a daughter-in-law' (strong forms).

Regarding the use of the short, long, and redundant forms, the following observations will suffice. The short form is the usual one. It is the one found in the dictionary. The long form is used either in a non-honorific sense or to give definiteness. Thus घोड़ा *ghoṛá* (short form), '*a* horse,' but घोड़वा *ghŏr'wá*, '*the* horse.'

The redundant form is used much in the same sense as the long form, but only by the vulgar. The vulgar indeed use both the long and redundant forms, as caprice dictates, in the sense of the short form; and in connection with this it may be noted that while to use the long form in the sense of the short form is vulgar, to use the redundant form in this sense is very vulgar.

SECTION 39. There are two numbers in Bihárí, the singular and plural. The plural may be either simple or periphrastic.

Number.

Directions for the formation of the plural will be found in each Grammar.

Case.

SECTION 40. There are (including the vocative) eight cases,—the nominative, accusative, instrumental, dative, ablative, genitive, locative, and vocative. Their power is the same as in Bangálí. They can all be formed by adding postpositions; but some dialects, such as Maithilí, show signs of organic declension in the instrumental or locative, or both.

Gender.

SECTION 41. This will be found treated under the head of Adjectives.

CHAPTER IV.

ADJECTIVES.

Gender.

SECTION 42. Gender is little observed in Bihárí: hence few adjectives change for gender, and it is difficult to make any general rules.

Adjectives, like nouns, have weak, strong, long, and redundant forms. Except in South Bhágalpúr (see special Grammar), *tadbhava* adjectives ending in आ *á*, as मीठा *míṭhá*, 'sweet,' form their feminines by changing आ *á* to ई *í*: as मीठा *míṭhá*, *fem.* मीठी *míṭhí*. Long and redundant forms in ॰वा *'wá* form their feminines in इया *iyá*. Thus हलुक॰वा *haluk'wá*, 'light,' *fem.* हलुकिया *halukiyá*; मिठक॰वा *miṭhak'wá*, 'sweet,' *fem.* मिठकिया *miṭhakiyá*.

All other adjectives remain unchanged for gender. Thus भारी *bhárí*, 'heavy,' *fem.* भारी *bhárí*; हलू *halú*, 'light,' *fem.* हलू *halú*.

Maithilí exceptions.

SECTION 43. In Northern Maithilí some adjectives ending in a silent consonant form their feminines in इ *i*, which is pronounced very lightly, like a mere breath. Thus बड़ *baṛ*, 'great,' *fem.* बड़ि *baṛi*, pronounced *baṛ'*; and सुंदर *sundar*, 'beautiful,' *fem.* सुंदरि *sundari*, pronounced *sundar'*.

The rules for the formation of the feminine of nouns are the same as those for the formation of the feminine of adjectives.

Numeral adjectives.

SECTION 44. These are treated of separately in each Grammar.

CHAPTER V.

PRONOUNS.

No general rules.

SECTION 45. These are treated of separately in each Grammar.

CHAPTER VI.

VERBS.

General rules.

SECTION 46. Treated of separately in each Grammar.

Verbs, how quoted.

SECTION 47. Verbs are generally quoted in the form of their infinitive or verbal noun. In all the dialects of Bihárí there are at least two forms of the verbal noun—one in ल *l* and one in ब *b*: thus देखल *dekhal* and देखब *dekhab*, 'to see.' In most of the dialects the verbal noun is quoted in the former of these two forms, but in North Maithilí and in Mágadhí it is usual to quote it in the latter. This custom is followed throughout these Grammars. Some of the dialects, *e.g.* Southern Maithilí, have a form in ना *ná*, corresponding to the High Hindí infinitive in ना *ná*. It is, however, never used in the sense of a verbal noun, but only in that of the future participle passive. Thus हमरा एक बकरी लेना अछ *ham'rá ék bak'rí lená achh; lit.* 'to me a goat is *necessary to be got*,' *i.e.* 'I want a goat.'

Multiplicity of forms.

SECTION 48. In one respect the conjugation of verbs is very simple. Once given the stem-form of any particular tense, it is easy to conjugate it throughout, for the personal terminations are nearly always the same for all tenses. Verbs, however, in Bihárí have one difficulty, which is unknown to students of Hindí; it is the multiplicity of personal terminations for each person. Sometimes there are as many as six terminations for one person, any of which may be used at option. It is not necessary to give examples of this here, as they will be found on every page of the Verbal Paradigms.

CHAPTER VII.

INDECLINABLES.

Indeclinables.

SECTION 49. It is not necessary to treat of these at length, as the subject belongs rather to vocabulary than to accidence. The following notes regarding the more common indeclinables may be found useful.

Adverbs.

SECTION 50. The more usual pronominal adverbs are given with the pronouns in each Grammar. Note the following:—

काल *kál*, or काल्ह *kálh*, or काल्ही *kálhí*, 'yesterday' or 'to-morrow.'

बिहान *bihán*, 'to-morrow.'

आगू *ágú*, 'before.'

पाछू *páchhú* or पीछू *píchhú*, 'behind.'

फुन *phun* or फिन *phin*, 'again.'

निदान *nidán*, 'lastly.'

संजोग *sañjog*, 'accidentally.'

नीमन *níman* or नीक *ník*, 'well.'

आस्ते आस्ते *áste áste* or अस्ते अस्ते *aste aste*, 'slowly.'

जिन *jin*, जनु *janu*, जिनि *jini*, जनि *jani*, or जिमी *jimí*, 'like.'

Particles of prohibition used with the imperative only are—

जिन *jin*, जनु *janu*, जिनि *jini*, and जनि *jani*, 'do not.'

The Hindí मती *matí* (for *mat*) is also occasionally used.

The following are particles of emphasis meaning 'indeed':—ई *í* or ईं *ĩ* and ही *hí* or हीं *hĩ*. The following are particles of emphasis meaning 'also':—ऊ *ú* or ऊँ *ũ*, ओ *o* or ओं *õ*, हू *hú* or हूँ *hũ*. These particles of emphasis are always used enclitically, and are put after the word to which they refer. They often supersede the final vowel of the word emphasized. Examples of their use are हम-हीं *ham'hĩ*, 'even I;' हम-रो *ham'ro*, 'me also.'

Prepositions.

SECTION 51. The following may be noted:—

तरे *tare*, 'beneath.'

ले *le*, 'till.'

माँझ *mãjh*, 'amid.'

बाटे *báṭe*, बारे *báre*, बरे *bare*, or बदे *bade*, 'for,' 'by reason of.'

ले *le*, लै *lai*, 'for.'

लाग *lág*, लागी *lágí*, 'for.'

खातिर *khátir*, 'for,' 'by reason of.'

नाँईं *nâí*, 'like.'

Conjunctions. SECTION 52. Note,—

अउर *aür* or आओर *áŏr*, औ *au* or ओ *o*, 'and.'

बाकि *báki*, बरऽकि *bar'ki*, or बरुक *baruk*, 'but.'

पर *par*, पै *pai*, 'but.'

की *kí* or कि *ki*, 'or,' 'that.'

चाहे *cháhe*, 'or.'

जौ *jau*, 'if,' 'although.'

तौ *tau*, तैँ *tẽ*, 'then.' (Illatively.)

Interjections. SECTION 53. Interjections vary considerably in different districts.

हे *he* and हो *ho* are usual in addressing men.

गे *ge* and गै *gai* in addressing women.

Final. SECTION 54. The above list of indeclinables is of course in no way complete. A fuller list will be found in Hœrnle's Comparative Grammar, pp. 389 and following. The above indeclinables are nearly all used throughout Bihár, with slight varieties of spelling.

APPENDIX.

As promised in the last paragraph of § 23, the following selections in the Northern Maithilí dialect are here given, with translation. The translation will also serve for the selections appended to the various Grammars of the series.

CONVERSATION BETWEEN TWO VILLAGERS.

The following conversation is based on the similar one in Banáras Bhojpúrí in Dr. Hœrnle's Gaudian Grammar. It has been translated for me into Northern Maithilí by Bábú Srí Náráyaṇ Siñh, of Jogivárá, Darbhangá:—

१ प्रश्न कहू भाइ, कतय सँ अबैछी।

उत्तर पछिमा गाम सँ अबैछी।

२ प्र. ओतय सँ कहिआ चलल्हुँ।

उ. सबेरेक चलल छी।

३ प्र. कथी लय ओतय गेल छलहुँ।

उ. ओतय हमर खेत अछि, ओकरा देखै गेल छलहुँ।

४ प्र. ओहि मेँ की बाओग अछि।

उ. केवल राहडि बाओग कैल अछि।

५ प्र. कहू भाइ एहि फसिलक केहन रंग अछि।

उ. एहि फसिलक वार्ता की पुछैछी, पानि बरिसला बिना सब खाक भेल अछि।

६ प्र. आइकाल्हि अपनेक भाइ नहिँ देखि पड़ैछथि।

उ. हमर भाइ आइकाल्हि जिला मेँ नोकर छथि, एतय बहुत थोड़ काल अबैछथि।

प्र. अपनेक बड़की गाय केर की हाल अछि।

उ. ओ आइकाल्हि गाभिनि अछि, परंतु घरी नहिँ भेठल्हा सँ छूटि गेलि अछि।

८ प्र. कै मास सँ गाभिनि अछि।

उ. भेलैक तँ आठ मास, परंतु ओकर पेट उच नहिँ देखि पड़ैछैक।

९ प्र. कुमरन्वैति अछि, वा एखन नहिँ।

उ. हँ किछु २ बूझि पड़ैअछि।

१० प्र. ई कोन बिआन थिकैक, और कतेक दूध दैति अछि।

उ. ई एकर आठम बिआन थिकै। दुइ अढ़ाइ सेर दूध एक बेरि मेँ दैति अछि।

११ प्र. हमन्रा एक बकन्री लेबैक अछ, अपन्नेक गाम मेँ भेटति।

उ. हमन्रा गामोँ मेँ बकन्री सभ तँ अछि, परंतु दाम कड़ा छैक।

१२ प्र. अपन्नेक बकन्री की भेलि।

उ. हम घरैक लेल ओकन्रा गामन्हिँ पर छाड़न्लेँ रहैत छी।

१३ प्र. किच्छु दूध दैति अछि।

उ. नेना सभ केँ पिबैक भरि भै आइत छैक।

१४ प्र. एहि बेरि कुसिआर रोपन्लउँ अछि वा नहिँ।

उ. कुसिआर तँ रोपन्लउँ अछि, परंतु ओहि मेँ किच्छु लाभ नहिँ।

१५ प्र. अपन्नेक ओतय सँ इनार मोट मंगनी भेट सकैअछि।

उ. किऐ नहिँ, सभ दिन पटौनाइ पर लै लेल जाय।

१६ प्र. अपन्नेक ओतय कतेक मोट चलैअछि।

उ. तीनि मोट तँ लधन्लेँ छी।

१७ प्र. अपन्नेक आमक गाछी किछु फड़ैअछि, की नहिँ।

उ. एहि बेरि तँ बदरी सँ माह सबहि मेँ लाही लागि गेलैक, नहिँ तँ बहुत होइत छल।

१८ प्र. थोड़ेक आम हमन्रऊँ अचार लै देब।

उ. जखन अपन्ने चाही, तखन तोड़न्वा लेल जाय।

१९ प्र. अपन्नेक बालक किछु पढ़ैछथि, की नहिँ।

उ. हँ, गुरुक ओतय आइत अछि, अक्षर चीन्हि गेल अछि, आइकाल्हि पहाड़ा पढ़ैत अछि।

१० प्र. स्कूल मेँ किऐ नहिँ पढ़वैछिऐन्हि।

उ. किछु सीखि लेए, तँ पठाए दिऐक।

११ प्र. हम॰ऊँ अपन॰ा बालक कैँ स्कूल मेँ पठाबै चाहैछी

उ. बेस, हम॰रा बाल॰कक संग ओक॰रऊँ पठाए दिऔक ॥

FABLES.

The following fables have been also translated for me by Bábú Srí Náráyaṇ Siñh from Rádhá Lál's Hindí Reader, Part II, into the Northern Maithilí dialect :—

पहिल कथा।

एक मुर्गा गोबर॰क ढेरी कैँ चाँगुर सँ उक॰टि रहल छल। अचानक* ओहि सँ बड़॰का मोतीक दाना बहर॰ाएल। मुर्गा बाजल, बाह, केहन रूप रंग आओर चम॰की छैक, औहर॰री एक॰रा पबैत तँ अत्यन्त खुसी होइत। परंतु हम॰रा मेठक आगि एहि सँ नहिँ मिझाएत†। हा, एक अछरक दाना हम॰रा हाथ लगैत, तँ से मोती सभ सँ अधिक छल। सत्य‡ अछि —

जे अपन॰ा काज नहिँ आबै, से चूल्हा भार मेँ जाए।

दोसर कथा।

कंगालक पूछब आओर अतीथिक उत्तर देब।

एक कंगाल कोनो पहुँचल अतीथि सँ पुछ॰लक कि, हम तँ भूखेँ मरैछी, आओर हमर परोसी गद्दी तकेआ पर पड़ल लोटैत अछि। राति दीन चैन करैअछि। ओक॰रा मेँ कोन गुण छैक, जे दाता ओक॰रा नेहाल कैलन्हि, आओर हम॰रा कंगाल कैलन्हि। ई सुनि कँ अतीथि उत्तर देल॰थीन्हि। बाबा तोँ ई नहिँ सुन॰लेँ छह —

राम भरोसा बैसि कँ सब॰हिक भोज॰रा लेथि।
जेहन जनिकर भाक॰री तेहन्नेँ सन भरि देथि ॥

तेसर कथा।

कोनो भल॰मानुस एक गोसाँइ सँ कहल॰थीन्हि। महाराज देस २ आओर गाम २ घुम॰ला सँ की लाभ अछि। एक ठाम रहि कँ सामी मेँ लय किऐ नहिँ लग॰बैछह।

---

* Or देब जोगेँ † Also दताएत, but vulgar. ‡ Also सरूप, or साँच vulgar.

आओर कोनो मठ मेँ बैसि कँ दाताक गुन किऐ नहिँ गबैछह। जोगी कहलथीन्हि जे, बाबा ई सभ सद्रूप अछि। परंतु तोँ ई कहिनी नहिँ सुनलेँ छह—

ज्ञानी पानि बहन्तु सम बान्हल दुर्ज्जन तुच्छ।
धमितँहि भलमानूस भल दाग न लागय कुच्छ* ॥

चारिम कथा।

एक दीन जाड़क समय मेँ कोनो पैघ लोकक घर मेँ आगि लागल। सभ बस्तुजात † जरि कँ छाउर भै गेल। ओ बाहर ठाढ़ भेल हाथ मिड़ैत छल, कि एक गरीब परोसिआ जाड़क मारल थर २ कपैत घर सँ निकसि आएल, आओर हाथ सेदै लागल। तखन ओ धनवान बाजल, वाह वाह, ककरो घर जरै आओर केओ तापै।

पाँचम कथा।

बान्हल काठी ओ फुजल काठी।

एक गृहस्तक बेटा ‡ सभ अपना मेँ लड़ाइ झगड़ा करैत छल। कथा सभ सँ बड़ुत बुझौलन्हि परंतु केओ किछु नहिँ मानलन्हि। तखन गृहस्त अपना मन मेँ कहलक कि, जँ एकरा सभ कँ किछु कै देखाबी, तँ चाही जे बुझि जाय। एक दीन ओ अपना बेटा सभ कँ बजौलक आओर कहलक कि थोरेक काठी हमरा सोभा लै आबह। ओहि काठी सबहि कँ ओ गृहस्त जौड़ि सँ कसि कै बान्हलक। फेरि प्रत्येक सँ कहलक कि जौड़ि जनु फोयह, आओर काठी सबन्हि कँ तोड़ि देह। एक एक लागि पड़ल, परंतु किच्छु नहिँ भेल। फेरि गृहस्त फो कँ एक २ काठी देलन्हि। तखन ओ सभ ओकरा झट पट तोड़ि देलक। तखन ओकरा सभक बाप कहलन्हिक, कि, बेटा, जौँ तौँ बान्हल काठी सबहिक तरहेँ अपना मेँ मेलि कैकँ रहबह, तौँ सभ बैरीक दाँत खट्टा करबह। आओर जौँ बिछुरि गेलाह, तखन जानह कि बिगड़ि गेलाह।

बिछुरल § से बिगड़ल।

छठम कथा।

ऊँड़ार सभ आओर भेँड़ा सभक मिलाप।

एक बेरि ऊँड़ार सभ भेँड़ा सभ सँ कहाए पठौलन्हि कि आबह, हम तोँ अपना मेँ मिला कै लिअ। किऐ अपना मेँ लड़ब आओर एक दोसराक शोणितक पिआसल रहब। ई पाजी

* कुच्छ is Hindí for किच्छु, but is used for the sake of metre. † Also चीज वस्तु.
‡ छड़िका vulgar. § Also फुटल.

कुकुर सभ सभ झगड़ाक जड़ि अछि। ओहिना सदा भूकि १ कें हमरा सभ कें भड़कबैअछि। एकरा सबहि कें हमरा लग पठाए दैह। फेरि की झगड़ा अछि। हमरा तोहरा में सदा प्रीति आओर मिलाप रहत, तैं तोहरा सभक केसो टेढ़ नहिं हैतऊ। गमार भेँड़ा सभ एहि कपटी ऊँड़ार सभक कथा मानि लेलक। आओर कुकुर सभ कें ऊँड़ारक ओतय पठाए देलक। पहिलें तँ ऊँड़ार सभ कुकुर सभ कें खाए गेल, फेरि भेँड़ा सभक पाछा चाँगुर झाड़ि पड़ल। थोरबहि दीन में सभ भेँड़ऊ कें खाए गेल। सत्य अछि—

बेरी सदा धोखा देत अछि। ओ लोकनि गमार थिकाह, जे बेरी कें सत्यवादी बुझैछथि॥

सातम कथा।

बाघ, ऊँड़ार, आओर चित्ता।

एक बेरि बाघ, ऊँड़ार सभ, ओर चित्ता सभ अपना में ई ठहरौलक कि सभ मीलि कै शिकार मारी। फेरि अपना में बाँटि ली। ई ठानि कै जंगल में कूद फान करै लागल। आओर जखन एक बड़का टा कारी हरीन कें मारि लेलक, तखन बाघ बाजल कि, आबह, एकरा बाँटू, आओर झटद ओकर तीन खंड कै देलक, आओर गरजि कै बाजल कि, पहिल खंड हम लेब। किऐक तँ हम जंगलक राजा थिकऊँ। आओर दोसरो हम लेब। किऐक तँ हम एकरा मारबा में बहुत दौड़ धूप कैलें छी। आओर तेसर खंड ई घैल अछि। देखेछी ककर सक अछि जे हमरा सोझा सँ उठा लऽ जाएत। ई सूनि कें चित्ता आओर ऊँड़ार मौंगड़ि सुटकाए कँ पड़ाएल। आओर बाघ हरीन कें एकसरे खाए गेल। ई कहानी ठीक थीक

जकर लाठी तकर महीस।

आठम कथा।

माँटिक आओर पितड़क घैलक कथावार्त्ता।

एक बेरि कतऊ नदी चढ़लि, तँ एक पितड़क घैल आओर एक माँटिक घैल बहि चलल। पितड़क घैल माँटिक घैल सँ कहलक कि, हमरा संग लागल चलह, तँ हम तोहरा बचा लेबऊ। माँटिक घैल बाजल, ई अपने बहुत नीक कथा कहलें। हम अपनेक भल मानब आओर सदा गुन गाएब। परंतु सत्य पूछी, तँ हमरा ई डर अछि कि कतऊ पानिक लहरिक धक्का सँ अपनेक लग नहिं आ रही। किऐक तँ जौं अपने सँ फराक रहब, तौं एहिबा

हिलैत डुलैत बतङ्क मोर पर आए लागब। परंतु जौँ अपन॰ने सँ भेट भेल आओर बतङ्क चूकि सँ धक्का लागि गेल, तँ हम॰रो पेट फाटि जाएत। सत्य थीक

पैघ सबहि सँ आशा राखी, परंतु समीप नहिँ जाई ॥

नवम कथा।

एक मोन॰सी बजार मेँ बैसल चिट्ठी लिखैछल। एक बिदेशी आएल आओर बाजल, मोन॰सी जी, की लिखैछी। मोन॰सी उत्तर देल॰थीन्हि कि, भाइ चिट्ठी लिखैछी। ओ कहल॰कैन्हि हम॰रो* नमस्कार लिखि दिओन्हि। मोन॰सी कहल॰थीन्हि नहिँ हौ, अर्जी लिखैछी। ओ कहल॰कैन्हि तँ हम॰रो सही कै दिअ। मोन॰सी अगुताए कँ बज॰लाह कि, तम॰सुक लिखैछी। ओ बाजल हम॰रो गोआही लिखि दिअ। मोन॰सी बुझ॰लक ई तँ केओ अपूर्व ढंगक लोक देख पड़ैअछि। पुछल॰थीन्हि अहाँक नाम की थीक। ओ हँसल आओर बाजल, हमर नाम थीक

मानह, न हँ मानह, हम तोहर पाहुन।

दसम कथा।

एक पैघ लोकक घर मेँ रातिक समय आगि लागि गेलैन्हि। ओ तँ अपन नेना भुट॰का सभ सहित बह॰राए पड़ैलाह। आओर चाकर सभ कैँ हुकुम देलन्हि जे बस्तुजात निकासह। एत॰बा मेँ आगि बड़त छिरिआए† गेल। सौँसो घर धुआँ धाह भै गेल। चाकर सभ बाजल जे, हम की की निकासू। तखन ओ भल॰मानुस ठंढा साँस भरि बाजल, बाबा।

आगि लागल झोँप॰ड़ी, जे निक॰से, से लाभ।

एगार॰हम कथा।

एक अमारि‡ गोआरिनि माथ पर मट॰कुरी धैलैँ चलि जाइछलि। चलैति २ ओक॰रा मन मेँ ई तरंग उठ॰लै कि, हँ एहि दही कैँ बेचब॰गः आओर कंचा सब॰हि सँ आम कीनि लेब। ओरेक आम हम॰रा संग अछि, सभ मिलाए कँ तीनि से सँ किछु बढ़ि जाएत। एहि मेँ किछु सड़ि पचि जाएत। परंतु अढ़ाइ से तँ बच॰लो रहत। आओर ओहि मेँ सँ जे बाँचल निक॰सत, ओहि सभक नीक दाम भेँटत। तौँ दीवारी मेँ एक हरिअर साड़ी लेब। हँ हँ हरिअर साड़ी हम॰रा मुँह पर नीक खुलत। आओर बस, हम तँ हरिअरे साड़ी लेब, आओर

* हमरो is emphatic for हमर, 'of me also.' † Also खिड़ि गेल। ‡ Also गमैया.

ओकःरा पहिरि कँ मेला मेँ जाएब, आओर खूब अकड़ि अथन गहःना कपःड़ाक सुनरःताई आओर मुँहक चमक चिमक देखाएब। आओर एक २ आलि मैँ से २ बेरि झुकब। एहि सोच बिचार मेँ ओ गमैआ गोआरिनि जैह किछु चमक दिमक कैं टेढ़ि आलि चललि तँ मटःकुरी माथ सँ खसि टुकःरी २ भै गेलैक। आओर समःरो बनल बनाओल बर बिगड़ि गेल।

बारःहम कथा।

चिलःहोरि आओर कौआ।

एक चिलःहोरिक लोल मेँ एक घोँघा* छलै। कतेक भूमि पर दै दै पटःकलक परंतु घोँघा नहि फूटल। तखन एक कौआ ई रास्ता बतौलःकै जे एहि डोँका कँ लोल मेँ लैकँ बहुत ऊपर उड़ि जाउ, आओर ओतय सँ खसाए दैह तौँ डोँका फूटि जैतःऊ। चिलःहोरि बुझःलक जे ई बहुत नीक कथा अछि, आओर डोँका कँ लैकँ उड़लि। आओर बहुत ऊपर जाए कँ छाड़ि देलक। जैह डोँका धरःती पर खसल, टूक २ भै गेल। आओर कौआ ओकर गुदा खाए गेल। थोरःवा काल मेँ चिलःहोरि नीचा उतःरलि तँ खुँदुआ छाड़ि किछु नहिँ पौलक।

तेरःहम कथा।

अम्मत अंगूर।

एक खिखिरि कोनो फलःवारी मेँ जाए पड़लि†। देखःलक जे अंगूर सभक एहन गुच्छ सभ पाकल टट्टी मेँ लटःकि रहल अछि, कि जकःरा सँ रस चूबि रहल अछि। औ कोनो रखःवारो नहिँ अछि। ई देखि ओकःरा मुँह मेँ पानि भरि ऐलै। बहुतो उछिलछि कूदलि, परंतु अंगूर सभक गुच्छ लग नहिँ पहुँच सकलि। जखन कोनो तरःहेँ हाथो नहिँ लगःलै तखन ओ एना बड़ःबड़ाइति ओतय सँ चललि कि—

अम्मत अंगूर के खाओ।

चौदःहम कथा।

रसायनी।

एक रसायनी कोनो मनुष्य सँ कहःलक कि, जौँ तोँ किछु चानी हमःरा ओतय लै आबह, तँ हम एक एहन जड़ी मारी कि लगःले ओहि चानीक सोन भै जाय। ओ सोझ साझ मनुष्य ओकःरा दाओ मेँ आबि गेल। आओर कतःऊ सँ दुख सुख सहि दुर से रुपैआक

---

* Or डोँका।   † Also जाए निकःसलि।

चाँनी ओहि रसायनी कैँ आनि देल॰कै। रसायनी ओहि राति कँ ओछाओन उठाए कँ कत॰ऊ चलैत भेल। आब ओ बेचारा बिपत्तिक मारल ओहि कपन्टी रसायनीक खोज मैँ दौड़ धूप करै लागल। जंगल २ तक॰लक। परंतु ओहि रसायनीक कतऊ ठेकान नहिँ लागल। ओकरा एहि तर॰हेँ बब॰ड़ाएल देखि कँ एक मनुष्य कहल॰कै कि तोह॰रा सँ ई चूकि भेल॰ऊ जे ओहि कपन्टी अलौकिक जाल मैँ बभ॰लाह। परंतु आब पछ॰ताएब आओर ओक॰रा तक॰बा मेँ दौड़ धूप कैला सँ किछु नहिँ हैत। एहि कथा पर हम तोह॰रा एक कहिनी सुन॰बैछिअऊ, जक॰रा सभ दीन मन रखिअह।

पंद्॰हम कथा।

एक चड़ै कोनो गृहस्तक फुल॰बाड़ी मैँ जाए कँ. काँच पाकल फल सभ॰टा काटि जाइति छलि। गृहस्त सदा ओक॰रा ताक मैँ छल। एक दीन अंगूरक टाट पर जाल लगाए कँ ओक॰रा धैलक आओर मारै चाह॰लक। चड़ै गृहस्त सँ कह॰लक कि, जौँ तोँ हम॰रा छाड़ि दैह, तखन हम एहि उपकारक बद॰ला तोह॰रा कैएक कथा सभ सिखाए दिअऊ, कि जाहि मैँ तोह॰रा बड़॰का लाभ हैत॰ऊ। गृहस्त कह॰लक कि, तोँ पहिलेँ सिखाए दैह, तखन हम तोह॰रा छाड़ि देब। चड़ै ओक॰रा तीन कथा कहल॰कैक। एक तँ ई जे बेरी अपन॰ना बस मेँ आबि जाए, तोँ छाड़ैक नहिँ चाही। दोसर जे कथा ध्यान मेँ नहिँ आबे, ओ नहिँ मानै बूझि। तेसर गेल बस्तुसभक लेल पछ॰तैबाक नहिँ चाही। आओर चारिम एक कथा आओर अछि कि जखन तोँ हम॰रा छाड़ि देबह, तखन कह॰बऊ। गृहस्त एहि कथा सभ कैँ सुनि, जेह कहल॰कै से कैलक। आओर ओ ओहि चड़ै कैँ छाड़ि देलक। तखन चड़ै भीति पर बैसि कँ कह॰लक कि हम॰रा पेट मेँ मुर्गीक अंड॰ऊ सँ पैघ एक मोती छल। जौँ तोँ हम॰रा नहिँ छाड़ितह आओर मारि दितह, तखन ओ मोती तोह॰रा हाथ लगैत। गृहस्त पछताबै लागल। ओ कह॰लक, रे गमार, तोँ हमर तीनू कथा एखन॰हि बिस॰रि गेलेँ। किऐक हम तोहर बैरी छलिअऊ। जखन धै लेलेँ* छलेँ तखन छाड़ब की रहौ। आओर मुर्गीक अंडाक बराबरि तँ हम॰हिँ नहिँ छी। फेरि मुर्गीक अंडा सभ सँ पैघ मोती हम॰रा पेट मेँ हैब कहिआ ध्यान मेँ आबि सकैअछि। परंतु तोँ एहि कथा पर भरोसा कैलह। आओर आब जौँ हम तोह॰रा हाथ सँ निक॰सि गेलऊँ, तँ पछ॰तौला सँ की भै सकैअछि। एहि सँ ई फल बह॰राइअछि कि पूर्बहिँ सँ सभ काज कैँ बऊत सोच बिचाड़ि कै करैक चाही। आओर जौँ कोनो काज बिग॰ड़ि जाय तखन पछ॰तैबाक नहिँ चाही।

* Instead of लेलेँ, the vulgar would say लेनेँ or लेने.

सोड़हम कथा।

कोनो धनिक कैं दुइ बेटा रहैन्हि। जखन हुनक बाप मरि गेलथीन्हि तखन दूनू भाइ हुनक धन अपना में बाँटि लेलन्हि। जेठ भाइ अपन रुपैया पैसा सुख चैन आओर खेलि तमासा में उड़ावै लागल। आओर छोट भाइ बड्ड जतन सँ बनीज ब्यापार करै लागल। एक दीन जेठ भाइ छोट भाइ सँ हँसि हँसि कैं कहलथीन्हि कि, भाइ किऐक दीन भरि खट्ट तौल करैत रहैछह। हमरा संग रहह। खाह, पिबह, चैन करह। बहुत दीन पाछाँ, जखन छोटका भाइ लेन देन कैकैं बहुत रुपैया एकट्ठा कै लेलक, तखन ओकर जेठ भाइ जे रंग राग आओर खेलि तमासा में अपन सभ धन उड़ाए भिखारि भै गेल छल, ओकरा डेओढ़ी पर आबि कहै लागल कि, भाइ, हम तोहरा पहिलेँ हँसी से उड़ौने रहिअह। परंतु जौँ हमहुँ तोहरा जकाँ बनीज ब्यापार करितहुँ, आओर खट्ट तौलितहुँ तखन आइ पाओ भरि अन्न एम्हर ओम्हर सँ माँगि नहिँ लेतहुँ। सत्य अछि—

आलस्य एहन्ने कीरा अछि, जे धन कैँ चूरा कै देत अछि॥

सतरहम कथा।

लोभी कुकुर।

कोनो कुकुर नदीक तीर एक हाड़ पौलक, आओर मुँह में लेलक। जेँ ओकर परिछाँही पानि में देखलक, बूझलक कि दोसर हाड़ अछि। मारि लोभ सँ मुँह फोएलक कि ओकरहु पानि सँ बहार करी। ओ हाड़ जे मुँह मेँ रहैक; सेहो गमौलक। सत्य अछि

माछी बैसलि दूध पर पाँखि गेलै लपटाए।
हाथ, माँथ, मीड़ै, पिटै, लिप्सा मंद बलाए॥

TRANSLATION.

The following are primarily translations of the examples of Maithilí given above, but they will also serve as translations to the selections given at the end of the various Grammars of the series:—

Translation of a conversation between two villagers.

(1) Q. Tell me, brother, whence are you coming?

A. From the next village.

(2) Q. When did you start thence?
A. Early this morning.

(3) Q. Why did you go there?
A. I have some land there, and went to see it.

(4) Q. What is sown in it?
A. Only some *ráhaṛ*.

(5) Q. Tell me, brother, what are the prospects of this harvest?
A. Are you asking about this harvest? Why, there has been great loss for want of rain.

(6) Q. Your brother is not seen anywhere nowadays?
A. Nowadays he is at service in the fort. He comes here very seldom.

(7) Q. How is your big cow?
A. Nowadays she is in calf, but she has got very thin for want of food.

(8) Q. How many months is she gone in calf?
A. It's eight months, but she does not look big with young.

(9) Q. Are there any signs of pregnancy yet?
A. Yes, there are a few signs.

(10) Q. What calving of hers will this be? and how much milk does she give?
A. This is her eighth calving. She gives two or two and a half *seers* of milk at a time.

(11) Q. I want to get a goat: shall I find one in your village?
A. There are, indeed, goats in my village, but the prices are high.

(12) Q. What has become of your goat?
A. I have let it loose in the village to graze.

(13) Q. Does it give any milk?
A. Enough for the children's drinking.

(14) Q. Have you planted any sugarcane this year, or not?
A. I have, indeed, planted sugarcane, but there has been no produce.

(15) Q. Can I get on loan from your people a well-rope and leather bucket?
A. Why not? Take it any day when you want to irrigate.

(16) Q. How many buckets have you working?
A. There are three in use, irrigating.

(17) Q. Have your mango-trees borne fruit this year, or not?
A. This year, owing to the clouds, blight has attacked the trees, otherwise there would have been a great quantity (of fruit).

(18) Q. Will you give me a few mangos for pickles?
A. Whenever you want them, come and pluck them.

(19) Q. Does your son know how to read, or not?
A. Yes; I send him to the schoolmaster, and he has learnt his letters, and nowadays he is learning the multiplication table.

(20) Q. Why not send him to read at school?
A. Let him learn a little first, and then I'll send him.

(21) Q. I also want to send my boy to school.
A. Good: send him along with mine.

Translation of the Fables.

THE following are translations of the first seventeen lessons in Múnshí Rádhá Lál's Hindí Reader, Part II:—

FABLE I.

A COCK was scratching with his spurs on a dung-hill, when of a sudden a large pearl came out thereof. The cock said, "Ah! how lovely and brilliant it is. If a lapidary had found it, he would have been extremely pleased;* but the fire of my belly will not be extinguished with this. If one grain of rice had come to me, it would have been of more value than a hundred pearls. True it is that—

What is of no use to one, goeth into the oven."†

* In some versions, 'swollen with pleasure.'

† *Chúlhá* is a 'fireplace,' and *bhár*, *bhár*, or *bhāsár*, 'an oven.'

Fable II.

The Beggar's Question and the Pilgrim's Answer.

A beggar once asked a certain pilgrim, who had come to him, saying, "I am dying of hunger, and my neighbour lies upon pillows and cushions and night and day lives at ease. What are his virtues that the Giver has blessed him and made me a beggar?" When the pilgrim heard this he replied, "Sir, have you not heard this?—

Rám sitteth at an upper window and taketh cognizance of all,† and as each one's service is so he payeth him."*

Fable III.

A gentleman once asked a holy man, "Reverend sir, what is the benefit of wandering about from country to country and village to village? Why not revere the name of Rám in one place? Why not sit in some temple singing the goodness of the Giver?" The sage replied, "Sir, all this is true, but have you not heard this saying?—

Running water is clear, but confined water stinketh. Good men wander about and no taint affecteth them."

Fable IV.

One day, in the cold weather, a certain rich man's house took fire. All his goods and chattels were burnt and reduced to ashes. He stood outside wringing his hands,‡ when a poor neighbour, trembling and shivering with cold, came up and began to warm his hands (at the conflagration). Then the rich man said—

"*Wah, wah! one man's house burneth and another warmeth his hands!*"§

---

* In some versions simply 'on high.'

† *Muj'rá* is literally a kind of entertainment at which *nách* girls sing but do not dance. Here men's actions are compared to a *muj'rá*, of which Rám is represented as a spectator.

‡ In some versions 'lamenting.'

§ That is, 'what is one man's meat is another man's poison.'

Fable V.

Sticks in a faggot and sticks loosened.

The sons of a certain farmer used to quarrel amongst themselves. He remonstrated with them verbally, but none of them paid any attention to him. Then the farmer thought to himself that if he could explain to them by some action, they would certainly understand something.

One day he called* his sons, and told them to bring before him a few sticks. These sticks the farmer tied into a faggot with a string. Then he said to each (of his sons), "Do not open the string, but break the sticks." Each went at it with a will, but nothing came of it. Then the farmer untied the string and gave them the sticks one by one, which they broke immediately. Then their father said to them, "My sons, if you remain united like the faggot, you will set your adversaries' teeth on edge;† but if you separate, then know that you are ruined."

"*Separated is ruined.*"‡

Fable VI.

The Friendship between the Wolves and the Sheep.

Once upon a time the wolves sent word to the sheep, saying, "Come, let us make friends. Why should we fight amongst ourselves, and each remain thirsting for the blood of the other? These scoundrelly dogs are the root of the quarrel. They make us quarrel by their perpetual barking: send them all to us, and then what quarrel (can) there be? We shall always remain in love and friendship; not even a hair of you will be turned." The foolish sheep believed the words of these deceitful wolves, and sent the dogs to where the

---

* Maithilí *bajaulak*, causal of *bájal*, 'to speak,' just as in Hindi *buláná* is causal of *bolná*, 'to speak.'

† *Lit.* 'make them sour.' Some versions have 'your enemies will remain under your power.'

‡ That is, 'union is strength.'

wolves were staying. Well, first the wolves ate up all the dogs, and then fell with sharpened claws* upon the sheep. In a very few days they devoured all the sheep also.† True it is that—

> "*Enemies always deceive, and people are fools who believe that their enemy telleth the truth.*"

Fable VII.

Once upon a time a tiger, the wolves, and the hunting leopards, agreed amongst themselves to unite in a hunting expedition, and afterwards to divide (the) booty amongst themselves. Having thus agreed, they began to leap and spring in the forest, and killed a large black deer. Then the tiger said, "Come, let us divide it," and immediately dividing it into three parts said with a roar, "The first part I shall take, because I am king of the forest, and the second because I have spent much running and exertion in capturing it, and the third part I have placed here; let me see who is able‡ to take it up from before me." When the leopard and wolf heard this, they lowered their tails and ran away, and the tiger ate up the whole deer. This saying is true—

> "*Whose is the cudgel, his the buffalo.*"

Fable VIII.

The Conversation of the Earthen and Brass Pitchers.

Once upon a time somewhere a river rose, and an earthen pitcher and a brass one were floated away. The brass pitcher said to the earthen, "Come along close by me and I'll take care of you." The earthen said, "The words which you have spoken are excellent, and I shall always be grateful to you and sing your praises for them; but if you ask the truth, (I must confess to) this fear that from the motion of the waves I may perchance be knocked against you. Now, if I remain apart from you, while I am thus

* Other versions have, 'with washed hands,' *i.e.* 'eagerly.'

† *Hu*, in Maithil *bhẽṛ'hu*, means 'also.'

‡ This is the Maithil version. Other versions are, 'who will put forth his leg.'

washed hither and thither I will reach the bank somewhere; but if I meet you, and anywhere accidentally knock against you, my belly will be burst." True it is—

"Hope in the great, but go not near them."

Fable IX.

A scribe was sitting in the bazár writing a letter. Up came a stranger, who said, "Mr. Munshí, what are you writing?" The scribe replied, "Brother, a letter." The other said, "Send my compliments also." The scribe said, "No, I'm writing a petition." Said he, "Let me sign it too." Wearied at his importunity the scribe said, "It's a bond I'm writing." "Then," said he, "write me also down as a witness." The scribe thought to himself this is a queer kind of fellow, and asked him his name. The other laughed and said, "My name is—

* '*Whether you honour me or nay, still with you I mean to stay.*'"

Fable X.

A rich man's house once took fire by night. He escaped outside with his family, and told his servants to bring out his chattels. Just then the fire blazed up exceedingly, and the house became a mass of flames and smoke. His servants asked what special things they were to bring out, and he said with a deep† sigh—

"My men, when a hut's afire, whatever is saved is gain."

Fable XI.

An ignorant milkmaid was going along with a pot of curds upon her head. As she trudged along the pleasant idea came into her noddle, "I'll sell these curds; with the pice I get for them I'll buy some mangos. I have at home already a few mangos, and altogether there will be more

* That is, 'I am an importunate, but unwelcome guest.' The proverb is well known, and literally translated is '(whether) you honour me or do not honour me, I am still your guest.'

† *Lit.* cold.

than three hundred. Some of them will perhaps go bad, but at any rate I'll have two hundred and fifty, and for them I'll get a fine price. Then I'll buy a green *sári* at the *diwálí* festival. Yes, yes, a green *sári* will become my style of face beautifully. And then! I'll take it, and put it on for the fair, and step out proudly and show off the finery of my clothes and ornaments and the beauty of my face, bowing a hundred times at every step." As she imagined all these fine things, the foolish milk-maid in her stateliness gave a lurch, and the curd-pail fell from her head and was smashed to atoms, and all the fine castle* which she had built for herself was dissipated.

Fable XII.

The Kite and the Crow.

A kite once held a cockle in his beak, and kept knocking it against the ground, but it would not open. Then a crow showed him how to do it. "Fly up a great height with the cockle in your beak, and let it fall from there." The kite thought this excellent advice and flew up with the cockle, and when he had got very high up he let it go. The cockle fell to the earth and was immediately smashed in pieces. Thereupon the crow ate up the inside.† Shortly afterwards the kite came down, but could find nothing but the (broken pieces of) shell (and flew away).

Fable XIII.

Sour Grapes.

A fox one day found himself in a garden, and saw bunches of grapes hanging from the trellis so ripe that the juice was dripping from them. No one was even watching, and when he saw them his mouth filled with water. He jumped and leaped a great deal, but could not reach even near them. When in any way his efforts were not successful, he went away muttering—

"*Who eats sour grapes?*"

---

* *Lit.* 'house.'

† *Gúdá* is the edible interior of a fruit or shell-fish. Thus, the *gúdá* of a mango is the flesh as distinct from the stone or the rind.

Fable XIV.

The Alchemist.

An alchemist said to a certain man, "Do you bring to my house some silver, for I know a root so wonderful* that by merely extracting its juice the silver will straightway become gold." The simple fellow fell into the trap, and with all the trouble in the world got two hundred rupees in silver from somewhere, and brought them to the alchemist. The latter that very night took up his bed and departed thence. Then the unhappy fellow, stricken by misfortune, began to run everywhere in search of the cheating alchemist. He searched woods and forests, but nowhere could he find any trace of him. Seeing him thus distracted, a man said to him, "You have made one mistake in falling into the swindler's net, but now nothing will come of your lamenting and running hither and thither searching for him. On this account I'll tell you a story, which you must remember all your days." (And accordingly he told him)

Fable XV.

(*Sequel to the above Fable XIV.*)

A bird used to go into the garden of a certain farmer and break off his fruit, ripe and unripe. The farmer kept continually on the watch for it, and one day caught it in a net which he had fastened to a vine trellis, and proceeded to kill it. The bird said to him, " If you let me go, in return for the favour I will teach you certain things which will be of great use to you." The farmer said, " First teach me and then I'll let you go." The bird told him three things,—first, " When you have your enemy in your power, never let him go :" second, " When a thing is incredible, don't believe it :" and third, " Don't waste regrets on a thing that's gone for good :" " and," added he, " there is a fourth thing which I will tell you when you let me go." When the farmer heard this he did as he had promised, and let the bird go. It (flew away and) sat on the top of a wall and said, " In my belly there is a pearl as big as a hen's egg. If you had not let me go, but had killed me, you would have got it." Then the farmer began to regret

---

* *Lit.* " I extract (the juice from) such a root that the silver," &c.

(his kindness), and the bird went on to say, "You fool! You have already forgotten my three bits of advice; for I was your enemy. When you had caught me, why did you let me go? And I am myself not as big as a hen's egg; so how is it credible that a pearl bigger than me should be in my belly? Yet you fixed your hopes on what I said, and now that I have escaped from your hand what is the good of your regretting it?"

The moral* of this is that nothing should be done without previous great care and deliberation, and that when anything has gone wrong there is no good in regretting it.

Fable XVI.

A rich man had two sons. When their father died they divided his property between them. The elder brother wasted his money in pleasure and dissipation, and the younger began to work as a merchant with great energy. One day the elder brother ridiculed the younger, saying, "Brother, why do you spend the whole day weighing food? Come and live with me. Eat, drink, and enjoy yourself." Long afterwards, when the younger brother, by his traffic, had collected great wealth, the elder, who had wasted all his in dissipation, and who had become beggared thereby, came to his mansion and said, "Brother, I ridiculed you in sport formerly; but if, like you, I had traded and weighed out food, I would not to-day be eating myself a quarter of a *ser* of food begged here and there. True it is that—

"Idleness is a maggot that turneth wealth to dust."

Fable XVII.

The Greedy Dog.

A certain dog found a bone on the bank of a river, and took it up in his mouth. When he saw its reflection in the water he thought that it was another bone, and through greed opened his mouth to pick it out; but he lost the bone which was (really) in his mouth. True it is that—

"A fly sat upon milk and got its wings smeared therewith. He beateth his head and wringeth his hands, and saith, 'Greed is a great evil.'"

---

* *Lit.* 'the fruit comes out.'

Reg. No. 11866J—600—7-3-83.

SEVEN GRAMMARS

OF THE DIALECTS AND SUBDIALECTS OF THE

BIHÁRÍ LANGUAGE.

SPOKEN IN THE PROVINCE OF BIHAR, IN THE EASTERN PORTION OF THE NORTH-WESTERN PROVINCES, AND IN THE NORTHERN PORTION OF THE CENTRAL PROVINCES.

PART II.

BHOJPÚRÍ DIALECT

OF SHÁHABÁD, SÁRAN, CHAMPÁRAN, NORTH MUZAFFARPUR, AND THE EASTERN PORTION OF THE N. W. P.

Compiled under orders of the Government of Bengal.

By GEORGE A. GRIERSON, B.C.S.,
OFFG. JOINT-MAGISTRATE OF PATNA.

CALCUTTA:
PRINTED AT THE BENGAL SECRETARIAT PRESS.
1884.

CONTENTS.

DIVISION III.

INDECLINABLES.

APPENDIX I.

SELECTIONS IN THE BHOJPÚRÍ DIALECT.

APPENDIX II.

BHOJPÚRÍ SONGS.

INTRODUCTION.

§ 1. The following Grammar treats of the Bhojpúrí dialect as spoken in its purity in Sháhábád, Sáran, and Baliyá. It also deals with the dialect of Champáran and North Muzaffarpúr. In Champáran a tendency towards the Maithilí dialect is observed, which becomes still more marked in North Muzaffarpúr. In the latter tract, indeed, it is difficult to say decisively whether, say, near Sítámaṛhí, the dialect is Bhojpúrí strongly influenced by Maithilí or Maithilí strongly influenced by Bhojpúrí. In the present series of Grammars it has been found more convenient to treat it as the former. Bhojpúrí has a Western subdialect, spoken about A'zamgaṛh, Banáras, and Jaunpúr in the North-Western Provinces. This is the form of the dialect which is treated of by Dr. Hoernle in his Gauḍian Grammar and by Mr. J. R. Reid in the A'zamgaṛh Settlement Report. The main points of difference between this Western Bhojpúrí and the pure Bhojpúrí here treated of will be found noted in the following pages.

§ 2. The alphabet and rules for spelling will be found in the General Introduction to this series of Grammars, and the remarks therein found are not repeated here.

DIVISION I.

DECLENSION.

CHAPTER I.

NOUNS.

§ 3. For general remarks, see the General Introduction, § 38 and ff.

The following are the post-positions used in declining the noun in Bhojpúrí:—

		Power.
Nom.	*Wanting.*	
Acc.	*Wanting* or के *ke.*	
Instr.	सेँ, तेँ, संते, or करऽते, *sẽ*, *tẽ*, *sante*, or *kar'te.*	'By.'
Dat.	के *ke.*	'To.'
	ले, खातिर, लाग, or ला, *le*, *khátir*, *lág*, or *lá.*	'For.'
Abl.	सेँ or ले, *sê* or *le.*	'From.'
Gen.	क, के, or कै; का[1], *k*, *kĕ*, or *kaĭ*; *ká.*[1]	'Of.'
Loc.	मेँ, मोँ, *mẽ*, *mõ.*	'In.'
Voc.	*Wanting.*	

[1] क *k*, के *kĕ*, कै *kaĭ*, are direct terminations, used only before nouns in the direct form, and do not change for gender. का *ká* is an oblique termination, used only before nouns in the oblique form. It does not change for gender. क *k*, के *kĕ*, कै *kaĭ*, in fact, nearly correspond to the Hindí का *ká* (and की *kí*), while का *ká* nearly corresponds to Hindí के *ke* (and की *kí*). Further west, in Ázamgaṛh, Banáras, and Jaunpúr, the Hindí के *ke* is used instead of का *ká*.

All these post-positions will only be used in one example, that of घोड़ा *ghoṛá*, 'a horse;' but they can all be used with all nouns.

There are also special forms for the instrumental and locative singular, for the formation of which see § 6.

Except those for the genitive, they can also be used with all pronouns. In the genitive singular many pronouns do not take these post-positions, but have other forms having similar terminations, subject to the same rules.

The following are examples of declension :—

§.4. (a) Masculine Tadbhavas in आ *á*.

Example of the declension of a *tadbhava** masculine noun in आ *á* :–

घोड़ा *ghoṛá*, 'a horse.'

Short form, { Weak, घोड़ *ghoṛ*. Strong, घोड़ा *ghoṛá*. } Long form,† घोड़’वा *ghŏṛ'wá* or घोड़’वे *ghŏṛ'wē*. Redundant form, † घोड़ौवा *ghŏṛauwá*.

Singular.

Nom.	घोड़ा [1] *ghoṛá*,	'a horse.'
Acc.	घोड़ा *ghoṛá* or घोड़ा के *ghoṛá ke*,	'a horse.'
Instr.	घोड़ें *ghŏṛē*, घोड़ा सँ, तें, संते, or कर’ते, *ghoṛá sē*, *tē*, *sante*, or *kar'te*,	'by a horse.'
Dat.	घोड़ा के, or खातिर, लाग, ला, *ghoṛá ke*, or *khátir*, *lág*, *lá*,	'to' *or* 'for a horse.'
Abl.	घोड़ा सँ, ले, *ghoṛá sē*, *le*,	'from a horse.'
Gen.	घोड़क, घोड़ा के, or कै ; का, *ghoṛak*, *ghoṛá kĕ*, or *kaĭ* ; *ká*,[2]	'of a horse.'
Loc.	घोड़े *ghŏṛe*, घोड़ा मेँ, मोँ *ghoṛá mē* or *mō*,	'in a horse.'
Voc.	हे घोड़ा *he ghoṛá !* or हे घोड़ऊ *he ghŏṛaú !*	'O horse!'

[1] Or घोड़ *ghoṛ*, घोड़’वा *ghŏṛ'wá*, घोड़’वे *ghŏṛ'wē*, or घोड़ौवा *ghŏṛauwá*, and so throughout the singular.

[2] घोड़क *ghoṛak*, घोड़ा के *ghoṛá kĕ*, and घोड़ा कै *ghoṛá kaĭ*, do not change for gender, and are only used as direct genitives; घोड़ा का *ghoṛá ká* is only used as an oblique genitive. This distinction is, however, seldom observed by the uneducated. So also in the plural.

---

* See General Introduction, § 12. † See General Introduction, §§ 12, 38, and ff.

Plural.

Nom.	घोड़न[1] *ghoṛan*,	'horses.'
Acc.	घोड़न *ghoṛan*, घोड़न के *ghoṛan ke*,	'horses.'
Instr.	घोड़न सँ, तेँ, संते, or कर॰ते, *ghoṛan sẽ, tẽ, sante,* or *karte*,	'by horses.'
Dat.	घोड़न के, or खातिर, लाग, ला, *ghoṛan ke*, or *khátir, lág, lá*,	'to' or 'for horses.'
Abl.	घोड़न सँ, ले, *ghoṛan sẽ, le*,	'from horses.'
Gen.	घोड़नक, घोड़न के, or कै; का, *ghŏranak, ghoṛan kĕ*, or *kaĭ; ká*,[2]	'of horses.'
Loc.	घोड़न मेँ, मोँ *ghoṛan mẽ, mõ*,	'in horses.'
Voc.	हे घोड़न *he ghoṛan !*	'O horses!'

[1] Or घोड़न्ह *ghoṛanh*, घोड़नि *ghŏṛani*, or घोड़॰वन (-न्ह) *ghŏṛ'wan* (*-nh*) or घोड़ौवन (-न्ह) *ghŏrauwan* (*-nh*), and so throughout the plural. In Sáran and Champáran an optional non-honorific form of the plural ends in स॰ *sa* : thus घोड़ास॰ *ghoṛása*, घोड़ास॰ के *ghoṛása ke*, घोड़ास॰ सँ *ghoṛása sẽ, &c.*

[2] See note [2] to singular.

§ 5. (b) Masculine Nouns ending in Silent Consonants.

Example of the declension of a masculine noun ending in a silent consonant:—

घर *ghar*, 'a house.'

Short form, घर *ghar*. Long form,* घर॰वा *ghar'wá* or घर॰वेँ *ghar'wẽ*. Redundant form,* घरौवा *gharauwá*.

Singular.

Nom.	घर[1] *ghar*,	'a house.'
Acc.	घर, घर के *ghar, ghar ke*,	'a house.'
Instr.	घरेँ *gharẽ*, or घर सँ *ghar sẽ, &c.*,	'by a house.'
Dat.	घर के, or खातिर *ghar ke* or *khátir, &c.*,	'to' or 'for a house.'
Abl.	घर सँ *ghar sẽ, &c.*,	'from a house.'
Gen.	घरक *gharak*, घर के or कै; का *ghar kĕ* or *kaĭ; ká*,	'of a house.'
Loc.	घरे *ghare ;* or घर मेँ *ghar mẽ, &c.*,	'in a house.'
Voc.	हे घर *he ghar !*	'O house!'

[1] Or घर॰वा *ghar'wá*, घरौवा *gharauwá*, and so throughout the singular.

---

* See General Introduction, §§ 12, 38, and ff.

Plural.

Nom.	घरन [1] *gharan,*	'houses.'
Acc.	घरन *gharan* or घरन के *gharan ke,*	'houses.'
Instr.	घरन सेँ *gharan sẽ, &c.,*	'by houses.'
Dat.	घरन के or खातिर *gharan ke* or *khátir, &c.,*	'to' *or* 'for houses.'
Abl.	घरन सेँ *gharan sẽ, &c.,*	'from houses.'
Gen.	घरनक, घरन के, कै; का, *gharanak, gharan kĕ, kaĭ; ká,*	'of houses.'
Loc.	घरन मेँ *gharan mẽ, &c.,*	'in houses.'
Voc.	हे घरन *he gharan !*	'O houses!'

[1] Or घरन्ह *gharanh,* घरनि *gharani,* घरन्वन (-न्ह) *ghar'wan (-nh),* घरौवन (-न्ह) *gharauwan (-nh),* and so throughout the plural.

§ 6. It is not necessary to decline further any nouns in full, as the above examples suffice. All nouns ending in vowels are declined like घोड़ा *ghoṛá,* and all those ending in silent consonants like घर *ghar.*

NOET, however, that—

(1) Occasionally in the singular we find an instrumental in ऐं *ē* and a locative in ए *e*: thus हम बलेँ ले जाइब *ham balẽ le jáib,* 'I shall take away by force,' where बलेँ *balẽ* is the instrumental of बल *bal,* 'force;' घटे *ghaṭe,* 'at a landing stage,' locative of घाट *gháṭ,* 'a landing stage:' so also घरे घरे *ghare ghare,* 'in every house,' 'from house to house.' When the noun ends in आ *á* or in silent अ *a,* the final vowel is elided before these terminations: thus घोड़ा *ghoṛá,* 'a horse,' has its instrumental घोड़ेँ *ghŏṛẽ,* and घर *ghar,* its locative घरे *ghare.** Nouns ending in other long vowels shorten them before these terminations: thus from माली *máli, instr.* मलियेँ. (See Genl. Intr., § 36, as to the shortening of the first syllable, and § 34 as to the insertion of euphonic य् *y.*)

* If the word contains a long vowel, it is shortened in these cases, as in घटे *ghaṭe,* above mentioned. Other examples are दनेँ *danẽ,* instrumental दाना of *dáná,* 'grain,' and रजेँ *rajẽ* of राजा *rájá,* 'a king.'

Nouns ending in other short vowels are very rare, and I have never met instances of these terminations in their case. These terminations are most common in the case of nouns which, like घर *ghar*, are masculine and end in silent अ *a*. In Western Bhojpúrí the instrumental ends in अन *an;* e.g. डरन *ḍaran*, 'through fear,' भूखन *bhúkhan*, 'by hunger,' घामन *gháman*, 'by heat,' from डर *ḍar*, भूख *bhúkh*, and घाम *ghám* respectively.

(2) All nouns ending in a long vowel shorten it before the plural termination न *n*, न्ह *nh*, or नि *ni*, and in the genitive in क *k*, but preserve it long in the other forms of the genitive: thus घोड़न *ghoṛan*, घोड़क *ghoṛak*, but घोड़ा के *ghoṛá kĕ*, घोड़ा कै *ghoṛá kaĭ*, &c.

(3) Certain verbal nouns ending in ल *l* have an oblique form in ला *lá:* thus देखल *dekhal*, abl. देखला सँ *dĕkh'lá sē*, 'from seeing;' also verbal nouns in the form of the root have an oblique form in ए *ĕ:* thus देख *dekh*, dat. देखे ला *dekhĕ lá*, 'for seeing.' Full particulars concerning these nouns will be found in § 111.

(4) The final syllables of all long forms and redundant forms may optionally be nasalised by the addition of *anunásik:* thus घोड़वा *ghŏṛ'wá* or घोड़वाँ *ghŏṛ'wā̃;* घरौवा *gharauwá* or घरौवाँ *gharauwā̃;* मलिया *maliyá* or मलियाँ *maliyā̃*.

An example of each of the more common forms of nouns follows:—

§ 7. (c) Masculine Tatsamas* in आ *á*.

राजा *rájá*, 'a king.'

Short form, राजा *rájá*. Long form,* रजवा *raj'wá* or रजवेँ *raj'wē̃*. Redundant form,* रजौवा *rajauwá*.

* See General Introduction, §§ 12, 38, and ff., 34 and ff.

Gen. sing. राजक *rájak*, राजा के, का, *rájá kĕ, ká, &c.*
Instr. sing. रजेँ *rajē, &c.*
Loc. sing. रजे *raje, &c.*
Nom. plur. राजन, राजन्ह, *rájan, rájanh, &c.* Also in Sáran and Champáran राजासन *rájása.*

§ 8. (d) Masculine Nouns in ई *í.*

माली *málí,* 'a gardener.'

Short form, माली *málí.* Long form,* मलिया *maliyá* or मलियेँ *maliyē.* Redundant form,* मलियवा *maliyawá* or मलीवा *malíwá.*

Gen. sing. मालिक *málik*, माली के, का, *málí kĕ, ká, &c.*
Instr. sing. मलियेँ *maliyē, &c.*
Loc. sing. मलिये *maliye, &c.*
Nom. plur. मालिन, मालिन्ह, *málin, málinh, &c.* Also in Sáran and Champáran मालीसन *málisa.*

§ 9. (e) Masculine Nouns in ऊ *ú.*

नाऊ *náú,* 'a barber.'†

Short form, नाऊ *náú.* Long form,‡ नउआ *naüá* or नौआ *nauá*, नउएँ *naüē* or नौएँ. Redundant form,‡ नउअवा *naüawá* or नौअवा *nauawá.*

Gen. sing. नाउक *náük*, नाऊ के, का, *náú kĕ, ká, &c.*
Instr. sing. नौएँ *nauē, &c.*
Loc. sing. नौए *naue, &c.*
Nom. plur. नाउन, नाउन्ह, *náün, náünh, &c.* Also in Sáran and Champáran नाऊसन *náúsa.*

---

* See General Introduction, §§ 12, 38, and ff., 34 and ff.

† Kellogg in his Hindí Grammar incorrectly gives आँसू *ãsú* as an example of a feminine noun in ऊ. It is masculine. आँसू *ãsú* is not used in Bihárí, लोर *lor* being the word for 'a tear.'

‡ See General Introduction, §§ 12, 38, and ff., and 34 to 36.

§ 10. (f) Feminine Nouns in ई *í*.

पोथी *pothí*, 'a book.'

Short form, पोथी *pothí*. Long form,* पोथिया *pŏthiyá* or पोथियँ *pŏthiyĕ*.
Redundant form,* पोथियवा *pŏthiyawá* or पोथीवा *pŏthíwá*.
Gen. sing. पोथिक *pothik* or पोथी के, का, *pothí kĕ, ká, &c.*
Instr. sing. पोथियँ *pŏthiyĕ, &c.*
Loc. sing. पोथिये *pŏthiye*.
Nom. plur. पोथिन, पोथिन्ह, *pothin, pothinh, &c.* Also in Sáran and Champáran पोथीसठ *pothísa*.

§ 11. (g) Feminine Nouns ending in a Silent Consonant.

बात *bát*, 'a word.'

Short form, बात *bát*. Long form,* बतिया *batiyá* or बतियँ *batiyĕ*.
Redundant form,* बतियवा *batiyawá* or बतीवा *batíwá*.
Gen. sing. बातक *bátak* or बात के, का *bát kĕ, ká, &c.*
Instr. sing. बतँ *batĕ, &c.*
Loc. sing. बते *bate, &c.*
Nom. plur. बातन *bátan*, बातन्ह, *bátanh, &c.* Also in Sáran and Champáran बातसठ *bát'sa*.

§ 12. Periphrastic Plural.

With reference to the above plural forms, it must be noted that every noun can also form a periphrastic plural by the addition of a word signifying plurality, such as सभ *sabh*, 'all;' or, in the case of *rational* beings, such as लोग *log*, 'people.' Example: घर सभ *ghar sabh* instead of घरन *gharan*, and माली लोगक *málí logak* for मलिनक *malinak*. Sometimes even this plural affix is omitted, so that a plural noun appears under a singular form. An example occurs in the ninth of the following sentences, where बेटा *beṭá* is used for बेटा सभ *beṭá sabh*. This is the regular rule when a numeral adjective

* See General Introduction, §§ 12, 38, and ff., and 34 and 36.

precedes, as in Nos. 6 and 7 of the following sentences. Sometimes these plural affixes are added pleonastically to a word already in the usual form, *e.g.* **पोथिन सभ** *pothin sabh* for **पोथिन** *pothin.*

§ 13. Genitival Affixes.

The following examples have been specially designed to exhibit the use of the genitival affixes. As above pointed out, **-क** *-k*, **के** *kĕ*, and **कै** *kaĭ*, are direct terminations, while **का** *ká* is an oblique termination.

1. **ई राजा के मंदिर बाटे** (or **हवे**.) *Í rájá kĕ mandir báṭe* (or *hawe.*)	'This is the king's temple.'
2. **हम कन्स के लौंड़ी हवीं.** *Ham Kans kĕ lãũṛí hawí.*	'I am the maid-servant of King Kans.'
3. **मधुमाछिन**[1] **के झूँड़ उड़ गइल.** *Madhumáchhin*[1] *kĕ jhũṛ uṛ gaïl.*	'A swarm of bees flew away.'
4. **कपटी का मारला**[2] **के कुछुवो दोख नाहीं.** *Kap'ṭí ká már'lá*[2] *kĕ kuchhuwŏ dokh náhí.*	'There is no sin in slaying a deceiver.'
5. **मथुरा के मेहररुअन**[3] (nom. plur. of **मेहररुआ**, long form of **मेहरारू**) **रोअत चल गइली.** *Mathurá kĕ mĕh'raruan*[3] (nom. plur. of *mĕh'raruá*, long form of *mĕh'rárú*) *roat chal gaïlí.*	'The women of Mathurá departed weeping.'
6. **हर रंगक बात सुनल गइल.** *Har raṅgak bát sunal gaïl.*	'Matters of many kinds were heard.'
7. **असफटिक के चार गो फाटक टूट गइल.** *As'phaṭik kĕ chár go pháṭak ṭúṭ gaïl.*	'Four gates of crystal broke.'

[1] In Sáran and Champáran optionally **मधुमखीसन** *madhumakhisa.*

[2] **मारला** *már'lá* is the oblique form of the verbal noun **मारल** *máral* (see § 6, 3, and § 109). With regard to the long vowel in the antepenultimate, see General Introduction, § 36, exc. 1.

[3] In Sáran and Champáran optionally **मेहरारूसन** *mĕh'rárúsa.* In Sháhábád, optionally, **मेहरारू . . . . गइली सन** *mĕh'rárú . . . . gaïlí sa.*

CHAPTER II.

ADJECTIVES.

§ 14. Gender.

See General Introduction, § 42 and ff.

§ 15. Numeral Adjectives.

The cardinals are nearly the same as those in High Hindí. The following are the ones that present points of difference :—

1, एक *ĕk* or एगो *ego.*	73, तिहंतर *tihantar.*
2, दो *do* or दू *dú.*	74, चौहंतर *chaŭhantar.*
6, छो *chho.*	75, पछंतर *pachhantar.*
9, नो *no.*	76, छिहंतर *chhihantar.*
15, पन॰रह *pan'rah.*	77, सतंतर *satantar.*
16, सोरह *sorah.*	78, अठंतर *aṭhantar.*
71, एकंतर *ĕkantar.*	89, नोआसी *nŏásí.*
72, बहंतर *bahantar.*	10,000,000, कड़ोर *kaṛor* or करोड़ *karoṛ.*

§ 16. Ordinals.

The ordinals up to 'sixth' are as follows :—

1st, पहिल *pahil ; obl.* पहिला *pahilá* or पह॰ला *pah'lá.**
2nd, दोसर *dosar ; obl.* दोस॰रा *dŏs'rá.**
3rd, तेसर *tesar ; obl.* तेस॰रा *tĕs'rá.**
4th, चौठ *chauṭh.*
5th, पाँचों *pắchō̃.*
6th, छठों *chhaṭhō̃* or छठ॰वाँ *chhaṭh'wắ.*

* The first three ordinals follow pronominal genitives in the formation of oblique forms. See *post,* § 34.

The ordinals above 'sixth' are all formed by adding वाँ *wā́* or ओँ *ō* to the cardinals: as दसन्वाँ *das'wā́* or दसोँ *dasō*, 'tenth;' पचासन्वाँ *pachás'wā́* or पचासोँ *pachásō*, 'fiftieth.'

§ 17. Fractional Numbers.

These are—

¼, पाव *páw*, पौआ *pauá*.
⅓, तेहाई *těhái*.
½, अधिया *adhiyá*.
¾, or —¼, पौने *gaune*, गँउठ *gãüṭh*.
1¼, or +¼, सवाँ *sawā́*, सवाई *sawái*.
1½, डेढ़ *ḍeṛh*.
2½, अढ़ाइ *aṛhái*, अढ़ैया *aṛhaiyá*.
+½, साढ़े *sáṛhe*.

§ 18. Multiplicatives.

Multiplicatives, such as the English 'twice' and 'thrice,' are not found in this dialect. The Bihárí idiom is illustrated in such phrases as दू सते चौदह *dú sate chaudah*, 'two seven's, fourteen;' छो तीया अठारह *chho tíyá aṭhárah*, 'six three's, eighteen,' which correspond to the English idioms 'seven times two' and 'three times six.' Numbers thus used are called multiplicatives, and differ in some respects from the cardinals. The following are the multiplicative numbers up to 10, including fractions:—

× 1, एक्काँ *ěkkā́*.
× 1¼, सवा *sawá*, सवैया *sawaiyá*.
× 1½, ड्योढ़ा *ḍyoṛha*.
× 2, दूना, *dúná*, दूनी *dúní*, दोबरी *dobarí*, दूगुना *dúguná*.
× 2½, अढ़ाई *aṛhái*, अढ़ैया *aṛhaiyá*.
× 3, तीया *tíyá*, तीना *tíná*.
× 3½, हुंठा *hunṭhá*, हुठा *huṭhá*.
× 4, चौक *chauk*, चौका *chauká*, चौके *chauke*.
× 4½, ढौँचा *dhaũchá*, धौँचा *dhaũchá*.

× 5, पचे *pache*, पंचे *panche.*
× 5½, पहुंचा *pahunchá.*
× 6, छट्ठे *chhaṭṭhe*, छक्का *chhakká*, छक *chhak.*
× 6½, खौँचा *khãũchá.*
× 7, सते *sate.*
× 8, अट्ठे *aṭṭhe.*
× 9, नवाँई *nawãí.*
× 10, दहाँई *dahãí.*

§ 19. Definite Cardinals.

These are as follows :—

दुन्नो *dunno*, दूओ *dúo*, 'the two,' 'both ;'
तीनो *tíno*, 'the three ;'
चारो *cháro*, 'the four ;' and so on,

adding ओ *o* to the numerals, after omitting a final short vowel. Example: पाँचो भाई जौरे हथ *pãcho bhái jaure hath*, 'the five brothers are an undivided family.'

§ 20. Indefinite Cardinals.

The termination ओ *o* or ओँ *õ* added to the numbers 'one hundred,' 'one thousand,' and so on, always denotes an indefinite number of these aggregates. In this idiom सव *saw* is always substituted for सौ *sau*, 'one hundred.' Examples are सवो पेड़ *sawo peṛ*, 'hundreds of trees ;' हजारो *hajáro*, 'thousands ;' लाखो *lákho*, 'tens of thousands ;' हजारोँ अद्‌मी मर्‌लन *hajárõ ad'mí mar'lan*, 'thousands of men died.'

§ 21. Collective Numerals.

These—viz. जोड़ा *joṛá*, 'a pair,' गंडा *gaṇḍá*, 'a four,'—are the same as in High Hindí. NOTE also पन *pan*, 'twenty *gaṇḍás*,' 'four score.' In selling cow-dung fuel a पन *pan* equals 22 or 23 *gaṇḍás*, according to locality. In selling mangos, the word गाही *gáhi*, 'a five,' is used.

CHAPTER III.

PRONOUNS.

§ 22. The following tables show the declensional forms of the principal pronouns and pronominal forms.

The declension of pronouns presents some important points of difference from that of nouns, which must be carefully noticed.

While nouns frequently remain unchanged before post-positions, pronouns, with few exceptions, change to some other form, called the *oblique* or *inflected base*.

The accusative singular of pronouns is, with one or two exceptions, never the same as the nominative. The only exception is कछु *kuchhu*, 'anything,' 'some thing.' In circumstances corresponding to those in which the accusative of a noun takes the nominative form, the accusative of a pronoun takes the oblique form without any post-position.

The genitive form of pronouns ending in र *r* is also to be noticed. The genitive forms in रा *rá* and री *rí* have only been noted near Patna City. रा *rá* is used before masculine nouns without restriction of case, and री *rí* before feminine nouns. Other genitive forms not ending in र *r* can be used before any noun in any gender or case. (See § 34.)

Pronouns have the same form, whether referring to masculine or feminine nouns. With the exception of the pronouns of the second person, they all want the vocative case.

§ 23. Pronouns of the First Person and of the Second Person Non-Honorific.

These pronouns have each two forms, a shorter and a longer.

हम *ham*, 'I.'

Singular.

	Shorter form.	*Longer form.*
Nom.	*Wanting.*	हम *ham.*
Acc.	मोरा [1] *morá* or मोरा के *morá ke.*	हमरा [1] *ham'rá* or हमरा के *ham'rá ke.*
Instr.	मोरा सँ *morá sẽ.*	हमरा सँ *ham'rá sẽ.*
Dat.	मोरा लेल *morá lel.*	हमरा लेल *ham'rá lel.*
Abl.	मोरा सँ *morá sẽ.*	हमरा सँ *ham'rá sẽ.*
Gen.	मोर, or मोरा, मोरी *mor*, or *morá*, *morí* (*fem.*)	हम्मर, हमार, or हमरे; हमरा,[2] हमरी : *hammar*, *hamár*, or *ham'rĕ*; *ham'rá*[2], *ham'rí* (*fem.*)
Loc.	मोरा मेँ *morá mẽ.*	हमरा मेँ *ham'rá mẽ.*
Voc.	*Wanting.*	*Wanting.*

[1] मोरो *moro* and हमरो *ham'ro* may be used for मोरा *morá* and हमरा *ham'rá* in an emphatic sense: thus हमरो दऽ *ham'ro da*, 'give to me also.'

[2] A form हमरे *ham're* is sometimes used round about Patna, equivalent to, and borrowed from, the Hindí हमारे *hamáre*: *e.g.* हमरे बेटा सँ कहऽ *ham're beṭá sẽ kaha*, equalling Hindí हमारे बेटे से कहो *hamáre beṭe se kaho*, 'tell my son.'

Plural.

	Shorter form.	*Longer form.*
Nom.	हमनी [1] *hamaní.*	हमरनी [2] *ham'raní.*
Acc.	हमनी (के) *hamaní (ke).*	हमरनी (के) *ham'raní (ke).*
Instr.	हमनी सँ *hamaní sẽ.*	हमरनी सँ *ham'raní sẽ.*
Dat.	हमनी लेल *hamaní lel.*	हमरनी लेल *ham'raní lel.*
Abl.	हमनी सँ *hamaní sẽ.*	हमरनी सँ *ham'raní sẽ.*
Gen.	हमनी के, केर, or केरा, केरी *hamaní kĕ, ker*, or *kerá, kerí.*	हमरनी के, केर, or केरा, केरी *ham'raní kĕ, ker* or *kerá, kerí.*
Loc.	हमनी मेँ *hamaní mẽ.*	हमरनी मेँ *ham'raní mẽ.*
Voc.	*Wanting.*	*Wanting.*

[1] Or हमनिन्ह *ham'ninh*, हमनिन *ham'nin*, or हम सब *ham sab*, and so throughout.

[2] Or हमरन्ही *ham'ranhí*, हमरन्ह *ham'ranh*, हमरन *ham'ran*, or हमरा सब *ham'rá sab*, and so throughout.

तोँ *tõ* or तूँ *tú*, 'thou.'

Singular.

	Shorter form.	*Longer form.*
Nom.	तोँ or तूँ *tõ* or *tū̃*.	तोँ *tõ* or तूँ *tū̃*.
Acc.	तोरा,[1] तोरा के *torá* or *torá ke.*	तोहरा[1] or तोहरा के *tŏh'rá* or *tŏh'rá ke.*
Instr.	तोरा सेँ *torá sẽ.*	तोहरा सेँ *tŏh'rá sẽ.*
Dat.	तोरा लेल *torá lel.*	तोहरा लेल *tŏh'ra lel.*
Abl.	तोरा सेँ *torá sẽ.*	तोहरा सेँ *tŏh'rá sẽ.*
Gen.	तोर, or तोरा, तोरी *tor* or *torá, torí* (*fem.*)	तोहर, तोहार *or* तोहरे; तोहरा,[2] तोहरी, *tohar, tŏhár,* or *tŏh'rĕ; tŏh'rá, tŏh'rí* (*fem.*)
Loc.	तोरा मेँ *torá mẽ.*	तोहरा मेँ *tŏh'rá mẽ.*
Voc.	हे तोँ *he tõ* or हे तूँ *he tū̃.*	हे तोँ *he tõ* or हे तूँ *he tū̃.*

[1] तोरो *toro* and तोहरो *tŏh'ro* may be used for तोरा *torá* and तोहरा *tŏh'rá* in an emphatic sense: thus तोहरो देखैँ ही *tŏh'ro dekhĕ hí*, 'I see you also.'

[2] A form तोहरे *tŏh're* is sometimes used round about Patna, equivalent to, and borrowed from, the Hindí तुम्हारे *tumháre*: *e.g.* तोहरे बेटा सेँ कहैँ ही *tŏh're beṭá sẽ kahĕ hí*, equalling Hindí तुम्हारे बेटे से कहता हूँ *tumháre beṭe se kah'tá hū́*, 'I speak to your son.'

Plural.

	Shorter form.	*Longer form.*
Nom.	तोहनी[1] *tŏhani.*	तोहरनी[2] *tŏh'rani.*
Acc.	तोहनी (के) *tŏhani* (*ke*).	तोहरनी (के) *tŏh'rani* (*ke*).
Instr.	तोहनी सेँ *tŏhani sẽ.*	तोहरनी सेँ *tŏhrani sẽ.*
Dat.	तोहनी लेल *tŏhani lĕl.*	तोहरनी लेल *tŏh'rani lel.*
Abl.	तोहनी सेँ *tŏhani sẽ.*	तोहरनी सेँ *tŏh'rani sẽ.*

[1] Or तोहनिन्ह *tŏh'ninh*, तोहनिन *tŏh'nin*, तोहनियाँ *tŏh'niā̃* (long form), or तूँ सब *tū̃ sab*, and so throughout.

[2] Or तोहरन्ही *tŏh'ranhí*, तोहरन्ह *tŏh'ranh*, तोहरन *tŏh'ran*, or तोहरा सब *tŏh'rá sab*, and so throughout.

Gen.	तोहनी के, केर, or केरा, केरी, *tŏhaní kĕ, ker,* or *kerá, kerí.*	तोह॰रनी के, केर, or केरा, केरी, *tŏh'rani kĕ, ker,* or *kerá, keri.*
Loc.	तोहनी मेँ *tŏhaní mē.*	तोह॰रनी मेँ *tŏh'raní mē.*
Voc.	हे तूँ सब *he tū̃ sab.*	हे तूँ सब *he tū̃ sab.*

§ 24. Pronoun of the Second Person Honorific and Reflexive Pronoun.

आप *ap*, or अपने *ap'nĕ*, 'your honour,' 'self.'

Singular.

Nom. अपने[1] *ap'nĕ*, or आप *áp*.
Acc. अपने (के) *ap'nĕ* (*ke*), or आप (के)[1] *áp* (*ke*).
Instr. अपने सँ *ap'nĕ sē.*
Dat. अपने लेल *ap'nĕ lel.*
Abl. अपने सँ *ap'nĕ sē.*
Gen. अपने के *ap'nĕ kĕ, &c.*, or (reflexive only) अप्पन *appan*, आपन *ápan*.
Loc. अपने मेँ *ap'ne mē.*
Voc. *Wanting.*

Plural.

Nom. अपने सब *ap' nĕ sab*, or आप सब[1] *áp sab*.
Acc. अपने सब (के) *ap'nĕ sab* (*ke*).
Instr. अपने सब सँ *ap'nĕ sab sē.*
Dat. अपने सब लेल *ap'nĕ sab lel.*
Abl. अपने सब सँ *ap'nĕ sab sē.*
Gen. अपने सब के *ap'nĕ sab kĕ.*
Loc. अपने सब मेँ *ap'nĕ sab mē.*
Voc. *Wanting.*

[1] आप *áp* may be used for अपने *ap'nĕ* throughout the singular and plural. Another form of the plural is अपनन *ap'nan* or अपनन्हि *ap'nanhí* throughout all cases.

In the west of the district रौआँ *rauā̃*, plural रौअन्ह *rauanh*, is also used in the sense of 'your honour.'

§ 25. Demonstrative Pronouns.

These are (1) the proximate demonstrative ई *í*, 'this,' and (2) the remote demonstrative ऊ *ú*, 'that.'

Like the personal pronouns, they have each two forms, a shorter and a longer.

ई *í*, 'this.'

Singular.

	Shorter form.	*Longer form.*
Nom.	ई *í*.	ई *í*.
Acc.	एह (के) *ĕh* (*ke*).	एक॰रा (के) *ĕk'rá* (*ke*).
Instr.	एह सँ *ĕh sē*.	एक॰रा सँ *ĕk'rá sē*.
Dat.	एह लेल *ĕh lel*.	एक॰रा लेल *ĕk'rá lel*.
Abl.	एह सँ *ĕh sē*	एक॰रा सँ *ĕk'rá sē*.
Gen.	एह के, केर, &c., *ĕh kĕ, ker, &c.*	एकर *ekar*, एक॰रा,-री *ĕk'rá,-rí*.
Loc.	एह मँ, *ĕh mē*.	एक॰रा मँ *ĕk'rá mē*.

Plural.

Nom.	ई[1] *í*.	इन्ह॰कनी[2] *inh'kaní*.
Acc.	इन्ह (के) *inh* (*ke*).	इन्ह॰करा[3] (के) *inh'kará* (*ke*).
Instr.	इन्ह सँ *inh sē*.	इन्ह॰करा सँ *inh'kará sē*.
Dat.	इन्ह लेल *inh lel*.	इन्ह॰करा लेल *inh'kará lel*.
Abl.	इन्ह सँ *inh sē*.	इन्ह॰करा सँ *inh'kará sē*.
Gen.	इन्ह के, केर, &c., *inh kĕ, ker, &c.*	इन्ह॰कर *inh'kar*, इन्ह॰करा,-री *inh'kará,-rí*.
Loc.	इन्ह मँ *inh mē*.	इन्ह॰करा मँ, *inh'kará mē*.

[1] ई (सब) *í* (*sab*), इन्ह (सब) *inh* (*sab*), इन्हन (सब) *inhan* (*sab*), इन्हनी (सब) *inhaní* (*sab*), in which the word सब *sab* may be optionally omitted, and इख॰निन *ikh'nin*, अख॰नी *akh,ní* or एख॰नी *ĕkh'ní*, may all be used throughout the plural instead of ई *í* or इन्ह *inh*.

[2] Or इन्ह॰कन्ही *inh'kanhí*.

[3] Other oblique forms are इन॰करा *inh'kará*, इन्ह॰का *inh'ká*, or इन॰का *in'ká*; so also in the genitive, omitting the final long vowel.

ऊ *ú*, 'that.'

The close analogy between the declension of this pronoun and that of ई *í*, 'this,' will be manifest from the following paradigm:—

Singular.

	Shorter form.	*Longer form.*
Nom.	ऊ *ú*.	ऊ *ú*.
Acc.	ओह (के) *ŏh* (*ke*).	ओकऽरा (के) *ŏk'rá* (*ke*).
Instr.	ओह सँ *ŏh sẽ*.	ओकऽरा सँ *ŏk'rá sẽ*.
Dat.	ओह लेल *ŏh lel*.	ओकऽरा लेल *ŏk'rá lel*.
Abl.	ओह सँ *ŏh sẽ*.	ओकऽरा सँ *ŏk'rá sẽ*.
Gen.	ओह के, केर, *&c.*, *ŏh kĕ, ker, &c.*	ओकर *okar*, ओकऽरा,-री *ŏk'rá,-rí*.
Loc.	ओह मेँ *ŏh mẽ*.	ओकऽरा मेँ *ŏk'rá mẽ*.

Plural.

Nom.	ऊ[1] *ú*.	उन्हऽकनी[2] *unh'kaní*.
Acc.	उन्ह (के) *unh* (*ke*).	उन्हऽकरा[3] (के) *unh'kará* (*ke*).
Instr.	उन्ह सँ *unh sẽ*.	उन्हऽकरा सँ *unh'kará sẽ*.
Dat.	उन्ह लेल *unh lel*.	उन्हऽकरा लेल *unh'kará lel*.
Abl.	उन्ह सँ *unh sẽ*.	उन्हऽकरा सँ *unh'kará sẽ*.
Gen.	उन्ह के, केर, *&c.*, *unh kĕ, ker, &c.*	उन्हऽकर, उन्हऽकरा,-री *unh'kar*, *unh'kará,-ri*.
Loc.	उन्ह मेँ *unh mẽ*.	उन्हऽकरा मेँ *unh'kará mẽ*.

[1] ऊ (सब) *ú* (*sab*), उन्ह (सब) *unh* (*sab*), उन्हन सब *unhan* (*sab*), उन्हनी (सब) *unhaní* (*sab*), in which the word सब *sab* may be optionally omitted, and उखऽनिन *ukh'nin* or ओखऽनी *ŏkh'ní* may all be used throughout the plural instead of ऊ *ú* or उन्ह *unh*.

[2] Or उन्हऽकन्ही *unh'kanhí*.

[3] Other oblique forms are उनऽकरा *un'kará*, उन्हऽका *unh'ká*, or उनऽका *un'ká*; so also in the genitive, omitting the final long vowel.

NOTE.—In the above two demonstrative pronouns, the shorter form may be used either adjectivally or substantivally; but the longer form can only be used as a substantive, and never as an adjective.

§ 26. Correlative Pronouns.

These are (1) the relative pronoun जे *je*, 'who;' (2) the correlative pronoun से *se*, 'that;' and (3) the interrogative pronoun के *ke*, 'who?'

The close analogy between their forms will best be shown by printing them in parallel columns. Like the personal and demonstrative pronouns, they have each a shorter and a longer form.

It is not necessary to give their declension in full, as it is on exactly the same lines as that of the demonstrative pronouns. I shall therefore give only the nominative, genitive, and general oblique forms for each number.

§ 27. Interrogative Pronoun.

SUBSTANTIVAL.

का *ká* or की *kí* 'what?'

This pronoun is really a neuter form of के *ke*, and can only refer to inanimate things. The form की *kí* is peculiar to South-East Patna. का *ká* can only be used as a substantive. Its plural is the same as that of के *ke*.

Singular.

		Optional Gayá forms.
Nom.	का *ká* or की *kí*.	कौँची *kaũchí*.
Acc.	काहे के *káhĕ ke*.	कौँची के *kaũchí ke*.
Instr.	काहे सेँ *káhĕ sẽ*.	कौँची सेँ *kaũchí sẽ*.
Dat.	काहे ला *káhĕ lá*.	कौँची ला *kaũchi lá*.
Abl.	काहे सेँ *káhĕ s* .	कौँची सेँ *kaũchí sẽ*.
Gen.	काहे के, केर, *káhĕ kĕ, ker, &c.*	कौँची के, *kaũchí kĕ, &c.*
Loc.	काहे मेँ *káhĕ mẽ*.	कौँची मेँ *kaũchí mẽ*.

§ 28. Indefinite Pronoun.

केऊ *kĕú*, 'anyone,' 'some one.'

When used as an adjective, this pronoun takes also the form कौनोँ *kaunõ* or कउनोँ *kaünõ*.

Singular.

Nom.	केऊ *kĕú*, कोई *koí*, or केहू *kehú*.
Acc.	केकरो के *kĕkarŏ ke* or कौनोँ* (के) *kaunõ ke*.
Instr.	केकरो सेँ *kĕkarŏ sẽ* or कौनोँ सेँ *kaunõ sẽ*.
Dat.	केकरो के *kĕkarŏ ke* or कौनोँ के *kaunõ ke*.
Abl.	केकरो सेँ *kĕkarŏ sẽ* or कौनोँ सेँ *kaunõ sẽ*.
Gen.	केकरो *kĕkarŏ* or कौनोँ के *kaunõ kĕ, &c.*
Loc.	केकरो मेँ *kĕkarŏ mẽ* or कौनोँ मेँ *kaunõ mẽ*.

Plural.—*Wanting.*

---

* कौनेँ *kaunẽ*, or कोई *koí*, or केहू *kehú*, and so throughout.

§ 29. The indefinite pronoun कुछु *kuchhu*, कुच्छो *kuchchhŏ*, or कुच्छओ *kuchchhaŏ*, 'anything,' 'something,' is declined regularly like a substantive: thus, कुच्छो के *kuchchhŏ ke*, कुच्छो सँ *kuchchhŏ sẽ*, &c.

§ 30. The indefinite pronoun सब *sab*, 'all,' 'every one,' is declined regularly like a substantive. It is frequently written सभ *sabh*. When plurality is to be emphasised, it has an oblique plural form सबन *saban* or सभन *sabhan*: thus, सभ के *sabh kĕ*, 'of all,' *taken as a whole*; but सभन के *sabhan kĕ*, 'of all,' *taken severally*.

§ 31. The indefinite pronouns जेकेउ *jekĕú*, 'whoever,' and जेकुच्छो *jekuchchhŏ*, 'whatever,' are compounds, and are declined regularly like their component parts: thus acc. sing. जेह केकरो *jĕh kĕkarŏ*, जेह कुच्छो *jĕh kuchchhŏ*; instr. जेह केकरो सँ *jĕh kĕkarŏ sẽ*, &c.

The indefinite pronominal adjective कइक *kaik* signifies 'several.'

§ 32. Derivative Pronominal Forms.

The following table gives the more usual pronominal adjectives and adverbs in a succinct form.

§ 33. Adjectival Pronouns.

The following sentences are designed to show the use of the various pronouns, both adjectivally and substantivally. Before doing so it is best to note here that colloquially the oblique forms एह *ĕh*, ओह *ŏh*, जेह *jĕh*, तेह *tĕh*, and केह *kĕh*, are frequently written and pronounced ए *e*, ओ *o*, जे *je*, ते *te*, and के *ke* respectively :—

(1) जे आएल हल, से गेल, *je áĕl hal, se gel :* 'he who had come, went.'

(2) जे जन आएल हल, से गेल, *je jan áĕl hal, se gel :* 'the man who had come, went.'

(3) जेकर खेत, तेकर धान, *jekar khet, tekar dhán :* 'he who owns the field, owns the paddy.'

(4) जेह (or जे) जन के खेत, तेह जन के धान, *jĕh* (or *je*) *jan kĕ khet, tĕh jan kĕ dhán :* 'the man who owns the field, owns the paddy.'

(5) के हल *ke hal ?* 'who was it ?'

(6) ऊ कउन लोक हइ *ú kaün lok haï ?* 'what caste is he ?'

(7) केकर घोड़ा हइ *kekar ghoṛá haï ?* 'whose is the horse ?'

(8) की हइ *kí haï*, or की हकइ *kí hakaï*, or का हइ, *ká haï ?* 'what is it ?'

(9) कउन पेड़ हइ *kaün peṛ haï ?* 'what tree is it ?'

(10) काहें में पानी लइलन्हू है *káhĕ mē pání laïl'hú hai ?* 'in what have you brought the water ?'

(11) कउन लोटा में पानी लइलन्हू है *kaün loṭá mē pání laïl'hú hai ?* 'in what *loṭa* have you brought the water ?'

(12) केऊ न० अइलइ *kĕú na aïlaï*, 'no one came.'

(13) केऊ (or कौनों) लड़िका न० अइलइ *kĕú* (or *kaunō*) *laṛiká na aïlaï*, 'no boy came.'

(14) ऊ गाँव में केकरो कुछु न० हइ *ú gāw mē kĕkarŏ kuchhu na haï*, 'in that village no one has anything.'

(15) ऊ गाँव के कउनों बनिया सें कुछु न० मिली *ú gāw kĕ kaünō baniyá sē kuchhu na mili*, 'in that village nothing will be got from any shopkeeper.'

(16) ऊ दवाई के कुच्छो में धरे के* होई *ú dawái ke kuchchhŏ mẽ dharĕ ke** *hoi*, 'it will be (necessary) to put that medicine into something.'

(17) कईक मर्‌दाना अइल्‌थिन *kaík mar'dáná aïl'thin*, 'several men came.'

§ 34. On the Pronominal Oblique Genitive.

The following are examples of pronominal genitives which end in र *r* or न *n*, and which have an oblique form ending in रा *rá* or ना *ná*. These oblique forms occur for all pronominal genitives ending in र *r*, and are used with nouns in any form except that of the nominative singular or plural:—

Direct Genitive.	Meaning.	Oblique form.
मोर *mor.*	'My.'	मोरा *morá.*
हम्मर *hammar.*	'My.'	हम्‌रा *ham'rá.*
तोर *tor.*	'Thy.'	तोरा *torá.*
तोहर *tohar.*	'Thy.'	तोह्‌रा *tŏh'rá.*
अप्पन *appan.*	'Own.'	अपना *ap'ná.*
एकर *ekar.*	'Of this.'	एक्‌रा *ĕk'rá.*
ओकर *okar.*	'Of that,' 'his.'	ओक्‌रा *ŏk'rá.*
जेकर *jekar.*	'Whose.'	जेक्‌रा *jĕk'rá.*
तेकर *tekar.*	'His.'	तेक्‌रा *tĕk'rá.*
केकर *kekar.*	'Whose?'	केक्‌रा *kĕk'rá.*

The following examples will show the use of the genitive in—(*a*) its direct form, (*b*) its oblique form.

* Dative of the verbal noun.

a.—GENITIVES AGREEING WITH NOUNS IN THE NOMINATIVE FORM, *i.e.* DIRECT GENITIVES.

ओकर मौगी कइसन बेस ! हइ *okar maugí kaïsan bes ! haï* 'how beautiful his wife is!'

केकर बेटा हइ *kekar beṭá haï ?* 'whose son is he?'

हम्मर धंधा बिगड़त *hammar dhandhá big'ṛat,* 'my profession will be ruined.'

ओकर रोइब सुन के *okar roib sun kĕ,* 'on hearing her lamentations.'

ओकर इकरार लिखऽ *okar ik'rár likha,* 'write a bond to that effect' (*lit.* of that).

अप्पन सब धनवाँ लुटा कर गरीब हो गेलइ *appan sab dhan'wā̃ luṭá kar garíb ho gĕlaï,* 'having wasted all his substance he became poor.'

b.—GENITIVES AGREEING WITH NOUNS NOT IN THE NOMINATIVE FORM, *i.e.* OBLIQUE GENITIVES.

ओकरा चढ़े के घोड़ा *ŏk'rá chaṛhĕ kĕ ghoṛá,* 'his riding-horse' (*lit.* the horse of his riding).

ऊ ओकरा फुलवारी में आएल *ú ŏk'rá phul'wárí mē áĕl,* 'he came into *his* (some one else's) garden.'

हमरा सरकी में *ham'rá sar'kí mē,* 'in my hovel.'

तोहरा घरे में *tŏh'rá gharĕ mē,* 'in your house.' तोरा हथवा से *torá hath'wá se,* 'from thy hand.'

हमरा दरवाजा से ओकर दरवाजा बाँस भर अलग हइ *ham'rá dar'wájá sē okar dar'wájá bā̃s bhar alag haï,* 'his doorway is a rod distance from mine.'

किसनवा अपना जिया मे कहलकइ *kisan'wá ap'ná jiyá me kahal'kaï,* 'the husbandman said in his heart.'

These oblique genitives must not be confounded with the Patna genitives in रा *rá* and री *rí*, mentioned in § 22. Sometimes, by the vulgar, the direct form is used instead of the oblique, but the oblique form is never used instead of the direct.

DIVISION II.

CONJUGATION.

CHAPTER IV.

INTRODUCTORY.

§ 35. It must be noted with respect to the following paradigms that colloquially the plural is commonly used in the place of the singular: thus तोँ हउ *tô ha*, 'thou art,' is commonly used instead of तोँ हही *tõ hahi*, which is the more correct form.

Note also that there is great laxity colloquially in regard to gender. The forms given for the feminine are only those which are specially confined to that gender; but instead of these, the masculine forms are often used colloquially. In the following paradigms when the masculine and feminine forms coincide, the latter are not given.

§ 36. With regard to the spelling of the various tense forms, it must be noted that अइ *aï* and अउ *aü* are frequently written ऐ *ai* and औ *au* respectively: thus such forms as देखन्तइ *dĕkh'taï* and देखन्तउ *dĕkh'taü* are often written देखन्तै *dekh'tai* and देखन्तौ *dekh'tau*. It has not boon thought necessary to put both these varieties of spelling into the paradigms: hence only देखन्तइ *dĕkh'taï*, देखन्तउ *dĕkh'taü*, &c., will be found therein. With regard to this and to the shortening of antepenultimate vowels, see General Introduction, §§ 34 – 37.

§ 37. Conjugational System.

The conjugation of the verb √ देख *dekh*, 'see,' being given in full, it is not necessary to give here the details of conjugation at length.

§ 38. There are three moods—the Indicative, Conjunctive, and Imperative. These may again be divided into *simple tenses*—formed from the root direct, and *periphrastic tenses*—formed with the aid of auxiliary verbs added to the verbal noun (in its oblique form), or the present or past participle, or to the conjugated preterite indicative.

§ 39. The *simple tenses* are as follows :—

INDICATIVE.	CONJUNCTIVE.	IMPERATIVE.
Preterite.	Present.	Present.
Future.	Preterite.	

Of these, the present imperative is always the same as the present conjunctive.

§ 40. The *periphrastic tenses* are as follows :—

a) From the oblique form of the verbal noun—

Indicative—

Indefinite present.
Indefinite preterite.

In these tenses the verbal noun is really in the locative case: thus हम देखे हो *ham dekhĕ hí*, 'I see,' means 'I am on seeing,' *i.e.* the vulgar English 'I am a-seeing.' These tenses are formed with the present and imperfect tenses of the defective auxiliary verb.

b) From the present participle, direct form—

Indicative—

Definite present with	auxiliary	present.
Imperfect	,,	preterite.
Durative future	,,	future.

Conjunctive—

Future with auxiliary present conjunctive.
Durative present „ preterite „

c) From the past participle: direct form in the neuter verb, oblique form in the active verb—

Indicative—

Future exact with auxiliary future.

Conjunctive—

Future exact with auxiliary present conjunctive.
Preterite „ preterite.

d) From the preterite indicative—

Indicative—

Perfect with auxiliary present.
Pluperfect „ preterite.

Concerning the use of the auxiliary in tenses formed from the past participle, see General Introduction, p. 13, cl. (4).

§ 41. The Simple Tenses.

The personal terminations of all these tenses are as follows. They are (with a few exceptions, which will be found in the paradigms) nearly the same for all tenses. They are added to a tense-stem, the formation of which will be described afterwards.

It will be observed that there are many optional forms of terminations for each person. They are all used with nearly equal frequency. They should be carefully committed to memory.

Table showing the Personal Terminations.

Person.	Singular.		Plural.	
	Masculine.	Feminine.	Masculine.	Feminine.
1st	ऊँ ū́.	इयोँ iyõ.	ई í, ईँ ī́.	इयोँ iyŏ.
			इअइ iaï, इअउ iaü.	
2nd	अँ ã, ऐँ ẽ.		अ a, हू hú.	ई í, ऊ ú.
	आ á, ए e, अइ aï.	ईँ ī́.	हूँ hū́, हुन hun, हो ho.	
	ही hí.		हीँ hí, हिन hin.	
3rd	ए e.		ईँ ī́, इन in.	
	अइ aï, अउ aü.		अथ, थी, थिन, ath, thí, thin.	थीन thín, थिनी thiní.
	कइ kaï, कउ kaü.		थू thú, थुन thun.	
	अस as.		ही hí, हिन hin.	
			खिन khin *.	खीन, खिनी. khín,* khiní.*

§ 42. These terminations are added to various tense-stems, and it is by these tense-stems that the tenses are distinguished. The tense-stems are formed as follows:—

§ 43. The Preterite Indicative.

The stem of this tense is formed by adding अल *al* to the root. Thus √ देख *dekh*, 'see,' preterite stem देखल *dekhal*, to which the terminations are added: thus देखलूँ *dĕkh'lū́*, 'I saw.' This tense has this peculiarity in the

* These terminations are much used by Kayasth women.

second and third persons, that it adopts special terminations for active and others for neuter verbs: thus active देखिस *dekhis* or देखलकइ *děkhal'kaï*, 'he saw,' but neuter गिरल *giral* or गिरलइ *gir'laï*, 'he fell.'

§ 44. The Future Indicative.

The stem of this tense is formed by adding अब *ab* to the root. Thus देखब; second person देखबें *děkh'bẽ*, 'thou wilt see.' The personal terminations in the first person are slightly altered in this tense, and the third person is not formed from the stem in अब *ab* at all, but is formed by adding the following terminations to the root direct:—

Future.

Person.	Singular.		Plural.	
	Masculine.	Feminine.	Masculine.	Feminine.
3rd	ई *i*. अत *at*. तइ *taï*, तउ *taü*.	ती *ti*.	इहें *ihẽ*. तन *tan*. अथ, थी, थिनी, *ath, thi, thiní*. थुन *thun*. खिन *khin*. अतथी *at'thi*, &c.	तिन *tin*. थीन *thín*, थिनी *thiní*. खीन *khín*, खिनी *khiní*. अतथीन *at'thín*, &c.

§ 45. The Present Conjunctive and Imperative.

In this tense the terminations are added to the root itself: thus, देखूँ *dekhũ*, 'let me see.'

§ 46. The Preterite Conjunctive.

In this tense अत *at* or इत *it* is added to the root. The personal terminations are then added: thus देखतूँ *děkh'tũ*, '(if) I had seen.'

CHAPTER V.

AUXILIARY VERBS.

§ 47. There are two classes of auxiliaries, the defective and the complete.

§ 48. There is one defective auxiliary verb formed from the √ अह *ah*, 'be.' It has a few optional forms, derived from a strengthened form of the above, viz. √ हक *hak*. The defective auxiliary verb is only used in the present and preterite tenses. In conjugation this root loses its initial अ *a*.

§ 49. The complete auxiliary verb is formed from the √ हो *ho*, 'become,' and is conjugated regularly throughout. Its preterite, however, is never used as an auxiliary, but only as a verb substantive. In the west of Gayá forms occur derived from the √ होख *hokh*. These, however, are properly Bhojpurí forms, and being found in the Sháhábád Grammar are not given here.

§ 50. Defective Auxiliary Verbs.

√ अह *ah*, 'be.'

There are only two tenses—the present and the preterite; the rest are borrowed from the complete verb √ हो *ho*, 'become.' Some forms of the present tense are formed from a strengthened form of the root, viz. √ हक *hak*.

NOTE that throughout the initial vowel अ *a* of the root has disappeared.

§ 51. Present: '*I am,*' *&c.*

Person.	Singular.		Plural.	
	Masculine.	Feminine.	Masculine.	Feminine.
1st	ही *hí.* हकी *hakí*, हिकूँ *hikű.*	हियौँ *hiyõ.*	ही, हीं, *hí, hí.* हिअइ, हिअउ, *hiaï, hiaü.*	हियौँ *hiyõ.*
2nd	हँ, हेँ, *hã, hẽ.* हे, है, हही, *he, hai, hahí.*	हीँ *hí.*	हऽ *ha.* हहू, हहूँ, हहुन, हहो, *hahú, hahű, hahun, haho.* हहीँ, हहिन, *hahí, hahin.* हकीँ, हकिन, *hakí, hakin.*	ही *hí.*
3rd	हइ, हउ, हे, हो, हऽ, हँ, *haï, haü, he, ho, ha, hã.* हस *has.* हकइ, हकउ, *hakaï, hakaü.*		हईँ, हइन, *haí, haïn.* हथ, हथी, हथिन, *hath, hathí, hathin.* हथू, हथुन, *hathú, hathun.* हहीँ, हहिन, हखिन, *hahí, hahin, hakhin.**	हथीन, हथिनी, *hathín, hathiní.* हखीन, हखिनी, *hakhín, hakhiní.*

* Forms such as this, containing ख *kh*, are much used by Kayasth women.

§ 52. Preterite: '*I was,*' *&c.*

Person.	Singular.		Plural.	
	Masculine.	Feminine.	Masculine.	Feminine.
1st	हलूँ *halū́.*		हली, हलीँ, *halī, halī́.* हलिअइ, हलिअउ, *haliaï, haliaü.*	
2nd	हलाँ, हलेँ, *halā̃, halẽ.* हला, हले, *halá, hale.* हल॰ही *hal'hī.*	हलीँ *halī́.* हली *halī.*	हल॰ *hala.* हल॰हू, हल॰हूँ, हल॰हुन. *hal'hú, hal'hū́, hal'hun.* हल॰हो, *hal'ho.* हल॰हीँ, हल॰हिन, *hal'hī́, hal'hin.*	हली, हलू, *halī, halú.*
3rd	हल, हलइ, हलउ *hal, halaï, halaü.*	हली *halī.*	हलन *halan.* हल॰थी, हल॰थिन, हल॰थुन, *hal'thí, hal'thin, hal'thun.* हल॰हीँ, हल॰हिन, *hal'hī́, hal'hin.* हल॰खिन, *hal'khin.*	हलिन *halin.* हल॰थीन, हल॰थिनी, *hal'thīn, hal'thinī.* हल॰खीन, हल॰खिनी, *hal'khīn, hál'khinī.*

§ 53. The Complete Auxiliary Verb.

√ हो *ho*, '*be*,' '*become*.'

INDICATIVE MOOD.

(*a*)—Preterite: '*I became*,' *&c.*

Form I.

Person.	Singular. Masculine.	Singular. Feminine.	Plural. Masculine.	Plural. Feminine.
1st	होलूँ* *holú.*		होली, होलीं, *holí, holí.* होलिअइ, होलिअउ, *hŏliaï, hŏliaü.*	
2nd	होलँ, होलेँ, *holã, holẽ.* होला *holá.* होलऽही *hŏl'hí.*	होलीं *holí.* होली *holí.*	होलऽ *hola.* होलऽहू, होलऽहूँ, होलऽहुन, *hŏl'hú, hŏl'hú̃, hŏl'hun.* होलऽहो, *hŏl'ho.* होलऽहीं, होलऽहिन, *hŏl'hí, hŏl'hin.*	होली, होलू, *holí, holú.*
3rd	होल, होलइ, होलउ, *hol, hŏlaï, hŏlaü.*	होली *holí.*	होलन *holan.* होलऽहीं, होलऽहिन, *hŏl'hí, hŏl'hin.* होलऽथी, होलऽथिन, होलऽथुन *hŏl'thí, hŏl'thin, holthun.* होलऽखिन *hŏl'khin.*	होलिन *holin.* होलऽथीन, -थिनी, *hŏl'thín,-thiní.* होलऽखीन, -खिनी, *hŏl'khín, -khiní.*

* Or होइलूँ *hŏilú*, and so throughout.

NOTE.—This tense is never used as an auxiliary, but only as a verb substantive.

There is also an irregular form of this tense, which is as follows:—

Form II.

Person.	Singular.		Plural.	
	Masculine.	Feminine.	Masculine.	Feminine.
1st.	भेलूँ *bhelű.*		भेली, भेलीँ, *bhelī, bhelí.* भेलिअइ, भेलिअउ, *bhĕliaï, bhĕliaü.*	
2nd.	भेलँ, भेलेँ, *bhelā, bhelē* भेला *bhelá.* भेलऽही *bĕhl'hi.*	भेलीँ *bhelí.* भेली *bhelí.*	भेलऽ *bhela.* भेलऽहू, भेलऽहूँ, भेलऽहुन, *bhĕl'hú, bhĕl'hű, bhĕl'hun.* भेलऽहो, *bhĕl'ho.* भेलऽहीँ, भेलऽहिन, *bhĕl'hí, bhĕl'hin.*	भेली, भेलू, *bhelí, bhelú.*
3rd.	भेल, भेलइ, भेलउ, *bhel, bhĕlaï, bhĕlaü.*	भेली *bhelí*	भेलन *bhelan.* भेलऽहीँ, भेलऽहिन, *bhĕl'hī, bhĕl'hin.* भेलऽथी, भेलऽथिन, भेलऽथुन, *bhĕl'thi, bhĕl'thin, bhĕl'-* [*thun.* भेलऽखिन *bhĕl'khin.*	भेलिन *bhelin.* भेलऽथीन, भेलऽथिनी, *bhĕl'thin, bhĕl'thiní.* भेलऽखीन, भेलऽखिनी, *bhĕl'khín, bhĕl'khiní.*

§ 54. (*b*)—Future: '*I shall be,*' *&c.*

Person.	Singular.		Plural.	
	Masculine.	Feminine.	Masculine.	Feminine.
1st	होब, * होबइ, होबउ, *hob, hŏbaï, hŏbaü.*		होब, होबइ, होबउ, *hob, hŏbaï, hŏbaü.*	होबी *hobí.*
2nd	होबँ, होबेँ, *hobã, hobẽ.*	होबीँ *hobī́.*	होबऽ *hoba.*	होबी, होबू, *hobí, hobú.*
	होबा, होबे, *hobá, hobe.*	होबी *hobí.*	होब॰हू, होब॰हूँ, होब॰हुन, *hŏb'hú, hŏb'hū́, hŏb'hun.*	
	होब॰ही *hŏb'hí.*		होब॰हो, होब॰हीँ, होब॰हिन, *hŏb'ho, hŏb'hī́, hŏb'hin.*	
			होइहऽ *hoiha.*	
3rd	होई *hoi.*		होइहेँ *hoihẽ.*	
			होथ, होथी, होथिन, होथुन, *hoth, hothí, hothin, hothun.*	होथीन, होथिनी, *hothín, hŏthiní.*
			होखिन *hokhin.*	होखीन, होखिनी, *hokhín, hŏkhiní.*
	होत, होतइ, होतउ, *hot, hŏtaï, hŏtaü.*	होती *hotí.*	होतन *hotan.*	होतिन *hotin.*
			होत॰थी, होत॰थिन, होत॰थुन, *hot'thí, hŏt'thin, hŏt'thun.*	होत॰थीन, होत॰थिनी, *hŏt'thín, hŏt'thiní.*

* होअब *hoab,* होइब *hoib,* or होएब *hoëb,* may be written throughout for होब *hob,* and होथ *oth* for होथ *hoth,* and होअत *hoat* or होइत *hoit* for होत *hot.*

CONJUNCTIVE MOOD.

§ 55. (*c*)—Present: '(*If*) *I be*,' &c.

Person.	Singular.		Plural.	
	Masculine.	Feminine.	Masculine.	Feminine.
1st	होऊँ *hoū́*.	होइयौं *hoiyõ*.	होई, होईं, *hoí*, *hoí*. होइअइ, होइअउ, *hŏiaï*, *hŏiaü*.	होइयौं *hoiyõ*.
2nd	हो, होए, *ho*, *hoe*. होआँ, होएँ, *hoã*, *hoẽ*. होअइ, होही, *hoaï*, *hohí*.	होईं *hoí*.	होअ *hoa*. होहु, होहुँ, होऊन, होहो, *hohú*, *hohú̃*, *hohun*, *hoho*. होहीं, होहिन, *hohí*, *hohin*.	होई, होऊ, *hoí*, *hoú*.
3rd	होए *hoe*. होअइ, होअउ, *hoaï*, *hoaü*. होअस *hoas*.		होईं, होइन, *hoí*, *hoin*. होथ, होथी, होथिन, होथुन, *hoth*, *hothi*, *hothin*, *hothun*. होहीं, होहिन, *hohí*, *hohin*. होखिन *hokhin*.	होथीन, होथिनी, *hothín*, *hŏthini*. होखीन, होखिनी *hokhín*, *hŏkhini*.

§ 56. (*d*)—Preterite: '*(If) I had been,*' &c.

Person.	Singular.		Plural.	
	Masculine.	Feminine.	Masculine.	Feminine.
1st	होतूँ* *hotū̃.*	होतियौं *hŏtiyō.*	होती, होतीं, *hoti, holí.* होतिअइ, होतिअउ, *hŏtiaï, hŏtiaü.*	होतियौं *hŏtiyō.*
2nd	होतँ, होतेँ, *hotã, hotẽ.* होता, होते, *hotá, hote.* होतही *hŏt'hi.*	होतीँ *hotí.* होती *hoti.*	होतऽ, *hota.* होतहू, होतहूँ, होतहुन, *hŏt'hú, hŏt'hū̃, hŏt'hun.* होतहो, *hŏt'ho.* होतहीँ, होतहिन, *hŏt'hí, hŏt'hin.*	होती, होतू, *hotí, hotú.*
3rd	होत, होता, *hot, hotá.* होतइ, होतउ, *hŏtaï, hŏtaü.*	होती *hoti.*	होतन *hotan.* होतथी, होतथिन, होतथुन; *htŏ'thí, hŏt'thin, hŏt'thun.* होतहीँ, होतहिन, *hŏt'hí, hŏt'hin.* होतखिन *hŏt'khin.*	होतिन *hotin.* होतथीन, होतथिनी, *hŏt'thin, hŏt'thiní.* होतखीन, होतखिनी, *hŏt'khin, hŏt'khiní.*

* होइत *hoit* or होअत *hoat* may be written for होत *hot* throughout.

§ 57. Present Participle, *'being.'*

Singular and Plural.

Masc.	Fem.
होत* *hot.*	होती *hotí.*

Past Participle, *'been.'*

Form 1.	होल † *hol.*	होली *holí.*
Form 2.	भेल *bhel.*	भेली *bhelí.*

§ 58. Infinitive, *'to be.'*

होएब *hoĕb*, होअब *hoab*, or होइब *hoib*.

---

* होइत *hoit* or होअत *hoat* may be written for होत *hot* throughout.

† होइल *hoil* may be written for होल *hol* throughout.

CHAPTER VI.

THE REGULAR ACTIVE VERB.

§ 59. There is only one conjugation of active verbs, if we except a few irregular verbs to be noted further on. The conjugation of neuter verbs differs from that of active verbs only in certain of the past tenses, and these will be treated of in a future page. Verbs whose roots end in vowels also exhibit slight variations, which will be explained at the proper place. For the sake of uniformity the tenses are given in the same order and under the same names as those in Dr. Hœrnle's Grammar.

Reference is again made to General Introduction, §§ 34 to 36, with regard to the changes of the root vowel.

§ 60. √देख *dekh*, 'see.'

INFINITIVE: देखब *dekhab*.

PRESENT PARTICIPLE: *Masc.* देखित *dekhit*, देखत *dekhat*, or देखइत *dĕkhaït*. *Fem.* देख॰ती *dĕkh'tí* or देखिती *dĕkhití*.

PAST PARTICIPLE: *Masc.* देखल *dekhal*. *Fem.* देख॰ली *dĕkh'lí*.

COMPLETE PAST PARTICIPLE: *Masc.* देखल भेल *dekhal bhel*. *Fem.* देखल भेली *dekhal bhelí*.

(A)—Simple Tenses.

INDICATIVE MOOD.

§ 61. (*a*)—Preterite: '*I saw,*' *&c.*

Person.	Singular.		Plural.	
	Masculine.	Feminine.	Masculine.	Feminine.
1st	देख॰लूँ *dĕkh'lú̃.*		देख॰ली, देख॰लीं, *dĕkh'li, dĕkh'lí̃.* देख॰लिअइ, देख॰लिअउ, *dĕkh'liaï, dĕkh'liaü.*	
2nd	देख॰ले *dĕkh'le.*	देख॰ली *dĕkh'li.*	देख॰ल॰ *dĕkh'la.*	देख॰ली, देख॰लू, *dĕkh'li, dĕkh'lú.*
	देख॰लँ, देख॰लेँ, *dĕkh'lã, dĕkh'lẽ.*	देख॰लीँ *dĕkh'lĩ.*	देखल॰हू, देख॰लहूँ,-हुन,-हो, *dĕkhal'hú, dĕkhal'hú̃,-hun,* [*-ho.*	
	देखल॰ही *dĕkhal'hí.*		देखल॰हीं, देखल॰हिन, *dĕkhal'hí̃, dĕkhal'hin.*	
3rd	देखिस *dekhis.*		देख॰लन, देखल॰कन, *dĕkh'lan, dĕkhal'kan.*	देख॰लिन, देखल॰किन, *dĕkh'lin, dĕkhal'kin.*
	देख॰कइ, देख॰कउ, *dĕkh'kaï, dĕkh'kaü.*		देखल॰थी, देखल॰थिन, *dĕkhal'thí, dĕkhal'thin.*	देखल॰थीन, देखल॰थिनी, *dĕkhal'thín, dĕkhal'thiní.*
	देख॰लक *dĕkh'lak.*			
	देखल॰कइ, देखल॰कउ. *dĕkhal'kaï, dĕkhal'-* [*kaü.*	देख॰ली *dĕkh'li.*	देखल॰थू, देखल॰थुन, *dĕkhal'thú, dĕkhal'thun.*	
			देखल॰हीं. देखल॰हिन, *dĕkhal'hí̃, dĕkhal'hin.*	
			देखल॰खिन, देखल॰कथिन, *dĕkhal'khin, dĕkhal'kathin.*	देखल॰खीन, देखल॰खिनी, *dĕkhal'khín, dĕkhal'-* [*khiní.*

§ 62. (*b*)—Future: '*I shall see,*' *&c.*

Person.	Singular.		Plural.	
	Masculine.	Feminine.	Masculine.	Feminine.
1st	देखब, देख॰बइ, देखबउ, *dekhab*, *dĕkh'baï*, *dĕkh'baü*. देख॰बो, देख॰बौं, *dĕkh'bo*, *dĕkh'baũ*.		देखब, देख॰बइ, देख॰बउ, *dekhab*, *dĕkh'baï*, *dĕkh'baü*.	देख॰बी *dĕkh'bí*.
2nd	देख॰बँ, देख॰बें, *dĕkh'bã*, *dĕkh'bẽ*. देख॰बा, देख॰बे, *dĕkh'bá*, *dĕkh'be*. देखब॰ही *dĕkhab'hí*.	देख॰बीं *dĕkh'bí*. देख॰बी *dĕkh'bí*.	देख॰बऽ *dĕkh'ba*. देखब॰हू, -हूँ, -कुन, -हो, *dĕkhab'hú*,-*hū́*,-*kun*,-*ho*. देखब॰हीं,-हिन, *dĕkhab'hí*,-*hin*. देखिहऽ *dĕkhiha*.	देख॰बी, देख॰बू, *dĕkh'bí*, *dĕkh'bú*.
3rd	देखी *dekhí*. देखत *dekhat*. देख॰तइ, देख॰तउ, *dĕkh'taï*, *dĕkh'taü*.	देख॰ती *dĕkh'tí*.	देखिहें *dĕkhihẽ*. देख॰खिन *dĕkh'khin*. देख॰तन *dĕkh'tan*. देखत॰थी,-थिन,-थुन, *dĕkhat'thí*,-*thin*,-*thun*. देखथ, देख॰थी, -थिन,-थुन, *dekhath*, *dĕkh'thí*,-*thin*, [-*thun*.	देख॰खीन, देख॰खिनी, *dĕkh'khín*, *dĕkh'khiní*. देख॰तिन *dĕkh'tin*. देखत॰थीन, देखत॰थिनी, *dĕkhat'thín*, *dĕkhat'thiní*. देख॰थीन, देख॰थिनी, *dĕkh'thín*, *dĕkh'thiní*.

Conjunctive (Conditional) Mood.

§ 63. (*c*)– Present : '(*If*) *I see* ;' rarely '*I see*,' or '*I shall see*,' &c.

Person.	Singular. Masculine.	Singular. Feminine.	Plural. Masculine.	Plural. Feminine.
1st	देखूँ *dekhū́.*	दॆखियौं *děkhiyō̃.*	देखी, देखीं, *dekhí, dekhī́.* दॆखिअइ, दॆखिअउ, *děkhiaï, děkhiaü.*	दॆखियौं *děkhiyō̃.*
2nd	देख, देखे, *dekh, dekhe.*		देखऽ, देखह, *dekha, dekhah.*	देखी, देखु, *dekhí, dekhú.*
	देखँ, देखेँ, *dekhā̃, dekhē̃.*	देखीं *dekhī́.*	दॆख॰हू, दॆख॰हूँ, दॆख॰हुन, *děkh'hú, děkh'hū̃, děkh'hun,* दॆख॰हो *děkh'ho.*	
	दॆखइ, दॆख॰ही, *děkhaï, děkh'hí.*		दॆख॰हीं, दॆख॰हिन, *děkh'hí, děkh'hin.*	
3rd	देखे *dekhe.*		देखीं, देखिन, *dekhí, dekhin.*	
	दॆखइ, दॆखउ, *děkhaï, děkhaü.*		देखथ, दॆख॰थी, दॆख॰थिन, *dekhath, děkh'thí, děkh'thin.* दॆख॰थू, दॆख॰थुन, *děkh'thú, děkh'thun.*	दॆख॰थीन, दॆखथिनी, *děkh'thín, děkh'thiní.*
	देखस *dekhas.*		दॆख॰हीं, दॆख॰हिन, *děkh'hí, děkh'hin.* दॆख॰खिन *děkh'khin.*	दॆख॰खीन, दॆख॰खिनी, *děkh'khín, děkh'khiní.*

§ 64. (*d*)—Preterite : '(*If*) *I had seen*,' *&c.*

Person.	Singular.		Plural.	
	Masculine.	Feminine.	Masculine.	Feminine.
1st	देखइतूँ,* *děkhaïtű.*	देखइतियों *děkhaïtiyõ.*	देखइती, देखइतीं, *děkhaïtí, děkhaïtí.*	देखइतियों *děkhaïtiyõ.*
			देखइतिअइ, देखइतिअउ, *děkhaïtiaï, děkhaïtiaü.*	
2nd	देखइता, देखइते, děkhaïtá, děkhaïte.	देखइती *děkhaïtí.*	देखइतऽ *děkhaïta.*	देखइती, देखइतू, *děkhaïtí, děkhaïtú.*
	देखइतँ, देखइतेँ, *děkhaïtã, děhkaïtẽ.*	देखइतीं *děkhaïtí.*	देखइत॰हू, देखइत॰हूँ, děkhaït'hú, děkhaït'hű, -हुन, -हो, -hun, -ho.	
	देखइत॰ही *děkhaït'hí.*		देखइत॰हीं, देखइत॰हिन, *děkhaït'hí, děkhaït'hin.*	
3rd			देखइतन *děkhaïtan.*	देखइतिन *děkhaïtin.*
	देखइत, देखइता, *děkhaït, děkhaïtá.*	देखइती *děkhaïtí.*	देखइत॰थी, देखइत॰थिन, *děkhaït'thí, děkhaït'thin.*	देखइत॰थीन,-थिनी, *děkhaït'thín,-thiní.*
	देखइतइ, देखइतउ, *děkhaïtaï, děkhaïtaü.*		देखइत॰ही, देखइत॰हिन, *děkhaït'hí, děkhaït'hin.*	
	देखइतइ हल *děkhaïtaï hal.*		देखइत॰खिन *děkhaït'khin.*	देखइत॰खीन,-खिनी, *děkhaït'khín,-khiní.*
	देखइतउ हल *děkhaïtaü hal.*		देख॰थी, देख॰थिन, *děkh'thí, děkh'thin.*	देख॰थीन,-थिनी, *děkh'thín,-thiní.*

* Or देख॰तूँ *děkh'tű* or देखितूँ *děkhitű*, and so throughout. As in the third person, so हल *hal* may be added throughout to emphasise the preterite character of the tense.

IMPERATIVE MOOD.

§ 65. (*e.*)—Present.—Same as Present Conjunctive.

Precative Forms.

Person.	Singular.		Plural.	
	Masculine.	Feminine.	Masculine.	Feminine.
1st	*Wanting.*	*Wanting.*	*Wanting.*	*Wanting.*
2nd	*Wanting.*	*Wanting.*	देखबꣻहू *dĕkhab'hú.* देखिहꣻ *dĕkhiha.* *or* देखी *dekhí.*	*Wanting.*
3rd	*Wanting.*	*Wanting.*	*Wanting.*	*Wanting.*

(B)—Periphrastic Tenses.

INDICATIVE MOOD.

§ 66. (*f*)—Present : '*I see.*'

Person.	Singular.		Plural.	
	Masculine.	Feminine.	Masculine.	Feminine.
1st	देखꣻ* हो† *dekha hi*, &c.	देखꣻ हियोँ *dekha hiyõ.*	देखꣻ हीँ *dekha hí*, &c.	देखꣻ हियोँ *dekha hiyõ.*
2nd	देखꣻ हँ *dekha hã*, &c.	देखꣻ हीँ *dekha hí.*	देखꣻ हꣻ *dekha ha*, &c.	देखꣻ ही *dekha hi.*
3rd	देखꣻ हइ, *dekha haï*, &c.		देखꣻ हईँ *dekha haí*, &c.	देखꣻ हथीन, &c. *dekha hathín*, &c.

* For देखꣻ *dekha*, देखे *dekhĕ* may be written throughout.

† Any other form of the present of the defective auxiliary verb may be used throughout.

§ 67. (*g*)—Indefinite Preterite: '*I saw,*' *&c.*

Person.	Singular.		Plural.	
	Masculine.	Feminine.	Masculine.	Feminine.
1st	देख०* हलूँ † *dekha halū̃.*		देख० हलीं *dekha halí.*	
2nd	देख० हलँ *dekha halã.*	देख० हलीं *dekha halí.*	देख० हल० *dekha hala.*	देख० हली *dekha hali.*
3rd	देख० हल *dekha hal.*	देख० हली *dekha halí.*	देख० हलन *dekha halan.*	देख० हलिन *dekha halin.*

* For देख० *dekha*, देखॆ *dekhĕ* may be written throughout.

† Any other form of the preterite of the defective auxiliary verb may be used instead.

§ 68. (*h*)—Definite Present: '*I am seeing,*' *&c.*

Person.	Singular.		Plural.	
	Masculine.	Feminine.	Masculine.	Feminine.
1st	देखइत *ही † *dĕkhaït hi.*	देखइत हियौँ *dĕkhaït hiyŏ̃*	देखइत हीं *dĕkhaït hí.*	देखइत हियौँ *dĕkhaït hiyŏ̃.*
2nd	देखइत हँ *dĕkhaït hã.*	देखइत हीं *dĕkhaït hí.*	देखइत ह० *dĕkhaït ha.*	देखइत ही *dĕkhaït hi.*
3rd	देखइत हइ *dĕkhaït haï.*		देखइत हइँ *dĕkhaït haí.*	देखइत हथीन, *dĕkhaït hathin.*

* देखैत *dekhait* or देखत *dekhat* may be used for देखइत *dĕkhaït* throughout.

† Any other form of the present of the defective auxiliary verb may be used throughout.

§ 69. (*i*)—Imperfect: '*I was seeing,*' *&c.*

Person.	Singular.		Plural.	
	Masculine.	Feminine.	Masculine.	Feminine.
1st	देखइत * हलूँ † *děkhaït halū̆.*		देखइत हलीं, *děkhaït halī̆.*	
2nd	देखइत हलँ *děkhaït halā̆.*	देखइत हलीं *děkhaït halī̆.*	देखइत हलऽ *děkhaït hala.*	देखइत हली *děkhaït halī.*
3rd	देखइत हल, *děkhaït hal.*	देखइत हली *děkhaït halī.*	देखइत हलन *děkhaït halan.*	देखइत हलिन *děkhaït halin.*

* देखैत *dekhait* or देखत *dekhat* may be used for देखइत *děkhaït* throughout.

† Any other form of the preterite of the defective auxiliary verb may be used throughout.

§ 70. (*j*)—Durative Future: '*I shall be seeing,*' *&c.*

Person.	Singular.		Plural.	
	Masculine.	Feminine.	Masculine.	Feminine.
1st	देखइत * होब † *děkhaït hob.*		देखइत होब *děkhaït hob.*	देखइत होबी *děkhaït hobī.*
2nd	देखइत होबँ *děkhaït hobā̆.*	देखइत होबीं *děkhaït hobī̆.*	देखइत होबऽ *děkhaït hoba.*	देखइत होबी *děkhaït hobī.*
3rd	देखइत होइ *děkhaït hoï.*	देखइत होती *děkhaït hotī.*	देखइत होइहेँ *děkhait hoihē.*	देखइत होथीन *děkhaït hothīn.*

* देखैत *dekhait* or देखत *dekhat* may be used for देखइत *děkhaït* throughout.

† Any other form of the future of the complete auxiliary verb may be used throughout.

§ 71. (*k*)—Perfect: '*I have seen,*' *&c.*

Person.	Singular.		Plural.	
	Masculine.	Feminine.	Masculine.	Feminine.
1st	देख॰लूँ* है† *dĕkh'lū̃ hai.*		देख॰लीं है *dĕkh'lī̃ hai.*	
2nd	देख॰लें है *dĕkh'lẽ hai.*	देख॰लीं है *dĕkh'lī̃ hai.*	देख॰लऽ है *dĕkh'la hai.*	देख॰ली है *dĕkh'lī hai*
3rd	देखिस है *dekhis hai.*	देख॰ली है *dĕkh'lī hai.*	देख॰लन है *dĕkh'lan hai.*	देख॰लिन है *dĕkh'lin h*

* Any of the other forms of the preterite may be used throughout.

† Or हइ *haï*, हउ *haü*, हऽ *ha*, or हँ *hã*, and so throughout.

§ 72. (*l*)—Pluperfect: '*I had seen,*' *&c.*

Person.	Singular.		Plural.	
	Masculine.	Feminine.	Masculine.	Feminine.
1st	देख॰लूँ* हल† *dĕkh'lū̃ hal.*		देख॰लीं हल *dĕkh'lī̃ hal.*	
2nd	देख॰लें हल *dĕkh'lẽ hal.*	देख॰लीं हल *dĕkh'lī̃ hal.*	देख॰लऽ हल *dĕkh'la hal.*	देख॰ली हल *dĕkh'lī h*
3rd	देखिस हल *dekhis hal.*	देख॰ली हल *dĕkh'lī hal.*	देख॰लन हल *dĕkh'lan hal.*	देख॰लिन हल *dĕkh'lin hal.*

* Any of the other forms of the preterite may be used throughout.

† Or हलइ *halaï* or हलउ *halaü*, and so throughout.

§ 73. (*m*)—Future Exact: '*I shall have seen,*' *&c.*

Person.	Singular.		Plural.	
	Masculine.	Feminine.	Masculine.	Feminine.
1st	देखल्ले होब * *dĕkh'lĕ hob.*		देखल्ले होब *dĕkh'lĕ hob.*	देखल्ले होबी *dĕkh'lĕ hobī.*
2nd	देखल्ले होबँ *dĕkh'lĕ hobā̃.*	देखल्ले होबीं *dĕkh'lĕ hobī́.*	देखल्ले होबऽ *dĕkh'lĕ hoba.*	देखल्ले होबी *dĕkh'lĕ hobī́.*
3rd	देखल्ले होइ *dĕkh'lĕ hoī.*	देखल्ले होती *dĕkh'lĕ hotī.*	देखल्ले होइहैं *dĕkh'lĕ hoihē̃.*	देखल्ले होथीन *dĕkh'lĕ hothī́n.*

* Any other form of the future of the complete auxiliary verb may be used instead throughout.

CONJUNCTIVE (CONDITIONAL) MOOD.

§ 74. (*n.*)—Future Conditional: '(*If*) *I be seeing,*' *&c.*

Person.	Singular.		Plural.	
	Masculine.	Feminine.	Masculine.	Feminine.
1st	देखइत* होऊँ† *dĕkhaït hoū̃.*	देखइत होइयौं *dĕkhaït hoïyō̃.*	देखइत होईं *dĕkhaït hoī́.*	देखइत होइयौं *dĕkhaït hoiyō̃.*
2nd	देखइत होअँ *dĕkhaït hoā̃.*	देखइत होईं *dĕkhaït hoī́.*	देखइत होअ *dĕkhaït hoa.*	देखइत होई *dĕkhaït hoī́.*
3rd	देखइत होअइ *dĕkhaït hoaï.*		देखइत होईं *dĕkhaït hoī́.*	देखइत होथीन *dĕkhaït hothī́n.*

* देखैत *dekhait* or देखत *dekhat* may be used for देखइत *dĕkhait* throughout.

† Any other form of the present of the complete auxiliary verb may be used instead throughout.

§ 75. (*o*)—Durative Present Conditional: '(*If*) *I were seeing*,' *&c.*

Person.	Singular.		Plural.	
	Masculine.	Feminine.	Masculine.	Feminine.
1st	देखइत* होतूँ† *dĕkhaït hotū̃.*	देखइत होतियौँ *dĕkhaït hŏtiyõ.*	देखइत होतीँ *dĕkhaït hotī́.*	देखइत होतियौँ *dĕkhaït hŏtiyõ.*
2nd	देखइत होतँ *dĕkhaït hotã.*	देखइत होतीँ *dĕkhaït hotī́.*	देखइत होतऽ *dĕkhaït hota.*	देखइत होती *dĕkhaït hotī́.*
3rd	देखइत होत *dĕkhaït hot.*	देखइत होती *dĕkhaït hotī.*	देखइत होतन *dĕkhaït hotan.*	देखइत होतिन *dĕkhaït hotin.*

* देखैत *dĕkhait* or देखत *dekhat* may be used for देखइत *dĕkhaït* throughout.

† Any other form of the preterite conditional of the complete auxiliary verb may be used instead throughout.

§ 76. (*p*)—Future Exact Conditional: '(*If*) *I have seen*,' *&c.*

Person.	Singular.		Plural.	
	Masculine.	Feminine.	Masculine.	Feminine.
1st	देखऽले होऊँ * *dĕkh'lĕ hoū̃.*	देखऽले होइयौँ *dĕkh'lĕ hoiyõ.*	देखऽले होईं *dĕkh'lĕ hoī́.*	देखऽले होइयौँ *dĕkh'lĕ hoiyõ.*
2nd	देखऽले होआँ *dĕkh'lĕ hoã.*	देखऽले होईं *dĕkh'lĕ hoī́.*	देखऽले होअ *dĕkh'lĕ hoa.*	देखऽले होई *dĕkh'lĕ hoí.*
3rd	देखऽले होअइ *dĕkh'lĕ hoaï.*		देखऽले होईं *dĕkh'lĕ hoī́.*	देखले होथीन *dĕkh'lĕ hothī́n.*

* Any other form of the present of the complete auxiliary verb may be used instead throughout.

§ 77. (*q*.)—Preterite Conditional: *'(If) I had seen, &c.*

Person.	Singular.		Plural.	
	Masculine.	Feminine.	Masculine.	Feminine.
1st	देखले होतूँ* *dĕkh'lĕ hotū̃.*	देखले होतियौँ *dĕkh'lĕ hŏtiyõ.*	देखले होतीँ *dĕkh'lĕ hotī.*	देखले होतियौँ *dĕkh'lĕ hŏtiyõ.*
2nd	देखले होतँ *dĕkh'lĕ hotā̆.*	देखले होतीँ *dĕkh'lĕ hotī.*	देखले होतऽ *dĕkh'lĕ hota.*	देखले होती *dĕkh'lĕ hotī.*
3rd	देखले होत *dĕkh'lĕ hot.*	देखले होती *dĕkh'lĕ hotī.*	देखले होतन *dĕkh'lĕ hotan.*	देखले होतिन *dĕkh'lĕ hotin.*

* Any other form of the preterite conditional of the complete auxiliary verb may be used instead throughout.

§ 78. Participles.

Adjectival.

	Masculine.	Feminine.	Oblique.
Present, 'seeing'	देखित *dekhit.*	देखिती *dĕkhitī.*	देखिते *dĕkhitĕ.*
	देखत *dekhat.*	देखती *dĕkh'tī.*	देखते *dĕkh'tĕ.*
	देखइत *dĕkhaït.*	देखइती *dĕkhaïtī.*	देखइते *dĕkhaïtĕ.*
Past, 'seen'	*a*) देखल *dekhal.*	देखली *dĕkh'lī.*	देखले *dĕkh'lĕ.*
	b) देखल भेल *dekhal bhel.*	देखल भेली *dekhal bhelī.*	

Conjunctive.

'Having seen' . . . . देख के *dekh kĕ* or देख कर *dekh kar.*

§ 79 Infinitives or Verbal Nouns, *'to see,' 'the act of seeing.'*

Nominative.	Oblique.
देख * *dekh.*	देखे *dekhĕ.*
देखल *dekhal.*	देख॰ला *dĕkh'lá.*
देखब *dekhab.*	*Not used.*†

* This form of the verbal noun is always the same as the root.

† The oblique form of this verbal noun is not used. Judging from analogy of other dialects, we should expect देख॰बा *dĕkh'bá.*

§ 80. Noun of Agency, *'one who sees.'*

Masculine.	Feminine.
देखिन॰हार or देखिनीहार *dĕkhin'hár* or *dĕkhiníhár.*	देखिन॰हारी or देखिनीहारी *dĕkhin'hárí* or *dĕkhiníhárí.*

CHAPTER VII.

THE REGULAR NEUTER VERB.

§ 81. This verb differs from the active verb only in the formation of certain of its past tenses. The three more usual past tenses are here given; the conjugation of the rest of the verb can be learnt from the conjugation of the √ देख *dekh*.

NOTE that throughout the periphrastic tenses of the neuter verb, in which the past participle occurs, the past participle takes the direct form गिरल *giral*, not the oblique form गिर्‌ले *gir'lĕ*, which might be expected: thus हम गिरल होब *ham giral hob*, 'I shall have fallen,' and not हम गिर्‌ले होब *ham gir'lĕ hob*, 'I shall have fallen.'

§ 82. √ गिर *gir*, 'fall.'

PAST PARTICIPLE: *Masc.* गिरल *giral.* *Fem.* गिर्‌ली *gir'lī*, '*fallen.*' *Obl.* गिर्‌ले *gir'lĕ.*

INDICATIVE MOOD.

§ 83. (*a*)—Preterite '*I fell,*' &c.

Person.	Singular.		Plural.	
	Masculine.	Feminine.	Masculine.	Feminine.
1st	गिर॰लूँ *gir'lú̃.*		गिर॰ली, गिर॰लीँ, *gir'lí, gir'lí̃.* गिर॰लिअइ, गिर॰लिअउ, *gir'liaï, gir'liaü.*	
2nd	गिर॰लेँ, गिर॰लेँ, *gir'lã, gir'lẽ.* गिर॰ला, गिर॰ले, *gir'lá, gir'le.* गिरल॰ही *giral'hí.*	गिर॰लीँ *gir'lí̃.* गिर॰ली *gir'lí.*	गिर॰ल॰ *gir'la.* गिरल॰हू,-हूँ,-हुन,-हो, *giral'hú,-hú̃,-hun,-ho.* गिरल॰हीँ,-हिन *giral'hí̃,-hin.*	गिर॰ली, गिर॰लू, *gir'lí, gir'lú.*
3rd	गिरल *giral.* गिर॰लइ, गिर॰लउ, *gir'laï, gir'laü.* गिर॰लक *gir'lak.*	गिर॰ली *gir'lí.*	गिर॰लन *gir'lan.* गिरल॰थी,-थिन,-थुन, *giral'thí,-thin,-thun.* गिरल॰हीँ, हिन, *giral'hí̃,-hin.* गिरलौ॰खिन *giral'khin.*	गिर॰लिन *gir'lin.* गिरल॰थीन,-थिनी *giral'thín,-thiní.* गिरल॰खीन,-खिनी, *ral'khín,-khiní.*

§ 84. (*k*)—Perfect: '*I have fallen,*' *&c.*

Person.	Singular.		Plural.	
	Masculine.	Feminine.	Masculine.	Feminine.
1st	गिर॰लूँ* है *girlú hai.*		गिर॰लीं है *gir'lí hai.*	
2nd	गिर॰ला है *girlá hal.*	गिर॰लीं है *gir'lí hai.*	गिर॰ल॰ है *gir'la hai.*	गिर॰ली है *gir'lí hai.*
3rd	गिरल है *giral hai.*	गिर॰ली है *gir'lí hai.*	गिर॰लन है *gir'lan hai.*	गिर॰लिन है *gir'lin hai.*

* Any of the other forms of the preterite may be used throughout.
† Or हइ *haï,* &c., throughout, as in the conjugation of √ देख *dekh.*

§ 85. (*l*)—Pluperfect: '*I had fallen,*' *&c.*

Person.	Singular.		Plural.	
	Masculine.	Feminine.	Masculine.	Feminine.
1st	गिर॰लूँ* हल *gir'lú hal.*	गिर॰लूँ हली *gir'lú halí.*	गिर॰लीं हल *gir'lí hal.*	गिर॰लीं हली *gir'lí halí.*
2nd	गिर॰ला हल *gir'lá hal.*	गिर॰लीं हली *gir'lí halí.*	गिर॰ल॰ हल *gir'la hal.*	गिर॰ली हली *gir'lí halí.*
3rd	गिरल हल *giral hal.*	गिर॰ली हली *gir'lí halí.*	गिर॰लन हल *gir'lan hal.*	गिर॰लिन हली *gir'lin halí.*

* Any of the other forms of the preterite may be used throughout.

CHAPTER VIII.

VOCALIC ROOTS.

§ 86. Many verbs have roots ending in vowels, and the junction of the root with the termination frequently causes some slight apparent irregularity.

For this reason the following examples are given of the conjugation of verbs having roots ending in vowels. They are here conjugated in the masculine gender, and through the four radical and participial tenses. From these the periphrastic tenses can easily be formed. It has not been thought necessary to give the conjugation in full for each person.

With regard to the shortening of the root vowel, see General Introduction, § 36.

§ 87. Example of a verb whose root ends in आ *á*:—

The conjugation of these verbs should be carefully studied, as a large class of active and causal verbs follows it.

In the preterite indicative these verbs insert a junction vowel between the root and the ल *l* of the termination: thus ख* + इ + लूँ *kha* + *i* + *lú*, 'I ate,' where इ *i* is the junction vowel; and प* + उ + लूँ *pa* + *u* + *lú*, 'I got,' where उ *u* is the junction vowel.

The following rules show when इ *i* and when उ *u* is the junction vowel:—

1) All active (including causal) verbs take उ *u*: thus पउलूँ* *paülú*, 'I got;' चढ़उलूँ *chaṛhaülú*, 'I caused to ascend.'

Exception.—The root √ खा *khá*,* 'eat,' always takes इ *i*: thus खइलूँ *khaïlú*, 'I ate.'

---

* With regard to the shortening of the root vowel, see General Introduction, § 36.

2) ALL neuter verbs take इ i: thus अघइलूँ aghaïlú, 'I was satiated;' आइलूँ aïlú, 'I came.'

Exception.—The √ गा gá, 'sing,' always takes उ u: thus गउलूँ. 'I sang.'

It is usual to add the letter व w to the end of all roots which take उ u, in order to distinguish them from those which take the letter इ i: thus √ पाव paw, √ गाव gaw, &c., which take उ u; but √ अघा aghá, √ आ á, &c. which take इ i.

All verbs which take a उ u in the preterite indicative insert a व w in the past participle; and similarly all verbs which take इ i, insert a य y in the past participle and in that form of the 3rd singular preterite which is the same as the past participle.

The following examples will make the above remarks clear.

The easiest way of remembering these changes is to note the form of the past participle of each verb; and then, as explained in General Introduction, § 37, the व *wa* or य *ya* is weakened in certain cases to उ *u* and इ *i* respectively.

It must, however, be noted that even in active verbs there is a tendency to substitute य *ya* for व *wa*, so that we sometimes find forms like पइलूँ *païlú* instead of पउलूँ *paülú*. This tendency is most marked in the east of the district; and in the adjoining Maithil-Mágadhí of South Munger (Monghyr) we find that it has become the rule and not the exception, and that the junction vowel उ *u* never occurs, but only forms like पइलूँ *païlú*, बजइलूँ *bajaïlú*, चढ़इलूँ *chaṛhaïlú*, &c.

88. Many people write ए *ĕ* instead of इ *i*: thus अएलूँ *aĕlú* instead of अइलूँ *aïlú*. The word for 'he came' is always आएल *áĕl*, and never आइल *áïl*. See § 96.

Many people also write ए *ĕ* instead of य *ya*, and ओ *ŏ* instead of व *wa*, in the past participle. Thus, it is quite common to find the words in the second column of the opposite table spelt पाओल *páŏl*, बजाओल *bajáŏl*, चढ़ाओल *chaṛháŏl*, गाओल *gáŏl*, खाएल *kháĕl*, अघाएल *agháĕl*, घबड़ाएल *ghab'ṛáĕl*, हड़बड़ाएल *haṛ'baṛáĕl*, and आएल *áĕl*.

§ 89. √ पा *pá*, 'get.'

INFINITIVE (1ST FORM): पा *pá* ; obl पाए *páĕ*, पावे *páwĕ*, पावऽ *páwa*, or पा *pá*.
„ (2ND FORM): पावल *páwal* ; obl. पउला *paülá*. (See General Introduction, § 37.)
„ (3RD FORM): पाअब *páab*, पाएब *páĕb*, *or* पायब *páyab*, 'to get.'

INDICATIVE MOOD.

Person.	Preterite. (See remarks above.) Singular.	Preterite. Plural.	Future. Singular.	Future. Plural.
1st	पउलूँ (or पइलूँ) *paülũ* (*païlũ.*)	पउलीं or पौलीं *paülí*, *paulí*.	पाएब or पायब *páĕb*, *páyab*.	
2nd	पउले or पौले, *paüle*, *paule*.	पउलऽ or पौलऽ *paüla*, *paula*.	पइबे *païbe*, पाबे *pábe*.	पइबऽ or पाबऽ *païba*, *pába*.
3rd	पाइस or *páis*. ; पउलक *paülak* or पौलक *paulak*.	पउलन or पौलन *paülan*, *paulan*.	पाई *páí*.	पइहें *païhẽ*.

CONDITIONAL MOOD.

Person.	Present. Singular.	Present. Plural.	Preterite. Singular.	Preterite. Plural.
1st	पाऊ *páú*.	पाईं or पावीं *páí*, *páví*.	पइतूँ* or पउतूँ *païtũ*, *paütũ*.	पइतीं *païtí*.
2nd	पावँ *páwã*.	पावऽ *páva*.	पइता *païtá*.	पइतऽ *païta*.
3rd	पावै *pávai*.	पावीं *páví*, पावथ or पाथ *pávath*, *páth*.	पाइत *páït*.	पइतन *païtan*.

* पउत *paüt* or पौत *paut* may be substituted for पइत *paït* throughout.

90. Example of a verb whose root ends in ई *í*:—

√ पी *pí*, 'drink.'

Infinitive: पीअब *píab*, 'to drink.'

INDICATIVE MOOD.

Person.	Preterite.		Future.	
	Singular.	Plural.	Singular.	Plural.
1st	पीलूँ * *pílū́*.	पीलीँ *pílī́*.	पीअब *píab*.	
2nd	पीले *píle*.	पील० *píla*.	पीबे *píbe*.	पीब० *píba*.
3rd	पीहिस or पीलक *píhis*, *pílak*.	पीलन *pílan*.	पीही *píhí* or पी *pí*.	पिहिहेँ or पीहेँ- *pihihẽ* or *píhẽ*.

* Or पिह०लूँ *píh'lū́*, and so throughout.

CONDITIONAL MOOD.

Person.	Present.		Preterite.	
	Singular.	Plural.	Singular.	Plural.
1st	पीहूँ *píhū́*.	पीहीँ *píhí*.	पिह०तूँ* *pih'tū́*.	पिह०तीँ *pih'tī́*.
2nd	पीअँ *píā̃*.	पीअ *pía*.	पिह०ता *pih'tá*.	पिह०त० *pih'ta*.
3rd	पीऐ *píai*.	पीहीँ *píhí*.	पीहित *píhit*.	पिह०तन *pih'tan*.

* Or पिहितूँ *pihitū́* or पीतूँ *pítū́*, and so on throughout.

§ 91. Example of a verb whose root ends in ऊ ú:—

√ चू chú, 'drip.'

Infinitive: चूअब *chúab*, 'to drip.'

INDICATIVE MOOD.

Person.	PRETERITE.		FUTURE.	
	Singular.	Plural.	Singular.	Plural.
1st	चूलूँ *chúlũ.*	चूलीँ *chúlí̃.*	चूअब *chúab.*	
2nd	चूला *chúlá.*	चूलऽ *chúla.*	चूबे *chúbe.*	चूबऽ *chúba.*
3rd	चूअल *chúal.*	चूलन *chúlan.*	चूई *chúí.*	चूइहेँ *chúihẽ.*

CONDITIONAL MOOD.

Person.	PRESENT.		PRETERITE.	
	Singular.	Plural.	Singular.	Plural.
1st	चूऊँ *chúũ.*	चूईँ *chúĩ.*	चूतूँ * *chútũ.*	चूतीँ *chútĩ.*
2nd	चूअँ *chúã.*	चूअ *chúa.*	चूता *chútá.*	चूतऽ *chúta.*
3rd	चूऐ *chúai.*	चूईँ *chúĩ.*	चूइत *chúit.*	चूतन *chútan.*

* Or चूइतूँ *chúitũ*, and so on throughout.

§ § 92. Example of a verb whose root ends in ओ *o*:—

√ रो *ro*, 'weep.'

Infinitive: रोअब *roab*, 'to weep.'

INDICATIVE MOOD.

Person.	PRETERITE.		FUTURE.	
	Singular.	Plural.	Singular.	Plural.
1st	रोलूँ * *rolū̃*.	रोलीँ *rolī̃*.	रोअब † *roab*.	
2nd	रोला *rolā*.	रोलऽ *rola*.	रोबे *robe*.	रोबऽ *roba*.
3rd	रोअल *roal*.	रोलन *rolan*.	रोई *roī*.	रोइहेँ *roihẽ*.

* Or रोअलूँ *roalū̃* or रोइलूँ *roilū̃*, and so throughout.

† Or रोइब *roib*, रोऍब *roĕb*, or रोब *rob*, and so throughout the first and second persons.

CONDITIONAL MOOD.

Person.	PRESENT.		PRETERITE.	
	Singular.	Plural.	Singular.	Plural.
1st.	रोऊँ *roū̃*.	रोईँ *roī̃*.	रोतूँ* *rotū̃*.	रोतीँ *rotī̃*.
2nd	रोअँ *roã*.	रोअ *roa*.	रोता *rotā*.	रोतऽ *rota*.
3rd	रोए *roai*.	रोईँ *roī̃*.	रोअत *roat*.	रोतन *rotan*.

* Or रोइतूँ *roïtū̃* or रोअतूँ *roatū̃*, and so on throughout.

For further examples of verbs of this class, see conjugation of √ हो *ho*, § 53 & ff.

CHAPTER IX.

IRREGULAR VERBS

§ 93. The following verbs are irregular only in their preterite tense indicative :— √ कर *kar*, 'do ;' √ धर *dhar*, 'seize' or 'place ;' √ मर *mar*, 'die ;' √ हो *ho*, 'become ;' and √ जा *já*, 'go.' Their conjugation is therefore given in that tense only.

The conjugation of √ हो *ho* has been already given in § 53 and ff., and is not given here.

Besides, the irregular forms √ कर *kar*, √ धर *dhar*, and √ मर *mar*, have each a regular form of the preterite indicative, which is also given.

The verbs √ दे *de*, 'give,' and √ ले *le*, 'take,' are also somewhat irregular in all the tenses, especially the preterite indicative and present conditional. The verb √ दे *de* is therefore given conjugated throughout the four radical and participial tenses. The verb √ ले *le* is conjugated precisely like the verb √ दे *de*.

§ 94. √ कर *kar*, 'do.'

Infinitive : करब *karab*, 'to do.'

INDICATIVE MOOD.

Person.	PRETERITE, Form I.		PRETERITE, Form II.	
	Singular.	Plural.	Singular.	Plural.
1st	कर॰लूँ *kar'lû.*	कर॰लीं *kar'lí.*	कइलूँ * *kaïlû.*	कइलीं *kaïlí.*
2nd	कर॰ले *kar'le.*	कर॰लऽ *kar'la.*	कइले *kaïle.*	कइलऽ *kaïla.*
3rd	कर॰लक *kar'lak.*	कर॰लन *kar'lan.*	कइलक *kaïlak.*	कइलन *kaïlan.*

* Or कैलूँ *kailû*, and so on throughout all forms. Similarly is conjugated the root √ धर *dhar*, 'place,' 'seize,' the letter ध *dha* being substituted for the letter क *ka*.

§ 95. √ मर *mar*, 'die.'

INDICATIVE MOOD.

Person.	PRETERITE, Form I.		PRETERITE, Form II.	
	Singular.	Plural.	Singular.	Plural.
1st	मरलूँ *mar'lū́.*	मरलीं *mar'lí.*	मुइलूँ *muïlū́.**	मुइलीं *muïlí.*
2nd	मरला *mar'lá.*	मरलऽ *mar'la.*	मुइला *muïlá.*	मुइलऽ *muïla.*
3rd	मरल *maral.*	मरलन *mar'lan.*	मुअल *mual.*	मुइलन *muïlan.*

* Or मुलूँ *múlū́*, and so throughout.

§ 96. √ जा *já*, 'go.'

This root is conjugated like √ पा *pá* in all tenses but the preterite indicative, which is therefore here given. With it is given the same tense of √ आ *á*, 'come,' for the sake of comparison.

Person.	√ आ *á*, PRETERITE INDICATIVE.		√ जा *já*, PRETERITE INDICATIVE.	
	Singular.	Plural.	Singular.	Plural.
1st	अइलूँ * *aïlū́.*	अइलीं *aïlí.*	गेलूँ *gelū́.*	गेलीं *gelí.*
2nd	अइला *aïlá.*	अइलऽ *aïla.*	गेला *gelá.*	गेलऽ *gela.*
3rd	आएल or अइलइ *áël* or *aïlaï.*	अइलन *aïlan.*	गेल *gel.*	गेलन *gelan*

* Or ऐलूँ *ailū́* or आएलूँ *aëlū́*, and so on throughout, except in third singular, which makes only आएल *aël*; but other forms are आएलइ *aëlaï*, अइलइ *aïlaï*, or ऐलइ *ailaï*. (See § 88.)

§ 97. √ दे *de*, 'give.

Infinitive: देब *deb*, 'to give.'

Obl. form of 1*st variety of verbal noun :* दे *de*, देवे *dewě*, *or* देअ *dea*.

INDICATIVE MOOD.

Present: हम देही *ham de hí*, &c.

Person.	PRETERITE.		FUTURE.	
	Singular.	Plural.	Singular.	Plural.
1st	देलूँ* *delũ*.	देलीं *delí*.	देब *deb*.	
2nd	देले *dele*.	देलऽ *dela*.	देबे *debe*.	देबऽ *deba*.
3rd	देलक or दीहिस *delak*, *díhis*.	देलन *delan*	दीही *díhí*.	दिहिहें or दीहें *dihihẽ* or *díhẽ*.

* Or दिह'लूँ *dih'lũ*, and so on throughout.

CONDITIONAL MOOD.

Person.	PRESENT.		PRETERITE.	
	Singular.	Plural.	Singular.	Plural.
1st	दीऊँ *díũ*.	दीं, दिहीं *dí*, *dihí*.	देतूँ* *detũ*.	देतीं *detí*.
2nd	दँ *dã* or दे *de*.	दऽ or देहू *da*, *dehú*.	देता *detá*.	देतऽ *deta*.
3rd	देइ *dei* or दे *de*.	देईं or देथ *deí*, *deth*.	देत *det*.	देतन *detan*.

* Or दिह'तूँ *dih'tũ* or दिहितूँ *dihitũ*, and so on throughout.

PRECATIVE, दीहऽ *díha*, दीही *díhí*.

Similarly is conjugated the √ ले *le*, 'take', the letter ल *la* being substituted for the letter द *da* throughout.

CHAPTER X.

THE PASSIVE VERB.

§ 98. The passive verb is formed by conjugating the verbal noun ending in अल *al* with the verb जाएब *jáĕb*, 'to go:' thus देखल जाएब *dekhal jáĕb*, 'to be seen.' This verbal noun is not altered for gender, number, person, or tense, only the verb जाएब *jáĕb* being conjugated. Thus—

हम देखल जा ही *ham dekhal já hí*, 'I am seen.' (*Masc.*)

हम देखल जा हियोँ *ham dekhal já hiyõ*, 'I am seen.' (*Fem.*)

हम सब देखल गेली *ham sab dekhal gelí*, 'we were seen.'

ऊ सब देखल गेलन *ú sab dekhal gelan*, 'they were seen.'

§ 99. This verbal noun in अल *al* must be carefully distinguished from the past participle having the same termination. The former even in irregular verbs is sometimes quite regular, while the latter is in them almost always irregular.

Thus the verbal noun of जाएब *jáĕb* is जायल *jáyal* or जावल *jával*, but the past participle is गेल *gel*. In other irregular verbs, however, such as करब *karab*, 'to do,' the verbal noun, like the past participle, may be either regular or irregular: thus कइल *kaïl* or करल *karal*, like the past participle. Hence the passive voice of जाएब *jáĕb*, 'to go,' used impersonally, is जायल जाएब *jáyal jáĕb* or जावल जाएब *jával jáĕb*: e.g. जायल जा है *jáyal já hai*, 'it is gone,' *itum est;* similarly ऊ कइल गेलइ *ú kaïl gĕlaï* or करल गेलइ *karal gĕlaï*, 'that was done.'

§ 100. Another common form of the passive is made by adding to the direct form of the first variety of the verbal noun (which is the same in form as the root) the verb पड़ब *paṛab*, 'to fall;' the whole then forms an intensive compound. (See § 114.)

Examples of this form are—

कुछु कुछु जान पड़ऽ हइ *kuchhu kuchhu ján paṛa haï*, 'a little is evident,' *i.e.* 'it is slightly apparent.'

एकऽरा से ई बूझ पड़ऽ हइ *ĕk'rá se í búјh paṛa haï*, 'from this, this is understood.

कुछु उमऽड़ल नऽ देख पड़ऽ हइ *kachhu um'ṛal na dekh paṛa haï*, 'it is not seen to be at all increased in size.'

The Potential Passive Voice.

§ 101. This voice, mentioned by Hœrnle in his Gauḍian Grammar, does not exist, so far as I am aware, in Mágadhí.

The Periphrastic Passive Voice.

§ 102. A very common kind of passive voice is formed by placing the verb √ आ *á* after the shortest form of a verbal noun in the locative case: thus देखेँ मेँ आएब *dekhĕ mẽ áĕb*, 'the coming into seeing,' *i.e.* 'to be seen.' The person by whom the action is done is put in the oblique genitive form of the noun or pronoun when there is one: thus तोँ हमऽरा देखेँ मेँ ऐला *tõ ham'rá dekhĕ mẽ ailá*, 'you came into my seeing,' 'you were seen by me.' The following example shows a verb in this voice conjugated in the preterite indicative masculine:—

	Singular.	Plural.
1.	देखेँ मेँ ऐलूँ *dekhĕ mẽ ailú̃.*	देखेँ मेँ ऐलीं *dekhĕ mẽ ailí.*
2.	देखेँ मेँ ऐला *dĕkhĕ mẽ ailá.*	देखेँ मेँ ऐलऽ *dekhĕ mẽ aila.*
3.	देखेँ मेँ आएल *dekhĕ mẽ áĕl.*	देखेँ मेँ ऐलन *dekhĕ mẽ ailan.*

EXAMPLE.—हमनी तोहऽरा देखेँ मेँ ऐलीं *hamaní tŏh'rá dekhĕ mẽ ailí*, 'we were seen by you.'

CHAPTER XI.

CAUSAL VERBS.

§ 103. A causal verb is formed by adding आव *áw* or आय *áy* to the root of the simple verb, and a double causal by adding वाव *wáw* or वाय *wáy*. The stems thus formed are conjugated exactly like verbs whose roots end in आ *á*. (See § 87). The long vowel of आव *áw* or आय *áy* and वाव *wáw* or वाय *wáy* is, as usual, liable to be shortened in the antepenultimate (see General Introduction, § 36); and if the व *wa* or य *ya* is followed by the neutral vowel, it becomes उ *u* or इ *i* respectively (see General Introduction, § 37), which, with a preceding अ *a* (see General Introduction, § 35), may be written औ *au* or ऐ *ai* respectively.

Thus, taking the simple verb √ उठ *uṭh*, 'rise,' and using the affixes आव *áw* and वाव *wáw*, the first plural definite present indicative of its causal would be regularly उठावैत छीं *uṭháwait hí*. But the first plural preterite would be उठवल्हीं *uṭhaw'lí*, which (as व *wa* is followed by the neutral vowel) becomes (General Introduction, § 37) उठउली *uṭhaülí* or उठौलीं *uṭhaulí*. Again for the double causal the forms would be उठ्वावैत छीं *uṭh'wáwait hí* and उठ्वउलीं *uṭh'waülí*, or उठ्वौलीं *uṭh'waülí*.

Similarly, if we use the affixes आय *áy* and वाय *wáy*, we get in the present definite उठायैत छीं *uṭháyait hí* and उठ्वायैत छीं *uṭh'wáyait hí*, and in the preterite उठइली *uṭhaïlí* or उठैलीं *uṭhailí* and उठ्वइलीं *uṭh'waïlí* or उठ्वैलीं *uṭh'wailí*.

The following are examples of the regular formation of causals and double causals. It may be remarked that the forms containing व *wa* are the usual ones. (See § 87). Only the forms in व *wa* are given below; the forms in य *ya* can be formed by substituting a final य *y* for a final व *w*:—

Simple Verb.	Causal.	Double Causal.
√ उठ *uṭh*, 'rise.'	उठाव *uṭháw*, 'raise.'	उठ्वाव *uṭh'wáw*, 'cause to raise.'
√ छिप *chhip*, 'be hidden.'	छिपाव *chhipáw*, 'hide.'	छिप्वाव *chhip'wáw*, 'cause to hide.'
√ लुक *luk*, 'be hidden.'	लुकाव *lukáw*, 'hide.'	लुक्वाव *luk'wáw*, 'cause to hide.

Simple Verb.	Causal.	Double Causal.
पक *pak*, 'be cooked.'	पकाव *pakáw*, 'cook.'	पकवाव *pak'wáw*, 'cause to cook.'
मिल *mil*, 'meet.'	मिलाव *miláw*, 'mix.'	मिलवाव *mil'wáw*, 'cause to mix.'
सुन *sun*, 'hear.'	सुनाव *sunáw*, 'tell.'	सुनवाव *sun'wáw*, 'cause to tell.'
कह *kah*, 'say.'	कहाव *kaháw*, 'cause to speak.'	कहवाव *kah'wáw*, 'cause to cause to speak.'
घुर *ghur*, 'be turned.'	घुराव *ghuráw*, 'turn.'	घुरवाव *ghur'wáw*, 'cause to turn.'

§ 104. If the simple root contains a long vowel it is shortened, viz. आ *á* to अ *a*, ई *í* to इ *i*, ऊ *ú* to उ *u*, ए *e* to ए *è*, ओ *o* to ओ *ŏ*, ऐ *ai* to ऐ *aĭ*, and औ *au* to औ *aŭ*.

Similarly, if a root ends in a double consonant, it is made single: thus—

जाग *jág*, 'be awake.'	जगाव *jagáw*, 'awaken.'	जगवाव *jag'wáw*, 'cause to awake.'
जीत *jít*, 'conquer.'	जिताव *jitáw*, 'cause to conquer.'	जितवाव *jit'wáw*, 'cause to cause to conquer.'
सीख *síkh*, 'learn.'	सिखाव *sikháw*, 'teach.'	सिखवाव *sikh'wáw*, 'cause to teach.'
पी *pí*, 'drink.'	पिआव *piáw*, 'cause to drink.'	पिअवाव *piawáw*, 'cause to cause to drink.'
भींज* *bhíj*, 'be wet.'	भिँजाव *bhĩjáw*, 'moisten.'	भिँजवाव *bhĩj'wáw*, 'cause to moisten.'
घूम *ghúm*, 'be turned.'	घुमाव *ghumáw*, 'turn.'	घुमवाव *ghum'wáw*, 'cause to turn.'
सूत *sút*, 'sleep.'	सुताव *sutáw*, 'put to sleep.'	सुतवाव *sut'wáw*, 'cause to put to sleep.'
बूड़ *búṛ*, 'sink.'	बुड़ाव *buṛáw*, 'immerse.'	बुड़वाव *buṛ'wáw*, 'cause to immerse.'

* See General Introduction, § 28.

Simple Verb.	Causal.	Double Causal.
√ देख *dekh*, 'see.'	देखाव *dĕkháw*, 'show.'	देखनवाव *dĕkh'wáw*, 'cause to show.'
√ पैर *pair*, 'swim.'	पैराव *pa͡iráw*, 'cause to swim.'	पैरनवाव *pa͡ir'wáw*, 'cause to cause to swim.'
√ बैठ *baiṭh*, 'sit.'	बैठाव *ba͡iṭháw*, 'seat.'	बैठनवाव *ba͡iṭh'wáw*, 'cause to sit.'
√ दौड़ *daur*, 'run.'	दौड़ाव *da͡uṛáw*, 'cause to run.'	दौड़नवाव *da͡uṛ'wáw*, 'cause to cause to run.'
√ लुक *lukk*, 'be hidden.'	लुकाव *lukáw*, 'hide.'	लुकनवाव *luk'wáw*, 'cause to hide.'

Note in connection with the above :—

Simple Verb.	Causal.
√ कह *kah*, 'speak.'	कहनलाव *kah'láw*, also regular.
√ खा *khá*, 'eat.'	खिआव *khiáw* or खिलाव *khiláw*, also regular.
√ पी *pí*, 'drink.'	पिलाव *piláw*, also regular.
√ देख *dekh*, 'see.'	देखनलाव *dĕkh'láw*, also regular.
√ सीख *sikh*, 'teach.'	सिखनलाव *sikh'láw*, also regular.

§ 105. Some primitive neuter verbs, having a monosyllabic root enclosing a short vowel, form the first causal by simply lengthening that vowel. The double causal is formed in the usual way, *e.g.*—

Simple Verb.	Causal.
√ कट *kaṭ*, 'be cut.'	काट *káṭ*, 'cut.'
√ बंध *bandh*, 'be tied.'	बाँध * *bǎdh*, 'tie.'
√ लद *lad*, 'be loaded.'	लाद *lád*, 'load.'
√ खिंच *khiṅch*, 'be dragged.'	खींच * *khích*, 'drag.'

§ 106. Sometimes a cognate diphthong is substituted for the long vowel, *e.g.*—

खुल *khul*, 'be open.'	खोल *khol*, 'open.'
घुल *ghul*, 'melt' (*neut.*)	घोल *ghol*, 'melt' (*act.*)

* When the vowel is lengthened *anuswár* becomes *anunásik*. (Compare General Introduction, § 28.)

§ 107. The verb √ निकस *nikas* or निकल *nikal*, 'come out,' makes its causal निकास *nikás* or निकाल *nikál*, 'take out,' on the analogy of the above. So also √ पसर *pasar*, 'be scattered,' makes पसार *pasár*, 'scatter,' 'extend,' √ ससर *sasar*, 'slip,' ससार *sasár*, 'cause to slip,' √ उपर *upar*, 'be rooted up,' उपार *upár* 'root up,' and √ उखर *ukhar*, 'be rooted up,' उखार *ukhár*.

§ 108. The following are irregular :—

Simple Verb.	Causal.	Double Causal.
√ अठ *aṭ*, 'be stopped.'	आड़ *áṛ*, 'stop.'	अड़ाव *aṛáw*.
√ फट *phaṭ*, 'be torn.'	फाड़ *pháṛ*, 'tear.'	फड़ाव *phaṛáw*.
√ छुट *chhuṭ*, 'be separated.'	छोड़ *chhoṛ* or छाड़ *chháṛ*, 'separate.'	छोड़ाव *chhŏṛáw*.
√ जुट *juṭ*, 'be joined.'	जोड़ *joṛ*, 'join.'	जोड़ाव *jŏṛáw*.
√ टुट *ṭuṭ*, 'be broken.'	तोड़ *toṛ*, or तोर *tor*, 'break.'	तोड़ाव *tŏṛáw* or तोराव *tŏráw*.
√ फुट *phuṭ*, 'be burst.'	फोड़ *phoṛ*, 'burst.'	फोड़ाव *phŏṛáw*.
√ बिक *bik*, 'be sold.'	बेँच *bẽch*, 'sell.'	बेँचाव *bẽcháw*.
√ रह *rah*, 'remain.'	राख *rákh*, 'place.'	रखाव *rakháw*.
√ भीग *bhíg*, 'be wet.'	भिँगो *bhĩgo*, 'wet.'	भिँगव्वाव *bhĩg'wáw*.
√ डूब *ḍúb*, 'sink.'	डुबो *ḍubo*, 'immerse.'	डुबव्वाव *ḍub'wáw*.

CHAPTER XII.

COMPOUND VERBS.

§ 109. Compound verbs are either intensives, potentials, completives, frequentatives, desideratives, continuatives, staticals, inceptives, permissives, or acquisitives.

§ 110. Compound verbs may be classed as—(1) those formed with the verbal noun, and (2) those formed with the participles.

(1) Those formed with the verbal noun are—

a) Intensives.	*e*) Desideratives.
b) Potentials.	*f*) Inceptives.
c) Completives.	*g*) Permissives.
d) Frequentatives.	*h*) Acquisitives.

(2) Those formed with the participles—

a) Continuatives.	*b*) Staticals.

Class I.—Compounds formed with the Verbal Noun.*

§ 111. There are three varieties of the verbal noun—

a) In अ *a* (silent), oblique form, ए *ĕ*; as देख *dekh*, obl. देखे *dekhĕ*.

b) In अल *al*, oblique form, ॰ला *'lá*; as देखल *dekhal*, obl. देख॰ला *dĕkh'lá*.

c) In अब *ab*, oblique form *wanting*; as देखब *dekhab*, obl. *wanting*.

The direct first form is always the same as the root.

Compound verbs are either formed with the direct form of the first or second variety of the verbal noun, or with the oblique form of the first variety.

* Much of the succeeding matter is based on Kellogg's Hindí Grammar.

§ 112. *Intensives, Potentials,* and *Completives,* are always formed with the direct form of the first variety; *Frequentatives* are always formed with the direct form of the second variety; and *Desideratives* are generally so. *Inceptives, Permissives,* and *Acquisitives,* are always formed with the oblique form of the first variety.

113. *Intensive* compounds intensify or otherwise modify the meaning of the verb whose root stands first in the compound. They are formed by adding to a verbal noun of the first variety in the direct form one of certain other verbs, which latter verb in conjunction with the verbal noun is then conjugated as usual. This second conjugated member does not, however, retain its separate character and significance, but only modifies, in accordance with the general idea which it embodies, the meaning of the unconjugated verbal noun to which it is annexed. Examples are—

फेँकब *phēkab*, 'to throw.'	फेँक देब *phēk deb*, 'to throw away.'
तोरब *torab*, 'to break.'	तोर डालब *tor ḍálab*, 'to break in pieces.'
बनब *banab*, 'to be made.'	बन आएब *ban áĕb* or बन जाएब *ban jáĕb*, ['to be completed.'
खाएब *kháĕb*, 'to eat.'	खा जाएब *khá jáĕb*, 'to eat up.'
बोलब *bolab*, 'to speak.'	बोल उठब *bol uṭhab*, 'to speak suddenly.'
काटब *káṭab*, 'to cut.'	काट लेब *káṭ leb*, 'to cut for oneself.'
राखब *rákhab*, 'to place.'	राख लेब *rákh leb*, 'to lay by.'

§ 114. The auxiliary verbs usually employed to form intensives are—

देब *deb*, 'to give,'	implying	*intensity.*
डालब *ḍálab*, 'to throw,'	"	*violence.*
आएब *áĕb*, 'to come,' } जाएब *jáĕb*, 'to go,' }	"	*completion.*
पड़ब *paṛab* or परब *parab*, 'to fall,'	"	*chance.*
उठब *uṭhab*, 'to rise,'	"	*suddenness.*
लेब *leb*, 'to take,'	"	*reflexiveness.*

पड़ब *paṛab* is also used in intensive compounds to form passives of transitive verbs. (See § 100.)

§ 115. *Potentials* are formed by adding to the same form of the verbal noun of any verb the verb सकब *sakab*, 'to be able,' which may then be conjugated throughout. Examples are—

बोल सकब *bol sakab*, 'to be able to speak.'

ऊ दौड़ सकऽ हइ *ú daur̤ saka haï*, 'he can run.'

हम जा सकब *ham já sakab*, 'I shall be able to go.'

ऊ सब आ सकऽ हल॰थिन *ú sab á saka hal'thin*, 'they were able to come.'

हम नऽ जा सकऽ ही *ham na já saka hí*, 'I cannot go.'

§ 116. *Completives* are formed by adding to the same form of the verbal noun of a verb the verb चुकब *chukab*, which may then be conjugated throughout. This compound denotes the *completion* of the act denoted by the primary member of the compound. Examples are—

ऊ खा चुकल *ú khá chukal*, 'he has done eating.'

जब ऊ खा चुकी *jab ú kha chukí*, 'when he shall have eaten.'

ऊ तो जा चुकल है *ú to já chukal hai*, 'he is indeed already gone.'

§ 117. *Frequentatives* are formed by affixing to the direct form of the second variety of the verbal noun of any verb the verb करब *karab*, which may then be used in any tense. Examples are—

आवल करऽ *áwal kara*, 'come often.'

ऊ कहल करे है *ú kahal karĕ hai*, 'he is in the habit of saying.'

हम शास्त्र के पढ़ल करऽ ही *ham sástr ke par̤hal kara hi*, 'I am in the habit of reading the shástras.'

तों हम्मार बात मानल करऽ *tõ hammar bát mánal kara*, 'always obey my words.'

तों काहे अइसन कइल करऽ हऽ *tõ káhĕ aïsan kaïl kara ha*, 'why do you always do so?'

ऊ जायल करे है *ú jáyal karĕ hai*, 'he often goes.'

§ 118. *Desideratives* are formed, like frequentatives, with the direct form of the verbal noun in अल *al*, substituting the verb चाहब *cháhab* for

करब *karab* as the second or conjugated member. These denote primarily *desire* to do the action expressed of the principal member ; secondarily, the *immediate futurity* of that action. Examples are—

ऊ बोलल चाहे है *ú bolal cháhĕ hai,* 'he wishes to speak.'

ऊ मुअल चाहे है *ú mual cháhĕ hai* or मरल चाहऽ हइ *maral cháha haï,* 'he is about to die.'

Sometimes the principal verb is put in the oblique form of the first variety of the verbal noun with or without the dative postposition के *ke* or ला *lá*. Examples are—

घड़ी बाजे चाहऽ है *ghaṛí bájĕ cháha hai,* 'the clock is about to strike.'
ऊ बोले के चाहे है *ú bolĕ ke cháhĕ hai,* 'he wishes to speak.'
ऊ जाए चाहे है *ú jáĕ cháhĕ hai,* 'he wishes to go.'
भेजे ला चाहऽ ही *bhejĕ lá cháha hí,* 'I wish to send.'

The desiderative compound in the precative form with चाही *cháhí* is idiomatically used to express obligation or duty. Examples are—

ई पोथी के पढ़ल चाही *í pothí ke paṛhal cháhí,* '(one) ought to read this book.' (*Lit.* 'be good enough to wish to read.')

तोहँरा ऊठमाँ जायल चाही *tŏh'rá úṭhamã jáyal cháhí,* 'it is right for you (*i.e.* you ought) to go there.'

§ 119. *Inceptives* are formed by using the inflected form of the first variety of the verbal noun in construction with the verb लागब *lágab,* 'to be joined,' 'to begin,' and denote the action of the verbal noun as *beginning.* Examples are—

कहे लागल *kahĕ lágal,* 'he began to say.'
मारे लगल्लइ *márĕ lag'laï,* 'he began to beat.'
बाघ खाए लगल्लइ *bágh kháĕ lag'laï,* 'the tiger began to eat.'

§ 120. *Permissives* are formed by combining the same form of the verbal noun with the verb देब *deb,* 'to give,' and express *permission* to do the act denoted by the verbal noun. Examples are—

हमँरा जाए दऽ *ham'rá jáĕ da,* 'let me go.'

हमरा बोलें दीही *ham'rá bolĕ díhí*, 'be good enough to let me speak.'

ऊ ओकरा खाए देलकइ *ú ŏk'rá kháĕ dĕl'kaï*, 'he allowed him to eat.'

§ 121. *Acquisitives* are the exact converse of the preceding, and are formed in the same way, substituting पाएब *páĕb*, 'to get,' for देब *deb*. Examples are—

> तोँ ऊठमाँ जाए नऽ पइबऽ *tõ úṭhamā̆ jáĕ na païba*, 'you will not obtain permission to go there.'
>
> हम बैठे नऽ पौली *ham baiṭhĕ na paulí*, 'I was not allowed to sit.'

Class II.—Compounds formed with the Participles.

§ 122. *Continuatives* are formed by combining the present participle of any verb with the verbs जाएब *jáĕb*, 'to go', or रहब *rahab*, 'to remain.' The present participle is sometimes in the direct and sometimes in the oblique form. The compound with जाएब *jáĕb* expresses *steady progression*, and with रहब *rahab* the *continuance* of a complete action. Examples—

> ऊ लिखइत जा हइ *ú likhaït já haï*, } 'he is going on writing.'
> ऊ लिखन्ते जा हइ *ú likh'tĕ já haï*, }
>
> ऊ सब छोकड़ियन पढ़इत (or पढ़न्ते) जा हलथीन *ú sab chhŏk'ṛiyan paṛhaït (paṛh'tĕ) já hal'thín*, 'those girls were going on reading.'
>
> पानी बहन्ते जा हइ *páni bah'tĕ já haï*, 'the water keeps flowing away.'
>
> ऊ गाते रहऽ हइ *ú gátĕ raha haï*, 'she continues singing.'
>
> तोँ सब काहे हँसन्ते रहऽ हऽ *tõ sab káhĕ hā̃s'tĕ raha ha*, 'why do you keep laughing?'
>
> नदी के धार बहन्ते रहऽ हइ *nadi kĕ dhár bah'tĕ raha haï*, 'the stream of the river keeps flowing on.'

Closely connected with the above is a common combination in which the past instead of the present participle takes the first place and a verb of motion the second place. An example is—

> एक बाघ पड़ल फिरऽ हलइ *ĕk bágh paṛal phira halaï*, 'a tiger was prowling about.'

NOTE.—In Hindí the form चला जाना *chalá jáná*, 'to go away,' occurs under this rule; but in Mágadhí this form does not occur, the compound taking an intensive form. Example—

नौँड़ी चल जावऽ हली *nãuṛí chal jáwa halí*, 'the girl was going along.'

§ 123. *Staticals* denote motion in a state of doing anything. They are formed by combining a verb of motion with a present participle in the oblique form. Examples are—

ऊ कन्दऽते आवे है *ú kand'tĕ áwĕ hai*, 'he comes weeping.'
एक जन्नी गाते आवऽ हलइ *ĕk janni gátĕ áwa halaï*, 'a woman came singing.'

DIVISION III.

INDECLINABLES.

§ 124. See General Introduction.

APPENDIX I.

THE following selections are in the Mágadhí dialect. The conversation between two villagers is written by a guru of the Bihár subdivision of the Patna district; the fables have been provided by Paṇḍit S'iv Náráyaṇ Trivedí, Deputy Inspector of Schools, Gayá. A translation of the selections will be found in the General Introduction :—

SELECTIONS FROM THE MÁGADHÍ DIALECT.

CONVERSATION BETWEEN TWO VILLAGERS.

(In the dialect of South Patna.)

(१) प्रश्न। कहऽ भाई कहऽवाँ सेँ आवऽ हऽ।
उत्तर। परऽसिआ गाँव सेँ आवऽ ही॥
(२) प्र। ऊँआँ सेँ कखऽनी चलऽलऽ हल।
उ। बिहऽने के चलल ही॥
(३) प्र। काहे लेल ऊँआँ गेलऽहू हल।
उ। ऊँआँ हम्मर खेत हउ, ओकऽरा देखे गेलौँ हल॥
(४) प्र। ओइ मेँ की* सुनऽलऽ है।
उ। खाली राहर डुबल गेलइ है॥
(५) प्र। कहऽ भाई अब के फसिल के की रंग हउ।
उ। ई फसिल के हाल की पुछऽ हऽ। पानी बरऽसे बिहुँ बड़ हरऽजा हथ॥
(६) प्र। आज कल्ह अपऽने के भाई ना देख पड़ऽ हथू।
उ। हम्मर भाई आज कल्ह किला मे नोकर हथ। एम्मे बहुत कम आवऽ हथ॥
(७) प्र। आप केरी बड़ऽकी गाय के हाल की हकउ।
उ। ऊ आज कल्ह गाभिन हइ; बाकी चारा न मिले सेँ दुट गेलउ हइ॥
(८) प्र। कइ महिना सतौँ गाभिन हो।
उ। भेलइ तो आठ महिना, बाकी पेट ओकर कुछु उमऽड़ल नऽ देख पड़ऽ हइ॥

---

* Note the use of की *kí* instead of का *ká*, which is peculiar to South-Eastern Patna.

(९) प्र । पाहुर करऽ हइ की अभी ना ।

उ । हाँ, कुछु कुछु जान पड़ऽ हइ ॥

(१०) प्र । ई कौथा बीआन हइ, अउर केत्तेक दूध दे हो ।

उ । ई अठ॰वाँ बीआन हइ । दू अढ़ाइ सेर दूध एक बाजी दे हइ ॥

(११) प्र । हम॰रा एगो बक॰री लेवे के हइ । तोह॰रा गाँव मेँ मिली ।

उ । हम॰रा गाँव मेँ बकरिअन तो हइ, बाकी दाम कड़ा हइ ॥

(१२) प्र । तोहर बक॰री की भेलउ ।

उ । हम चरे लेल ओक॰रा गाँवे पर छाड़ल रहऽ ही ॥

(१३) प्र । कुच्छो दूध दे है ।

उ । लड़िकन के खाए भर हो जा हउ ॥

(१४) प्र । अब के केतारी बोल॰हू हइ, की नऽ ।

उ । केतारी तो बोलिअइ हइ. बाकी ओह मेँ कुच्छो फाएदा नऽ हइ ॥

(१५) प्र । तोह॰रा कने सेँ चार मोट मंग॰नी मिल सकऽ हइ ।

उ । काहे नऽ । पटावन हो जाए पर ले लऽ ॥

(१६) प्र । तोह॰रा हिँआँ केठो मोट चलऽ हउ ।

उ । तीन मोट नाध॰लीँ है ॥

(१७) प्र । तोहर आम बगीचा कुछु फल हो की नइँ ।

उ । अब॰की तो बद॰ली सेँ लाही लग गेलइ नऽ तो बहुत होत हलइ ।

(१८) प्र । थोड़ा आम हम॰रो* अचार लेल दीहऽ ।

उ । अख॰नी तोहर जी चाहे. आ के तोड़॰वा लेहू ॥

(१९) प्र । तोहर लड़िका कुच्छो पढ़ऽ हो, की नइँ ।

उ । हाँ, गुरु कने जा हइ । अच्छर तो चीन्ह गेल हइ, आज काल्ह पहाड़ा पढ़े हइ ॥

(२०) प्र । स्कूल काहे नऽ भेजऽ ।

उ । कुच्छो सीख ले, तब भेज दीँ ॥

(२१) प्र । हम॰हूँ अप॰ना लड़िका के स्कूल मे भेजे ला चाहऽ ही ।

उ । अच्छा हम॰रा लड़िका के साथे ओक॰रो* भेज देहू ॥

---

* Emphatic for हम॰रा *ham'rá*, ओक॰रा *ŏk'rá*—'me also,' 'him also.'

FABLES.

(In the dialect of Gayá.)

१

एक गो मुर्गा गोबरऽवा के ढेर के चँगुरऽवा से कोड़ब करत हलइ, पर अनऽचित्ते ओकऽरा मे से एगो बड़ऽगो मोती निकल अइलइ। तब मुरगऽवा कहलऽकइ कि, आहा कइसन अच्छा हइ। एकऽरा जौहरिया पइतइ हल तो बड़ा नितऽरैतइ। पर हमर भूख एकऽरा से नइ जइतइ। एगो हमऽरा चाउर मिलइत तो सौ मोती से बेस हल। सच्चे है जे अप्पन काम नइ आवे, ऊ चूल्हा भाँड़ मे जाए।

२

एगो दलिद्दर खूब पक्का फकीर से पुछऽलक कि, हम भूखेँ मरत ही, और हम्मर परोसिया तक्या तोसक लगा के पड़ल रहे हे; रात दिन चैन करे हे। ओकऽरा मे कौन अइसन गुन हइ, जे भगऽवान ओकऽरा अइसन बनउलऽकन, और हमऽरा दलिद्दर कइलऽकन। ई सुन के, बाबाजी कहलऽथिन कि, बाबा, तूँ नइ सुनलऽ हऽ। राम जी झरोखा पर बैस कर सब के हिसाब करत हथिन. और जेकऽरा जइसन कमाइ तेकऽरा तइसन दे हथिन।

३

कौनोँ अच्छा अदऽमी एगो गोसाँई से कहऽलक कि, महराज जी, मुलुक मुलुक, और गाँवे गाँव फिरऽला से का मिले हो, एक ठाँव रह के, भगऽवान मे काहे न मन लगावऽ, और कौनोँ मठ मे बैस के भगऽवान के गुन गावऽ। तब जोगी जी कहलऽकन कि, बाबा, सब सच हो, पर तूँ ई कहऽतूत नइ सुनलँ हँ कि, जे पानी बहे हे, से कच्छल रहे है, और जे बाँधल रहे हे, से कदोर रहे हे। ऐसऽने साधु फिरऽला, से अच्छा, और कौनोँ दाग नऽ लगे हे।

४

एक दिन जाड़ा मे एक तलेवर के घर मे आग लागल, और सब माल आल जर के खार हो गेल, और ऊ जब्बर मे जाड़ा हो के पकऽता हल, कि एतऽना मे. एक गरीब परोसिया जाड़ से कंपऽते २ ओजईं आएल और तापे लागल। तब ऊ तलेवरऽवा बोलल कि, हाँ २ केकऽरो घर जरे केउ तापे।

५

एगो किसान के लड़॰कन अपन्नन मे बड़ लड़ऽ हल॰थिन। बात से केतें समभ॰उल॰कइ पर कौनोँ नइ मनल॰थिन। तब किसनवा अपन्ना जिया मे कहल॰कइ कि, एख॰निन के कुछु कर के देखइअइ, तो चाहे कुछु समझ जाय। एक दिन ऊ अपन्ना बेट॰वन के बोलौलक; और कहन्लक कि, थोड़े से लकड़ी हम॰रा आगूँ मे ले आवऽ, तब ऊ किसन॰वा ऊ लक॰ड़ियन के कस के बाँधल्लक, और एक एक से कहन्लक कि रसिया मत खोल और लक॰ड़ियन के तोड़ डालऽ। एका एकी बल उम॰जैल॰थिन पर केकरो से कुछु नइ भेलइ। तब किसनवा खोल के, एक २ लक॰ड़िया ओख॰नन के देल॰कइ, तो तुर॰न्ते तोड़ देल॰थिन। तब ओकर बप्पा कहल॰कइ कि बेटा तोह॰निओं* बाँधल लकड़ी नियर मिलल रहबऽ. तो सब दुसन्मन के हरइबऽ, और जो फुटबऽ, तो जामलऽ कि बिगड़ गेलऽ।

६

एक बेरी ऊँड़॰रा भेड़ियन से कहन्ला पेठौलन्कइ कि, आवऽ हमनी दोनो मेल करीँ काहे अपन्नन मे लड़ल करीँ, और एक दोसन्रा के लेहू के प्यासल रहीँ। ई सबड़ कुतन्वन सब लड़ाई के घर हथुन. ऐसन्हि रोज रोज भूक कर हमनार भगावऽ हथिन, और हमन्रा तोरा लड़ावऽ हय। इखन्निन के हम॰रा हिंयाँ भेज दऽ तो फेर काहे ला लड़ाई रहत, हमन्रा तोहन्रा मे सब दिन मेल रहत, तो तोहर बारो टेढ़ नइ होतौ। गँवार भेड़ियन खराब ऊँड़न्रन के बतियन मान के, कुतन्वन के भेज देलन्कन। पहन्ले ऊँड़न्रा तो कुतन्वन के खा गेल्लइ, सब पीछू भेड़ियन पर जर॰जिद लगा के पड़लइ, और थोड़ि के दिन मे सब भेड़ियन के भी खा गेलइ।

दुसन्मन सदे दगा दे है। ऊ बड़ गँवार हे, जे दुसन्मन के आपन समन्भे।

७

बाघ ऊँड़ार औ कँदुआ, एक बेरी ई तीनो मिल के अपन्नन मे मत मेरौलन्कन, कि सब मिल के सिकार मारीँ और फेर अप॰नन मे बाँट लिहीँ। ई कह अँगलन्वा मे उछन्ले कूदे लगल॰थिन, औ जब एगो बड़न्गो करिया हरिन मार लेल॰कथिन. तब बघन्वा बोल उठन्लइ कि लावऽ एकन्रा बाँटिअउ, और तुर॰न्ते ओकर तीन कुड्डी कर के हंभर कर बोलन्लइ कि, पहिल कुदिया तो हम लेबउ, काहे कि हम बन के राजा हिअउ; दोसन्रो भी हमन्हीं लेबउ

* Emphatic for तोहनी *tŏhaní*, 'you also.'

काहे कि एकन्रा मारे मे बड़ मेहन्नत करन्लौँ हठ, और तेसर कुद्दी धरल हउ, देखिअउ जेकर दम चलत हउ, कि हमन्रा आगूँ से ले जा हठ। ई सुन के कँदुआ और ऊँडन्रा हेरा के भाग गेलन, और बघन्वा अकेले हरिनिया के खइलन्कइ। ई कहतूत सधे हे, कि जेकर लाठी ओकरे* भइस।

८

एक बेरी नद्दी मे बाढ़ अइलइ। तो एगो पीतर और एक गो माटी के घैला दह चलन्लन। पितन्रा के घलन्वा मटियक घैलन्वा से कहलन्कइ कि हमन्रा भीरी भीरी चल, तब तोरा हम बचा लेबउ। मटियक घड़न्वा कहलन्कइ कि, तोँ अच्छा कहइ हठ, हम तोहर बड़ भल मानन्बो, और सदे गुन गइबो, पर सचे पुछऽ, तो हमन्रा एही डर हे, कि कहीँ पानी के ढेहू के धक्का से तोहन्रा पास चल गेलूँ, तो हम फूट जाब, औ अलग रहब, तो ऐसन्हीँ डोलन्ते डालन्ते कहीँ किनारा मे लग जाब। सचे हे, बड़ के आस राखी पर भीरी नऽ जाई।

९

एगो मुन्सी बजार मे बैठल, चिट्ठी लिखब करत हलन। ऊँहाँ एगो परन्देसी आ गेल। कहन्लक कि, मुन्सी जी का लिखत हठ। तब मुन्सी कहलन्थिन कि, भाई चिट्ठी लिखत ही। तब ऊ कहलन्कइ कि, हमन्रो† सलाम लिख दीहठ। फेर मुन्सी जी कहलन्थिन कि, अर्जी लिखठ ही। तब ऊ कहलन्कइ कि, हमन्रो नाँव लिख दीहठ। मुन्सिया चिड़न्चिड़ा के बोलन्लइ कि, तमस्सुक लिखऽ ही। तब ऊ कहलन्कइ कि, हमन्रो गोआही लिख दीहठ। मुन्सिया बुझलन्कइ कि ई तो कौनौँ अजब तरह के अदन्मी बुझा हे, और पुछलन्कइ कि तोर नाम का हउ। तब ऊ हँस के कहलन्कइ कि हम्मर नाम हे, मानठ चाहे नठ मानठ, हम तोहर पऊना हिओ।

१०

एक तलेबर अदन्मी के घर रात खनी आगि लगन्लइ। आपन लड़न्का बाला ले के बाहर निकन्लल औ चकरन्वन से कहन्लक कि, चीज बस्त निकालठ। एतन्ना मे अगिया बऊत लहक गेलइ, सब घरन्वा धूँएँ २ हो गेलइ। तब चकरन्वन बोले लगलन्थिन कि, हम कौंची २ निकालिऔ। तब ऊ तलेबर अदन्मी ऊंकर कर बोललइ। आगी लगन्ला मेँ जे २ निकालबठ सेई रहो।

---

* Emphatic for ओकर *okar*.
† Emphatic for हमर *hamar*, 'my also.'

११

एगो बेकूफ गोआरिन माथा पर दही के बासन रखऽले चल जा हल। औ चलऽते २ ओकऽरा मन मे ई बतऽलइ कि, दहिया के बेँचब, औ जे पैसा होत तेकर आम मोल लेब। कुछु आम हमऽरो हे। सब मिला के ३०० सौ से बढ़ जात। एह मे से कुछु सड़ जात, पर हाँ २५० तो बचत, औ जे बचत तेकर बहुत दाम मिलत। तब सोहराई मे एगो हरिअर साड़ी लेब। हाँ, हरिअर साड़ी हमऽरा बेस सोहत। हम हरिअऽरे साड़ी लेब। ओकऽरा पहन कर मेला पर जाएब, और खुब ऐँट जोँट के अप्पन गहऽना और लुगन के सोभा और मुँह के झलऽकी देखाएब, औ चलऽते २ सौ १ दफे झूकब। अइसन सोचइते बेकूफ गोआरिन जे ऐँट के चल लगऽलइ, तो दही के बासन गिर के टुकऽरी २ हो गेलइ, औ सब बनल बनावल घर बिगड़ गेलइ।

१२

एगो चील्ह अपऽना ठोर मे एक घोँघा लेले हलइ, ओकऽरा तोड़े लगी भूआँ मे कईक दफेँ पटऽकलऽकइ पर घोँघऽवा नइ टुटऽलइ। तब एगो कौआ ई कहलऽकइ कि, एकऽरा ठोरऽवा मे ले के, बहुत उप्पर उड़ के गिरा देहीँ, तो घोँघऽवा टूट जइतौ। चिल्हिया कहलऽकइ कि, अच्छा कहलँ औ ऊ घोँघऽवा के ले के उड़ऽलइ, औ बहुत दूर उप्पर जा के छोड़ देलऽकइ। जैसऽही भूआँ मे घोँघऽवा गिरऽलइ, चूर २ हो गेलइ, औ कौअऽवा तुरऽन्ते ओकर गुदऽवा खा गेलइ। जरीसन के बाद चिल्हिया नीचूँ उतरऽलइ, तो छिलऽकोइया छोड़, औ कुछु न पउलऽकइ।

१३

एगो लोमऽड़ी कौनोँ बगीचा मे गेलइ, और देखलऽकइ कि अंगूर घौरे २ पकल ठटऽरी मे लटऽकल हइ और ओकऽरा मे से रस चूअब करऽ हइ। ई देख के ओकर मन चपऽचपा गेलइ। बहुत उकऽलल कूदल, पर अँगुरऽवा के ठटरिया तक नऽ पहुँचऽलइ। जब केऊ ढंग से दाओ नऽ लगऽलइ, तब ऐसऽही बरऽबराते ऊँआँ से चल गेलइ कि, अइ, खट्टा आँगुर के खाए।

१४

एगो रसायऽनी केऊ अदऽमी से कहलऽकइ कि, तोँ कुछु चाँदी ला देऽ, तो हम एक अइसन अड़ी गार के दिखउ कि तुरऽन्ते ऊ चाँदी से सोना हो जाई। तबऽ ऊ अदऽमी दमऽपट्टी मे आ गेलइ, औ बड़ जुगुत से २०० दू सौ भर चाँदी ला देलऽकइ। रसैनियाँ

ओही रतिया के अप्पन डेरा ऊँआँ से उठा के चल गेलइ। तब ऊ बेचारा दुख झेल ऊ बेइमान रसायन॰नी के खोज के धुन मे जंगल मे हरान होलइ पर, ओकर कहीँ सूग न० लगन॰लइ! ओक॰रा घबन॰राएल देख के, एगो अद॰मी अइसन कहलन॰कइ कि, तोरा से ई चूक भेलउ कि ऊ बेइमान फकीर के फंदा मे पड़ गेलँ, अब पछ॰तौला से का होतउ। ई बात पर एगो खिस्सा तोरा सुनावउ हियौ, जेकन॰रा सदे याद राखे के चाही।

१५

एगो चिरइ कौनोँ किसान के बागचा मे जा के काँच कोचिल फल जा के काट दे हलइ। किसन॰वा रोज ओक॰रा खूग मे लागल हलइ। एक दिन अँगुर॰वा के ठटरिया पर जाल लगा के ओक॰रा पकड़॰लक औ मारे लेल करलन॰कइ। तब चिरँया किसन॰वाँ से कहलन॰कइ कि, तोँ हमन॰रा छोड़ दे, तो हम तोरा एकन॰रा बदला कते बात बता दियौ कि जेकन॰रा से तोरा बड़ लाभ होतइ। तब किसन॰वाँ कहलन॰कइ कि हमन॰रा पहन॰ले बता देले, तब हम तोरा छोड़ दियौ। चिरँया ओक॰रा तीन बात कहलन॰कइ। एक तो दुसन॰मन अपन॰ना बस मे आ जाय, तो ओक॰रा नइ छोड़े के चाही, दोसर जौन बात अकिल मे नइ अटे, ओक॰रा माने के नइ चाही. तेसर गेल चीज के लेल खोजे के नइ चाही. चौठ औ एगो हइ, जब तोँ हमन॰रा छोड़ दे, तब कहबौँ। किसन॰वा ई बतिया के सुन के, जइसन कहलन॰कइ ओइसन कइलन॰कइ, और चिरँया के छोड़ देलन॰कइ। तब ऊ भीत पर बैठ के कहे लगलइ कि, हमन॰रा पेट मे मुर्गी के अंडा से एगो बड़॰गो मोती हलइ। जो हमन॰रा नइ छोड़॰तँ और मारन॰तँ हल, तो ऊ मोतिया तोरा हात लगतउ हल। किसन॰वाँ पछ॰तावे लगन॰लइ। तब ऊ कहलन॰कइ कि, हे बेकूफ तुरन॰ते हम्मर तीनो बतिया भूल गेलँ। हम तोर दुसन॰मन हलिअउ, जब हमन॰रा पकड़॰लँ हल, तो काहे छोड़॰लँ, और मुर्गी के अंडा बराबर तो हमन॰हूँ* नही; फेर मुर्गी के अंडा से बड़॰गो मोती हमन॰रा पेटन॰वा मे कने से परन॰तीत भेलउ। पर तोँ ई बतिया पर आसन॰रा कैलँ। औ जब हम तोरा हथन॰वा से निकल गेलिअउ, तब पछ॰तौला से का होतौ। एकन॰रा से एही बूझ पड़० हइ, कि कौनोँ काम करे, तो पहन॰ले खूब बूझ ले, तब करे। और पीछे काम बिगड़ जाए, तो पछ॰तावे के नइ चाही।

१६

कौनोँ तलेवर के दूगो बेटा हलइ। जब ओकर बप्पा मर गेलइ, तब दोनो भइवन ओकर धन॰वाँ अपन॰नन मे बाँट लेलन॰कन। बड़॰का भइवा अप्पन रुपैया सुख चइन मे उड़ावे पड़ावे लगन॰लइ, औ छोटन॰का बड़ जुगुत से लगावन बझावन करे लगन॰लइ। एक दिन बड़॰का भइवा छोटन॰का भइवा से परन॰तर दे के कहे लगन॰लइ कि, भाई काहे दिन भर अनाज तौलत

* Emphatic for हम *ham*.

हँ। हम·रा साथ रह, खा, पी चइन कर। बहुत दिन बित·ला पर छोट·का भइवा लगावन बझावन कर के ढेर रुपया जमा कइल·कइ। तब ओकर बड़·का भइवा, जे गाएब बजाएब खेल तमासा मे अप्पन सब धन·वाँ लुटा कर गरीब हो गेलइ हल, ओकर दुअरिया पर आ के कहे लग·लइ कि, भाई हम तोरा पहि·ले हँसी मे उड़ौलियौ हल, पर हम·हूँ तोरा अइसन लगावन बझावन कर·तूँ, औ अनाज तौल·तूँ, तो आज ई गत हमर नइ होइत। सचे है, असं·कत अइसन बिद्दत हे, जो धन के धूर कर दे हइ।

१७

एगो कुत्ता नदी किनारे चलल जा हल। आइत २ ओक·रा एक हाड़ मिल गेलइ। ओक·रा मुह मे लेले। जब पनियाँ मे हेलल, तब हड़·वा के पर·छहियाँ पनियाँ मे जनउलइ। कुत·वा बुझल·कइ कि एगो और पनियाँ मे दोसर हाड़ हइ, तब ऊ हड़·वा निकाले ला मुह खोल·लक, कि मुँह·वाँ वाला हड़·वा ओ पनिया मे बह गेलइ। कुत·वा बोले लग·लइ कि, हाय, लोभी के ऐस·न गत हो हइ। जइसन मक्खी के भेल हल। मक्खी दूध पर बैठल और ओकर पँख·वा लब·टा गेल। तब माथा पट·के लागल, और कहे लागल कि·लोभ नैध नइ होए।

APPENDIX II.

List of Mágadhí Words.

The following list has been compiled principally with the help of Paṇḍit S'iv Náráyaṇ Trivedí, of Gayá. It contains a large number of words peculiar to Mágadhí, few of which will be found in any extant Hindí Dictionary.

MÁGADHÍ VOCABULARY.

अखैना *akhainá* (*H.* **पाँचा**), a rake for stirring chaff on the threshing floor.

अखौत *akhaut* (*H.* **खंभा को लाठे के बीच की मेख**), the fulcrum of a well-lever (**लाठा**).

अग॰रा *ag'rá* (*H.* **अगौरा**), sugar-cane tips, which are useless for making sugar, as they possess no juice.

अंगारी *angárí* (*H.* **चिनगारी**), a spark, scintillation = **तित॰की**.

अगेठी *angeṭhí* [1](*H.* **आग रखने का लोहे का बरतन**), a vessel for holding fire; [2](*H.* **अंग का ऐँठना**), the action of stretching the arms, as in yawning.

अचंगा *achangá* (*H.* **टाँड़**), a stage, shelf.

अज॰गुत *aj'gut, adj.* (*H.* **अचरज**), wonderful.

अँड़ास *āṛás* (*H.* **कूएँ के ऊपर का पटवट**), the wooden frame over a well.

अड़ौत *aṛaut* (*H.* **ओट**), a screen.

अथ॰री *ath'rí*, [1]an earthen basin for holding water or washing clothes; [2]a vessel for roasting poppy-flowers in cakes.

अमारी *amárí* (*H.* **गोबर की करसी**), dried cowdung.

अर॰पा *ar'pá*, the space between the thumb and forefinger. Cf. **कोड़ी, गिभी**.

अर॰मेना *ar'mená* (*H.* **मन बहलाव**), amusement, pleasure.

अलान *alán*, a trellis for supporting a creeping plant.

अस॰गनी *as'ganí* (*H.* **अरगनी**), a clothes-horse made of rope or bamboo = **टंगनी**, *q.v.*

अस॰ठी *as'ṭhí* (*H.* **नदा**), the raised piece of ground below the eaves (**ओलारी**) in a courtyard (**आँगन**).

आइल *áïl*, a field boundary.

आगन्दाइन *ág'dáïn*, the fore ox among the oxen engaged in treading corn. Cf. मेहन्टा कुड़न्दहिना.

आँतर *ā̆tar* [1] (*H.* हराई फाँदना), the portion of land contained within a plough-circuit; [2] the intermission of fever; [3] *adv. & prep.* (*H.* अंतर), within.

आपा *ápá*, a pit for keeping fish in when caught in a चिलौँद, *q.v.*

आभी *ábhí* (*H.* काठ की खंती), a heavy kind of wooden spade tipped with iron, used for digging up soils.

आरन्सी *ár'sí* (*H.* मछली मारने का थिक), a kind of horn-shaped net made of bamboos for catching fish.

आलो *álo* [1] (*H.* औधी), a part of a crop which is reaped by a cultivator for present eating, before the whole is ripe; [2] (*H.* अगरासन), the first fruits of a field offered to the family priest.

उकिल बिकिल *ukil bikil*, *adj.* (*H.* व्याकुल), perplexed; distraught.

उटन्कन *uṭ'kan*, a poker, an instrument for stirring a fire.

उड़ाह *uṛáh* (*H.* अनवासना), to dedicate to family use an earthen vessel, —that is to say, for one of the family to use it first before making it over to servants, otherwise if it is first used by servants it is impure.

उमन्ताहा *um'táhá*, *adj.* (*H.* बौड़ाहा), mad.

उसन्की *us'kí* (*H.* नाहक छेड़ना), teasing.

उसन्ठाह *us'ṭháh*, *adj.* (*H.* रुखा), rough.

उसन्रा *us'rá* (*H.* ओसारा), a portico, verandah.

उसुक पुसुक *usuk pusuk*, *adj.* (*H.* चंचल), fickle.

ओका *oká*, a bag for catching fish, dragged along through the water by two or more men.

ओझन्राएल *ŏjh'ráĕl*, *adj.* (*H.* अरझुरायल), tangled, tossed.

ओत *ot*, to put new straw on a roof; to rethatch a roof.

ओतइ *ŏtaï*, *adv.* (*H.* वहाँ), in that place; there.

ओहारी *ŏhárí* (*H.* ओरी), the eaves of a house. Cf. असन्ठी.

औठाई *ăuṭhái* (*H.* बंगटई), naughtiness, wickedness.

औठाह *auṭháh*, *adj.* (*H.* बंगठ), naughty, wicked.

औराना *auráná* (*H.* सड़ा माँस), rotten flesh.

कचन्कच *kach'kach*, *adj.* [1] (*H.* कच्चा) unripe; [2] *subst.* (*H.* कलह), altercation, debate.

कचन्डंबर *kach'ḍambar, adj.* (*H.* ढेकसल), half-ripe.

कचन्वनियाँ *kach'waniyā̃* (*H.* कसार, पिन्नी), a kind of sweetmeat.

कजन्री *kaj'ri*, a worm which infests buds and plant-shoots.

कटुआ *kaṭuá* (*H.* भूसा), chaff, husk.

कठन्नही *kaṭh'nahi* (*H.* काठ का डोल), a wooden bucket for drawing water from a well.

कड़रू *kaṛarú* (*H.* पड़वा), a male buffalo calf = काड़ा.

कतन्री *kat'ri* [1] (*H.* हाथ का गहना), an ornament worn on the fore-arm by low-caste women; [2] (*H.* कोल्हू का पटरा) a wooden plate attached to an oil-mill on which the oilman sits.

कत्ता *kattá*, an instrument for cutting bamboos, used only by Ḍoms.

कत्ती *katti*, a round potsherd used to play with.

कनन्कन *kan'kan, adj.* (*H.* ठंढा), cold.

कनन्तोड़ *kan'toṛ*, a small box.

कनन्वह *kan'wah*, a drain, a safety pipe for running off excess water.

कनन्वाँ *kan'wā̃* (*H.* छटाँक), the sixteenth part of a *ser.*

कनेटा *kaneṭá* (*H.* पाखा), the gable-end of a house.

कनौसी *kanausí* (*H.* बारी), a kind of ear-ornament.

कंदन्री *kand'ri*, a well dug on the bank of a river for filtering the river-water.

कंदा *kandá* (*H.* बंडा), a kind of esculent root.

कंधैली *kandhaili*, a bullock saddle.

कन्नी *kanni*, a twig; a small branch of a tree.

कन्हौआ *kanhauá* (*H.* कान का खूँट), ear-wax.

कपन्टी *kap'ṭi* (*H.* प्याला, ढकनी), an earthen cup.

कबरिया *kabariyá*, one who roots up paddy seedlings for transplantation. (The √ कबार means 'to root up.')

कमियाँ *kamiyā̃* (*H.* कमेरा), a labourer; a ploughman. *Fem.* कमियइनी *kamiaini*, a ploughman's wife.

करन्छी *kar'chhi* (*H.* किनारा), edge, border.

करीन *karín*, a canoe-shaped lever for raising water for irrigation.

कलौआ *kalauá* (*H.* कलेवा), breakfast.

काकुट *kákuṭ* (*H.* गडाँसी), a kind of chopper for cutting straw.

काड़ा *káṛá* (*fem.* काड़ी), (*H.* पड़वा), a buffalo calf = कड़रू.

काँड़ा *kā̃ṛá*, a long leather rope to which the bullocks are tied when treading out corn.

काँड़ी *kā̃ṛí* (*H.* ढरका), a bamboo tube for forcing liquids down an animal's throat.

काँदू *kā̃dú* (*H.* भुजवा), a grain-parcher.

कादो *kádo* (*H.* कीचड़), clay, mud.

किच्ची *kichchí* (*H.* कीचर), the mucus of the eye.

कीया *kíyá* (*H.* सिंधौरा), a small box for keeping *sindur* (red lead).

कुगड़ *kugaṛh*, *adj.* (*H.* बे डौल), ugly.

कुड़न्दहिना *kuṛ'dahiná*, the left hand ox of a ahrrow. Cf. आगन्दाइन, पँचौट, फेरा, हथौधा: also the ox nearest the post of a threshing floor. They all go round from right to left, and hence the left hand ox is nearest to the centre, *i.e.* is near (कुड़) the centre, on the right (दहिना) of the centre. Cf. मेंहटा.

कुंडा *kunḍá* (*H.* कन्ना), rice-dust.

कुद्दी *kuddí* (*H.* भाग), a portion, share.

कुरूर *kurúr*, an instrument for turning sand.

कुल्हिया *kulhiyá* [1](*H.* लड़कों की छोटी टोपी), a small boy's cap; [2](*H.* चुक्का) a small earthen pot for holding water.

केका *keká* (*H.* बिलखना), to lament.

केड़ी *keṛí*, the space between the fore-finger and thumb. Cf. अरन्पा, गिब्बी.

कँचिया *kā̃chiyá*, a kind of toothed sickle.

कोचानी *kŏchání*, the top of a roof.

कोनी *koní* (*H.* कोना), a corner, angle.

कोर *kor* [1](*H.* किनारा), margin, edge; [2] *adj.* (*H.* नया), new.

कोहा *kohá* (*H.* पतिला), an earthen pot.

कौअल *kaual* (*H.* कैंची), two long bamboos crossing each other like a pair of scissors for supporting the ridge-pole of a house.

कौरी *kaurí* (*H.* पगुरी), the act of chewing cud (of a ruminating animal).

क्योँचा *kyõchá*, an instrument for barking wood.

खखन्नल *khakh'nal*, *adj.* (*H.* आतुर), distressed; restless.

खटन्खट *khaṭ'khaṭ* (*H.* आवाज), a rapping sound.

खँड़न्हू *khā̃ṛ'hú* (*H.* आहर अथवा क्यारी का खंड), a section of an *áhar* (embankment) or of a field.

खपन्खप *khap'khap*, *adj.* (*H.* बहुत कीड़ा पड़ा हुआ), full of worms.

खप॰रौड़ी *khap'rauṛi*, an earthen pot for removing the after-birth, &c., when a child is born.

✓ खभाव *khabháw* [1] (*H.* जानवरों का उठाना), to make an animal get up to drive; [2] (*H.* पानी देने पर कोड़ना) to get a wet field dug *(causal)*.

खर॰ऐ *khar'ue* (*H.* सूखे में बोना), sowing in a dry field.

खिच्चा *khichchá*, *adj.* (*H.* कच्चा), unripe.

खिनौरी *khiuauri* (*H.* पुराना वा छोटा घर), an old or small plough.

✓ खिल *khil* (*H.* ठढ़ियाना), *v. a.* to sew in a particular way, to run, tack.

खुक्खे *khukkhe*, *adj.* (*H.* खाली), empty.

खुटिला *khuṭilá* (*H.* काँप), a kind of ear-ring.

खुद॰नी *khud'ni* (*H.* खोदनी), a spade. Cf. खुर॰नी.

खुर॰नी *khur'ni* (*H.* खोदनी), a spade used for stirring the embers of a fire. Cf. खुद॰नी.

खुर॰हा *khur'há* (*H.* रोग), a cattle disease attacking the hoof; foot-and-mouth disease.

खुस॰खुसाहा *khus'khusáhá*, *adj.* (*H.* टुनुक), brittle = ठस.

खेढ़ी *kheṛhí* (*H.* खुड़ी), a staircase.

खेवा *khewá* (*H.* मरातिब), a time; a turn; an occasion.

खैनी *khainí* (*H.* खाने की तमाकु), chewing-tobacco. Cf. पीनी.

खैहन *khaihan* (*H.* खाने का अन्न), corn given as food to raiyats.

खोँधा *khõdhá* (*H.* खोता), a nest.

खोना *khoná* (*H.* दोना), leaves folded in the shape of a cup.

खोरा *khorá* (*H.* मटका, कुँड़ा), a large earthen jar.

खोरी *khorí* (*H.* छोटी थारी), a kind of small dish.

खौराहा *khaŭráhá*, *adj.* (*H.* अभागा), unfortunate.

गउत *gaüt* (*H.* चारा), forage, fodder.

गँउठ *gãüṭh*, *adj.* (*H.* पौना), less by a quarter; a quarter less than.

गज॰बज *gaj'baj*, *adj.* (*H.* मिलाजुला), mixed.

गट॰पट *gaṭ'paṭ* (*H.* मेल मिलाप), association.

गपर॰गपर *gapar'gapar* (*H.* जल्दी खाना), gobbling, devouring.

गम॰छा *gam'chhá* (*H.* अंगोछा), a towel; a body-cloth.

गम॰लक *gam'lak*, *adj.* (*H.* जान गया), known, understood.

गरन्दवानी *gar'dawání* (*H.* कनाई), a necklet.

गरँगट *garãgaṭ* (*H.* कंकर), limestone; gravel.

गरार *garár* [1] (*H.* गरियार), an alligator: hence [2]*adj.* (*H.* ढीठ) obstinate, perverse, firm.

गलन्सटन्का *gal'saṭ'ka* (*H.* टीक), a neck-ornament.

गारन *gáran* (*H.* छोआ) treacle, molasses.

गालू *gálú* (*H.* झूठा लिङ्कू), a liar: *adj.* false.

गियारी *giyárí* (*H.* गरदन), the neck.

गिरन्गिरा *gir'girá* (*H.* छोटा जाल), a small net.

गिल्ली *gillí*, the space between the thumb and forefinger. Cf. केड़ी, चरन्पा.

गुदन्नी *gud'ní* (*H.* तनिकसा), a little.

गुदारा *gudárá*, wages for reaping.

गँड़ारी *gẽṛárí* (*H.* क्यारी), a bed in a garden or field.

गँदन्रा *gẽd'rá* (*H.* कथरी), a garment of rags worn by mendicants.

गेदागेदी *gedágedí*, *adj.* (*H.* छोटेछोटे), little; an infant.

गैंता *gãĩtá* (*H.* डेवाँ), a kind of spade used by *beldárs.*

गोआम *gŏám* (*H.* पानी बाँधने के लिये गोहार), a gang of men employed in embanking a water-course in order to divert the water in any given direction.

गोटा *goṭá* (*H.* बीया), seed.

गोठौर *gŏṭhaur* (*H.* गोइठे का घर), a house for keeping dried cowdung.

गोड़न्पौरी *gŏṛ'paurí* (*H.* ढेकी दवाने का गड्हा), the pit into which the rear of the lever of a pounding-machine (*ḍhekí*) is depressed.

गोरन्खिया *gŏr'khiyá* (*H.* चरवाहा), a herd-boy.

गोरा *gorá* (*H.* खरी का घोड़ा हुआ), white ink made of chalk and water.

गोलन्वा *gŏl'wá* (*H.* छोटी तरकी), a small ear-ornament.

गोलन्हथ *gŏl'hath* (*H.* गीला भात), over-boiled rice.

घटन्ना *ghaṭ'ná* (*H.* भात का चलौना), a stirrer; a spoon for stirring.

घटन्रा *ghaṭ'rá* (*H.* माल पूआ), a kind of cake.

घट्ठा *ghaṭṭhá* (*H.* मकई का दर्रा), coarse meal made from maize.

घसर घसर *ghasar ghasar*, *adv.* at once.

घिरन्सिंडी *ghir'sinḍí* (*H.* घनौची), a platform for keeping water jars on.

घुकन्री *ghuk'ri*, *adj.* (*H.* घुकरी, सिकुड़ मुकुड़), frozen; congealed.

घुग्घा *ghugghá* (*H.* घूँघट) a veil; the action of veiling the face.

घुरके *ghur'ke, adv.* again.

घुरचीला *ghur'chílá* (*H.* गुरचीला), a coil of rope.

घोघा *ghogha,* an umbrella made of *táṛ* leaves.

घोघी *ghoghí* (*H.* थैली), a pocket; a bag.

घोड़मूँहा *ghǒṛ'múhá* (*H.* टोड़ा), a piece of wood shaped like a horse's mouth, used for sustaining a roof.

घोर *ghor* (*H.* मट्ठा), buttermilk.

घौद *ghaud* (*H.* गौद), a bunch; a clump of fruit.

चक्का *chakká* (*H.* चक्र), a wheel.

चटगर *chaṭ'gar* (*H.* सुस्वाद), relish, flavouring.

चड़ियार *chaṛiyár,* a pit in which a *chắṛ* is worked (*see* चाँड़).

चतरा *chat'rá* (*H.* खेत का रोग), a disease which attacks crops.

चरक *charak* (*H.* उजला), white.

चराँढ *charắṭ* (*H.* चरागाह), pasture.

चलौना *chalauná* (*H.* भौंती), the treadle of a spinning wheel.

चाँईं *chắí* (*H.* इमली का चीँयाँ), tamarind seed.

चाँड़ *chắṛ* (*H.* दोगला, बेड़ी), a kind of basket used for tossing up water (used in irrigation).

चाँपी *chắpí* (*H.* दुदहँड़), a milk-pot.

चाली *chálí,* a coarse kind of mat made of bamboo slips tied together.

चास *chás* (*H.* जोत), ploughing.

चिकना *chik'ná* (*H.* मैहु, मक्खन), butter.

चिकसा *chik'sá* (*H.* आँटा), flour; meal.

चिटुरा *chiṭurá* (बेदाना की ढेँढ़ी), poppy capsules which have not borne seeds.

चिलोही *chilohí* (*H.* पहसुल), a sickle.

चिलौंद *chilaũd* (*H.* मछली मारने का चिक), a kind of trap for catching fish. Cf. चापा.

चीची *chíchí* (*H.* बतिया), young fruit.

चुइयाँ *chuiyắ* (*H.* चूआँ), a pit (especially in the dry bed of rivers) from which water springs.

चुकनी *chuk'ní* (*H.* पुरवा), a small earthen jar.

चुक्केमुक्के *chukkemukke* (*H.* उठकुनिया बैठना), the position of sitting with both hands on the knees.

चुनेटल *chuneṭal* (*H.* चूना से पोता हुआ), white-washed.

चुल्हानी *chulhání,* a cookhouse.

चुहचुह *chuh'chuh, adj.* (*H.* चटकीला) splendid, glittering.

चेँगा *chẽgá* (*H.* लड़का), a child.

चेल्ह्वा *chĕlh'wá* (*H.* ग्वार की छूरी), a knife used by milkmen.

√ छगुन *chhagun* (*H.* कुछ विचारना), to meditate.

छछ्नल *chhachh'nal, adj.* (*H.* सिलकस), longing, eagerly desirous.

छाहुर *chháhur* (*H.* छाया), a shade, shadow.

छिछोह्रा *chhichhŏh'rá* (*H.* चटोरा, चहुआ), a glutton.

छीपा *chhípá* (*H.* थाली), a dish.

छीहर *chhíhar, adj.* (*H.* पतरा), thin.

छुच्छी *chhuchchhí*, a kind of nose-stud; an ornament for the nose.

छूहा *chhúhá, adj.* (*H.* सरियाया हुआ), arranged; classified.

√ छेव *chhew* (*H.* काटना), to cut.

छोनी *chhoní*, the hole in a sugar-press through which the juice oozes out.

छोपी *chhopí*, an umbrella made of leaves.

जनिऔरी *janiaurí* (*H.* औरत), a woman.

जब्रा *jab'rá* (*H.* छोटी कोठी), a small granary.

जाबी *jábí* (*H.* खोंती), a net of string for muzzling the mouth of an ox or calf.

जारन *járan* (*H.* इंधन), fuel.

√ जिआव *jiáw* (*H.* मारना), to kill.

जुकुर *jukur* (*H.* योग्य), able, fit.

जोर *jor* (*H.* रस्सी), a string.

√ जोर *jor* (*H.* सुलगाना), to kindle.

जोरन *joran* (*H.* जाँवन), a kind of rennet, used for curdling milk.

झग्गार *jhaggár*, kind of hook for pulling out any water-pot or *loṭa* which may have fallen into a well.

झटैनी *jhaṭainí*, the leafed branch of a date-tree; the branch with its leaves.

झन्कौट *jhan'kauṭ* (*H.* चुरगचना), a kind of native hinge for securing a door. (झन 'saving;' कवाट, 'a door.')

झप्झप *jhap'jhap, adv.* (*H.* जल्दी जल्दी), quickly.

झँसगर *jhãs'gar, adj.* (*H.* झारदार), pungent (like mustard). झाँस means 'pungency,' as distinct from झाल, 'the heat of pepper.'

झाखुर *jhákhur, adj.* hairy.

झिक्टी *jhik'ṭí* (*H.* ठिकरी), a pebble.

झुक झुक *jhuk jkuk, adj.* (*H.* निहुरा हुआ), bent downwards.

झुकुर झुकुर *jhukur jhukur*, when a man with long hair dives or sinks in water, and a portion of his hair is seen floating on the surface, that portion is named as above.

√ झोर *jhor* (*H.* पोतना, झारना), to brush or wash.

झोल *jhol* (*H.* कराइन, जाला), a cobweb.

झोलाँड़ *jhŏlāṛ* (*H.* निकुंज), an arbour, a bower.

झौराहा *jhauráhá, adj.* (*H.* मचला, रोनेवाला), perverse; cross; restive.

टंगन्नी *ṭang'ni* (*H.* अरगनी), a clothes-horse made of rope or bamboo: = असन्गनी, *q. v.*

टंट घंट *ṭanṭ ghanṭ* (*H.* सामान), preparation.

टँड़ुआ *ṭāṛuá* (*H.* छोटी पइन), a small canal.

टिकन्री *ṭik'ri* (*H.* छोटी रोटी), a small loaf, a roll.

टीक *ṭik* (*H.* चुरकी), a lock of hair on the crown of the head.

टुकन्टुक *ṭuk'ṭuk* (*H.* एकटकी), a fixed gaze, a stare.

टुपन्टुप *ṭup'ṭup, adj.* (*H.* भरा डुआ), full.

टूअर टापर *ṭúar ṭápar* (*H.* अनाथ), an orphan; helpless.

टूईं *ṭúí* (*H.* तुतुई), a kind of vessel with a spout.

टेकन्नस *ṭěk'nas* (*H.* गोबर छत्ता, कुकुर मुत्ता), a mushroom, a toad-stool.

टेंभी *ṭēbhí* [1] (*H.* अंकुरा), a sprout, shoot; [2] (*H.* दीया की टेंभ), the flame of a candle.

टेहन्रा *ṭěh'rá* (*H.* चुका, मँड़िया), an earthen pot.

टोकन्नी *ṭŏk'ni*, a kind of wicker-work basket used for covering the eyes of an oilman's ox.

टोना *ṭoná*, a piece of wood.

√ टोप *ṭop* (*H.* सीना), to sew.

ठकन्मकाना *ṭhak'makáná, adj.* (*H.* ठगमुरी), perplexed.

ठकन्मुरन्की *ṭhak'mur'kí, adj.* (*H.* हक्का बक्का), perplexed.

ठस *ṭhas, adj.* (*H.* तुनुक), brittle = खुसन्खुसहा.

ठिसुआएल *ṭhisuáěl, adj.* (*H.* लजायल), ashamed.

ठेकन्रा *ṭhěk'rá*, a stick for stirring grain while it is being pounded.

ठेकुआ *ṭhěkuá* (पूआ), a kind of cake.

ठेघा *ṭheghá*, a kind of mud flight of steps.

डगन्रा *ḍag'rá*, a large flat dish made of wood.

√ डढ़ *ḍaṛh* (*H.* जलना), to burn.

डुंडा *ḍunḍá, adj.* (*H.* अकेला), alone, single.

डफुआना *ḍaphuáná*, a sign of anger.

डबन्डबाएल *ḍab'ḍabáěl, adj.* (*H.* लोरलोर), tearful.

डुब्भा *ḍubbhá.*	दह *dah.*

डुब्भा *ḍubbhá* (*H.* बड़ा कटोरा), a large cup.

डभःकल *ḍabh'kal, adj.* (*H.* डभका ऊषा), grain when nearly completely boiled (*lit.* that which says "*ḍabh ḍabh ḍabh*").

डमःका *ḍam'ká* (*H.* ऊँची जमीन), high land.

डमःरू *ḍam'rú* (*H.* शेर का बच्चा), a tiger whelp.

डमारा *ḍamárá* (*H.* बिनुआ कंडा), dried cowdung; *specially*, cowdung picked up dry in the jangal and not made into cakes (गोइठा).

डहःजर *ḍah'jar, adj.* (*H.* डाही), envious.

डोँड़ी *ḍõṛí*, a kind of fishing net.

डोभःरा *ḍŏbh'rá* (*H.* डबःरा), a small ditch.

ढनःढनाना *ḍhan'ḍhanáná, adj.* (*H.* भटकना), astray.

ढसःराएल *ḍhas'ráĕl, adj.* (*H.* गदराना), half-ripe, unripe (of fruit, or corn).

ढाउस *ḍháüs* (*H.* बड़ा भेघा) a toad, a large frog.

ढिलुआ *ḍhiluá* (*H.* हिंडोला), a cradle.

ढुरःढुर *ḍhur'ḍhur, adj.* (*H.* कोमल) soft, tender.

√ ढूस *ḍhús*, to attack with the horns (of a horned animal).

ढेकःवाँस *ḍhĕk'wãs* (*H.* ढेलवाँस), a sling.

ढोनी *ḍhoní* (*H.* डाली), a present of fruit, &c.

तगःही *tag'hí* (*H.* पगहा), a tether; a hobble.

तँगिअइ *tãgiaï* (*H.* हठ), obstinacy.

तनीगो *tanígo* (*H.* थोडासा), a little.

तपावन *tapáwan* (*H.* शराब), wine.

तरःहत्थी *tar'hatthí* (*H.* हथेली), the palm of the hand.

तरेँगन *tarẽgan* (*H.* तारागण), stars.

तले *tale, adv.* (*H.* नीचे), below, down.

तितःकी *tit'kí* (*H.* चिनगारी), a spark, scintillation = चंगारी.

तीअन *tían* (*H.* तरकारी), vegetables.

√ तीर *tír* (*H.* खीँचना), to draw, drag.

तीलेतीले *tíletíle, adv.* (*H.* बारबार), often, frequently.

तुतुहूँ *tutuhũ* (*H.* सहनाई), a musical instrument; a kind of large hautboy.

तेखार *tekhár*, the third ploughing of a field. Cf. दोखार, पुरवे, फारन.

थेथर *thethar, adj.* (*H.* कुचुआ), shameless.

दंद *dand* (*H.* फिकिर), anxiety.

दरेची *darechí* (*H.* छोटी खिरकी), a small window.

दह *dah*, a ditch.

दादर *dádar* (*H.* दरका), a crack, a fissure.

दिनगरे *din'gare* (*H.* दिन रहते), before sunset.

दिनौरा *dinaurá*, wages for reaping.

दिंदिआल *dindiál* (*H.* बेग से), violently.

दीनी *díní* (*H.* कटनी), wages for reaping, the act of reaping a crop.

दुमुहियाँ *dumuhiyã́*, *adj.* (*H.* बड़ा चतुर), cunning, artful.

√ दूस *dús* (*H.* दोष लगाना), to blame.

देखनगर *dĕkhan'gar* (*H.* देखनौक), beautiful.

दोखार *dokhár*, the second ploughing of a field. Cf. तेखार, पुरवे, फारन.

दोगा *dogá*, the thatching along the ridge of a roof.

दोँगा *dõgá* (*H.* गौने के बाद की यात्रा), the second journey of a bride to her husband's house.

दोगाह *dŏgáh* (*H.* बथर घरा), a cattle-shed.

धंधौरा *dhandhaurá* (*H.* बड़ी ज्वाला), a violent flame, a blaze.

धरखा *dhar'khá* (*H.* ताखा), a small shelf or recess in a wall.

धुइयाँ *dhuïyã́* (*H.* धूँआँ), smoke.

धुंधुर *dhundhur* (*H.* धुमैल), twilight.

धूर *dhúr* (*H.* बैल), an ox, a bullock.

धोकड़ी *dhŏk'ṛí* (*H.* थैली), a bag.

धोँछा *dhõchhá*, *adj.* (*H.* खाराब), wicked.

नारा *nárá* (*H.* मड़ुआ का सँठा), *maṛuá*-straw.

नितराल *nit'rál*, *adj.* (*H.* इतराना), wanton.

नीपे *nípe* (*H.* लीपना), plaster.

नूनू *núnú* (*H.* लड़का), a child, an infant.

नेठो *netho* (*H.* गेँड़री), a platter made of straw or rags to support a water-jar on a woman's head.

नोँचा *nõchá* (गोड़इती का नेग), the perquisite of grain taken by the village *goṛait* out of each crop.

नोख *nokh*, *adj.* (*H.* अनोखा), uncommon, wonderful.

नोनगर *nŏn'gar*, *adj.* (*H.* नोनखर), salt, saline.

पचाठी *pacháṭhí*, a religious ceremony before transplanting seedlings.

पँचौट *pãchauṭ*, the left ox of a harrow. Cf. आगन्दाइन, कुड़न्दहिना, फेरा, हथौआ.

पटसे *paṭ'se*, *adv.* (*H.* तुरते), quickly.

पठरू *paṭh'rú*, a kid.

पतिला *patilá* (*H.* कोहा), an earthen jar.

पतौरा *pataurá* (*H.* तरकारी), vegetables : = तीअन.

पथिश्रा *pathiá* (*H.* दौरी), a basket.

पन *pan*, an aggregate numeral = 20 *gaṇḍás*. One *gaṇḍa* = 4. One *pan* therefore = 80.

पनऽछंदा *pan'chhandá*, a man whose duty it is to guard water.

पनऽसोखा *pan'sokhá* (*H.* इंद्रधनुष), a rainbow.

पनिहता *panihatá*, boiled rice mixed with water.

पँरऽगा *pãr'gá* (*H.* श्रारी, माँगी), the boundary of a field.

परऽझो *par'jho* (*H.* दृष्टाँत), an example.

परम *param*, the sprout of a palm-tree.

परऽवैती *par'waiti* or परऽवैतिन *par'waitin*, a woman when engaged in a religious ceremony.

परियाठा *pariyáṭhá*, the wooden framework over a well on which the person who draws water stands.

पसऽनी *pas'ní* (*H.* खुरपी), a scraper, a kind of hoe.

पाचर *páchar*, straw, &c., mixed with earth for building.

पाँजा *pájá*, a bundle of grain.

पातन *pátan*, the act of laying freshly cut rice out in the field, either to dry or to be softened by the dew.

पालट *pálaṭ* (*H.* हेंगाना), the act of harrowing.

पिच्छुल *pichchhul*, *adj.* (*H.* फिसलहर), slippery.

पिट्ठा *piṭṭhá* (*H.* फरा), a kind of boiled pudding made of *sattú*.

पिलऽपिलाहा *pil'piláhá* (*H.* डरपोक), a coward.

पीँड़ *píṛ* (*H.* श्राहर का घेरा), a high bank round a pond or tank.

पीनी *píni* [1](*H.* पिउनी), cleaned cotton fit for spinning ; [2](*H.* पीने की तमाकू), smoking tobacco. Cf. खैनी.

पुकऽठाल *puk'ṭhál*, *adj.* (*H.* गदराना), half-ripe.

पुत्ती *putti* (*H.* पखती), the spokes of a spinning wheel.

पुरवे *purawe*, the second ploughing of a field. See दोखार, तेखार, फारन.

पेँटऽकुनियाँ *pĕṭ'kuniyã* (*H.* पेटकुइँयाँ), sleeping on the face, with the belly underneath.

पैरा *pairá* (*H.* बधिया बैल), a castrated ox ; a bullock.

पोथानी *pŏthání* (*H.* पैताना), the foot of a bed.

पौती *pauti* (*H.* पेटारी), a kind of covered basket.

फरऽका *phar'ká*, [1]a pit for catching fish ; [2](*H.* मिरगी), epilepsy.

फारन *phāran* (*H.* पहिलवाह), the first ploughing of a field. Cf. दोखार, पुरवे, नेखार.

फुच्ची *phuchchí*, short hair, down.

फँटी *phẽṭi*, pieces of dried cowdung.

फेन *phen*, *adv.* (*H.* फिर), again.

√ फेन *phen* (*H.* फेंटना), to mix.

फेरा *pherá*, the right hand ox of a harrow. Cf. आगन्दाइन, कुड़न्दहिना, पँचौट, हथौआ.

फोकन्चा *phŏk'chá* (*H.* फफोला), a blister.

फोरन *phoran*, spices for seasoning food.

बटुरी *baṭuri*, a kind of leg-ornament.

बदन्हा *bad'há* (*H.* पौला), a wooden shoe.

बधन्वाहा *badh'wáhá*, one who guards a field (बाध); a *garde champêtre*.

बनियाती *baniyáti*, one who works in the forest (बन).

बनुसार *banusár*, the completion of the transplanting of rice seedlings from the nurseries to the fields; हम्मर बनुसार भेल 'I have finished transplanting my rice-seedlings.' Cf. कबरिया.

बरन्हा *bar'há* (*H.* बरियत), the rope for drawing up the leather bucket of a well.

बरिआर *bariár*, *adj.* (*H.* जबरदस्त), high-handed, powerful.

बरौंची *baraũchi* (*H.* झोटनी), a brush made of pig's bristles (used by goldsmiths).

बलन्ही *bal'hí* (*H.* लकड़ी का बोझ), a bundle of fuel.

बलुई *baluí*, an insect which infests grain when first in the ear.

बसन्नी *bas'ní* (*H.* कलस्सी), a water-pot.

बँसन्फेंटा *bãs'phẽṭá* (*H.* सोंटा), a stick, a cudgel.

बाँकी *bãkí*, a disease which attacks the leaves of trees (especially the pepper-tree) and causes them to curl up and wither.

बाध *bádh* (*H.* हार), the cultivated fields immediately round a village.

बिच्चा *bichchá* (*H.* बीआ), seed.

बिछरन्नी *bichhar'ní*, the washing of a cloth after it has had patterns printed on it.

बिंडा *binḍá*, a bundle of straw on the edge of the well on which the bucket rests when it is being emptied of water.

बिरन्वाई *bir'wái*, vegetable seedlings.

बीअर *bíar* (*H.* बिल), a hole.

बीझल *bíjhal* (*H.* घुना हुआ), weevil-eaten.

बीरी *bíri* (*H.* बजका, पतौरा), a kind of food made of leaves and flour fried in *ghí*.

बीरो *bíro* (*H.* दवा), medicine.

बीहन *bíhan*, seed-grain.

बुतन्रु *but'rú* (*H.* लड़का), an infant.

बेँग *bẽg* (*H.* मेँढक), a frog.

बेस *bes, interj.* (*H.* अच्छा), all right !

बैना पेहानी *bainá pĕhání*, a sweetmeat or cake distributed at a marriage or other ceremony.

बौधा *baudhá, adj.* (*H.* बेसमझ), senseless; an idiot.

भगन्जोगन्नी *bhag'jŏg'ní* (*H.* खद्योत), a firefly.

भगन्वा *bhag'wạ́* (*H.* लंगोटी), a small cloth worn between the legs.

भदन्राहा *bhad'ráhá, adj.* (*H.* अभागा), unfortunate.

भनर भनर *bhanar bhanar*, an obscure sound, a hum.

भनन्सा *bhan'sá*, a kitchen, a cook-room.

भरन्भर *bhar'bhar, adj.* (*H.* बेलस), wanting in viscosity, not tenacious..

भाँगल *bhãgal, adj.* (*H.* टुटा हुआ), broken.

भाँड़ा *bhãṛá* (*H.* चट्टी), a jar.

भास *bhás* (*H.* ज्ञान), sense, knowledge.

भिठारा *bhiṭhárá* (*H.* चौमास), a field reserved for *rabí* crops.

भीरे *bhire* or भीरू *bhirú, adj.* (*H.* नजदीक), near.

भुकुर भुकुर *bhukur bhukur* (*H.* जुगजुगाना), a twinkling.

भूँआँ *bhũã* (*H.* धरती), the earth, the ground.

भूँजा *bhũjá* (*H.* चबेना), parched grain.

भूँभुर *bhũbhur* (*H.* भौक), hot ashes, embers.

भूर *bhúr* (*H.* छेद), a hole.

भोकिला *bhŏkilá* (*H.* छोटी पइन), a small water-channel.

भोथर *bhothar, adj.* (*H.* गोँठिल), blunt.

भोरेँ *bhori* (*H.* गलती), an error, a mistake.

मँइयाँ *mãiyã* (*H.* लड़न्की), a girl.

मकन्री *mak'ri* (*H.* लाठा के नीचे की लकड़ी), a piece of wood fastened in the post of a well-lever (लाठा) to keep the latter in its place.

मँगन्नी *mãg'ní, adv.* (*H.* घलुआ), gratis; gratuitously; for nothing.

मँगन्रा *mãg'rá*, a large kind of tile laid along the ridge pole of a roof.

मटन्पर *maṭ'par* (*H.* छोटी बोरसी), an earthen pot for containing fire.

मड़न्सटन्का *maṛ'saṭ'ká* (*H.* मड़गर भात), rice-gruel.

मने मने *mane mane, adv.* (*H.* चुपे चुपे), quietly.

मरुआएल *maruáĕl, adj.* (*H.* मुरझायल), withered.

मल्हिया *malhiyá* (*H.* कसोलिया), a small cup for keeping oil.

माँईं *mấí* (*H.* लड़की), a girl.

माँजन *mấjan* (*H.* मुखिया), the chairman of a committee.

माँझा *mấjhá* (*H.* सिपावा के ऊपर की लकड़ी), the angle in which the front of a cart rests when supported on a *sipáwá* (the two crossed sticks used to support a cart when the bullocks are away): [2]ground-bait; food thrown into water to attract fishes before fishing: [3]a plaster of powdered glass applied to kite strings to enable them to cut the string of a rival kite.

✓ मिचन्कार *mich'kâr* (*H.* फीचना, मीसना), to rinse; grind.

मिँझाल *mĩjhál* (*H.* बुता ब्रुझा), extinguished.

मिरन्कुटाह *mir'kuṭáh, adj.* (*H.* दुबला), lean, thin.

मुड़न्वारी *muṛ'wárí*, the iron ferule of an oil-press.

मुँहन्गर *mũh'gar, adj.* (*H.* बाचाल), eloquent.

मुहन्चुर *muh'chur*, paddy when partially husked.

मजन *mejan* (*H.* मेलन), mixture; mingling.

मेमन्ना (*mĕm'ná*), a kid.

मेहन्टा *mĕh'ṭá*, the ox which when employed in treading out corn stands nearest the centre post (मेह). Cf. आगन्दाइन.

मैया *maiyá* (*H.* मा), a mother.

मोरी *morí* (*H.* बीहन), rice seedlings for transplantation.

मौगा *maugá* (*H.* मेहरा), womanhood.

मौनी *mauní* (*H.* कुरई), a very small kind of basket.

रावा *ráwá* (*H.* राव), syrup.

रेँगा *rẽgá* (*H.* लड़का), a boy.

रेस *res* (*H.* डाह), envy; jealousy.

लकन्पक *lak'pak, adj.* (*H.* लचीला), elástic; viscid; tenacious: = लुरन्लुर।

लगन्नी *lag'ní*, a general term for all the apparatus of a wedding.

लंगटन्फाट *laṅgaṭ'pháṭ* (*H.* सिफला), one who has no food in his house and dresses himself extravagantly; an extravagant coxcomb.

लछनन्गर *lachhan'gar, adj.* (*H.* सुलच्छनी), fortunate.

लजन्कोट *laj'koṭ* (*H.* लजाधुर), bashful.

लबन्लब *lab'lab, adj.* (*H.* जो वे समझ बऊत बोले), an ignorant prater.

✓ लंभ *lambh*, to drive cattle into another person's field.

लरन्हा *lar'há* (*H.* पतीला लाठा), a thin pole.

लराहा *laráhá, adj.* (*H.* लसदार), tenacious, viscid = लुरन्लुर

√ लहन्काव *lah'káw* (*H.* लेलवाना), to cause to blaze: *hence*, to incite, excite (as a dog to bite a person).

लुग्गा *luggá* (*H.* कपड़ा), cloth generally; a cloth for wearing.

लुरन्गर *lur'gar, adj.* (*H.* समरन्दार), intelligent; witty.

लुरन्लुर *lur'lur, adj.* (*H.* लचीला), elastic; viscid; tenacious: = लकन्पक, लराहा.

लुहन्चुह *luh'chuh, adj.* (*H.* चहचह), variegated, bright-coloured.

लूर *lúr* (*H.* सजर), wit; *especially* cleverness and expertness in some particular trade or art.

लूरूखूरू *lúrúkhúrú*, the doing a little work; acting lazily or half-heartedly.

लेदन्गुदाह *lĕd'gudáh*, a disease in which the belly swells (? dropsy).

लेदा *ledá*, the mud counterpoise of a well-lever.

लेदाल *lĕdál* (*H.* लसेटा), plaster.

लेरू *lerú* (*H.* बछवा), a calf.

लेवा *lewá* (*H.* खोदे में बोना), sowing in a wet field.

लेहू *lehú* (*H.* रक्त), blood.

लोढ़ा बिच्छा *loṛhá bichchhá* (*H.* भिखा), gleaning.

लोँदा *lõdá*, a lump of kneaded clay, a clod.

लोर *lor* [1](*H.* आँसू), tears; [2](*H.* मालपुवा का आँटा), a thin paste of flour for preparing the sweetmeat called *málpúá*; [3](*H.* कान का कर्णभूषण), an ear-ornament worn by men of the gowálá caste.

लोँहन्ड़ा *lõh'ṛá*, the first day of the *chhaṭh* festival.

लोहँड़िया *lŏhãṛiyá*, one whose caste prevents his eating with another.

सनेस *sanes* [1](*H.* भेँट), recognition; [2](*H.* उपहार), a complimentary present.

समन्धर *sam'dhar*, the wedge which holds the three parts of a plough together.

समाँठ *samãṭh* (*H.* मूसर), a pestle.

समैला *samailá*, the two pegs of wood or metal at each end of a yoke.

समौआ *samauá* (*H.* ढेकी का मूसर), the wooden pestle of a pounding-machine.

सर *sar* (*H.* नाँद), a basket used for raising water for irrigation.

सरन्सुर *sar'sur, adj.* (*H.* बराबर), equal.

सलन्सल *sal'sal* (*H.* मोटाई चढ़ना), getting fat.

सँसिहीन sãsihín, *adj.* (*H.* कमपैदगार), without prosperity, unlucky.

सिक्का *sikká* (*H.* सिकहर), three or more strings forming a kind of sling for carrying anything, such as are used by *bahngí-bardárs*.

सिराएल *siráël*, *adj.* (*H.* ठंडा), cold.

सिरौर *siraur*, a furrow: = सेवात.

सुघर *sughar*, *adj.* (सुघर, सुंदर), beautiful.

सुनगुन *sun'gun* (*H.* पता), a person's address; news about a person.

सुपरी, *sup'ri* (*H.* मेठिया), a small jar.

सुरखुरू *sur'khurú*, *adj.* (*H.* तेजी), influential.

सेवात *sëwát*, a furrow: = सिरौर।

सोई *soí* [1] (*H.* पसेवा), a spring of water; anything which oozes out naturally without artificial pressure; [2] (*H.* पसीना), perspiration.

सोझराएल *sõjh'ráël*, *adj.* disentangled (of string, &c.)

सोहना *sõh'ná* (*H.* सोनार की चिमटी), a goldsmith's tongs.

हकबक *hak'bak*, *adj.* (*H.* ठकमुरकी), motionless.

हथैला *hathailá*, an earthen vessel for ladling the juice out of a sugar-press.

हथौवा *hathauá*, one of the oxen of a harrow; the one next the कुड़न्दरिया, *q. v.*; also *v.* बागन्दारन, पँचौट, and घेरा.

हबगब *hab'gab* (*H.* चपसोच), a precaution.

हराठा *haráthá* *adj.* (*H.* मोटा ताजा), hard-working; vigorous.

हलचुल्ली *hul'chullí* [1] (*H.* जलदबाज), expeditious; [2] (*H.* चंचल), fickle, restless.

Reg. No. 2356J -460-7-4-83.

SEVEN

GRAMMARS

OF THE DIALECTS AND SUBDIALECTS OF THE

BIHÁRÍ LANGUAGE.

SPOKEN IN THE PROVINCE OF BIHAR, IN THE EASTERN PORTION OF THE NORTH-WESTERN PROVINCES, AND IN THE NORTHERN PORTION OF THE CENTRAL PROVINCES.

PART III.

MAGADHÍ DIALECT

OF SOUTH PATNA AND GAYA.

Compiled under orders of the Government of Bengal

By GEORGE A. GRIERSON, B.C.S.,

OFFG. JOINT-MAGISTRATE OF PATNA.

CALCUTTA:

PRINTED AT THE BENGAL SECRETARIAT PRESS.

1883.

CONTENTS.

APPENDIX I.

SELECTIONS IN THE MAGADHI DIALECT.

APPENDIX II.

MAGADHI VOCABULARY.

INTRODUCTION.

§ 1. The following Grammar* treats of the Mágadhí dialect as spoken in its purity in South Patna and Gayá. In North Patna a variety of the Maithilí dialect is spoken, and round the City of Patna a debased form of the Hindústání language is also much used.

§ 2. The alphabet and rules for spelling will be found in the General Introduction to this series of Grammars, and the remarks therein found are not repeated here.

* I have to thank Paṇḍit Śiv Náráyaṇ Trivedí, Deputy Inspector of Schools, Gayá, Munshí Jadunandan Saháy and Munshí Diláwar Alí, Sub-Inspectors of Schools, Patna, for assistance rendered to me in the preparation of the work.

DIVISION I.

DECLENSION.

CHAPTER I.

NOUNS.

§ 3. For general remarks, see the General Introduction, § 38 and ff.

The following are the post-positions used in declining the noun in Mágadhí:—

		Power.
Nom.	*Wanting.*	
Acc.	*Wanting* or के *ke.*	
Instr.	से, सेँ, सतौँ, *se*, *sē*, or *satí*,	'by.'
Dat.	के *ke*,	'to.'
	ला. लेल, खातिर, or लागी, *lá*, *lel*, *khátir*, or *lági*,	'for.'
Abl.	से, सेँ, or सतौँ, *se*, *sē*, or *satí*,	'from.
Gen.	क, के, केर, *k*, *kĕ*, *ker*, or (rarely and only near Patna City) केरा, केरी, *kerá*, *kerí*,	'of.'
Loc.	मे, मेँ, मोँ, *me*, *mē*, *mō*,	'in.'
Voc.	*Wanting.*	

All these post-positions will only be used in one example, that of घोड़ा *ghoṛá*, 'a horse;' but they can all be used with all nouns.

Except those for the genitive, they can also be used with all pronouns. In the genitive singular many pronouns do not take these post-positions, but have other forms having similar terminations subject to the same rules.

The following are examples of declension:—

§ 4. (a) Masculine Tadbhavas in आ *á*.

Example of the declension of a *tadbhava** masculine noun in आ *á*:—

घोड़ा *ghoṛá*, 'a horse.'

Short form { Weak, घोड़ *ghoṛ*. Strong, घोड़ा *ghoṛá*. } Long form,* घोड़वा *ghŏṛ'wá*. Redundant form, † घोड़ौवा *ghŏṛauwá*.

Singular.

Nom.	घोड़ा [1] *ghoṛá*,	'a horse.'
Acc.	घोड़ा *ghoṛá* or घोड़ा के *ghoṛá ke*,	'a horse.'
Instr.	घोड़ा से, सेँ, or सतेँ *ghoṛá se, sẽ*, or *satí*,	'by a horse.'
Dat.	घोड़ा के, or ला, लेल, खातिर, लागी *ghoṛá ke*, or *lá, lel, khátir, lágí*,	'to' *or* 'for a horse.'
Abl.	घोड़ा से, सेँ, or सतेँ *ghoṛá se, sẽ*, or *satí*,	'from a horse.'
Gen.	घोड़क, घोड़ा के, or घोड़ा केर, केरा, केरी [2] *ghoṛak, ghoṛá kĕ*, or *ghoṛá ker, kerá, kerí*,	'of a horse.'
Loc.	घोड़ा मे, मेँ, मोँ *ghoṛá me, mẽ*, or *mõ*,	'in a horse.'
Voc.	ऐ घोड़ा *ai ghoṛá !*	'O horse!'

[1] Or घोड़ *ghoṛ*, घोड़वा *ghŏṛ'wá*, or घोड़ौवा *ghŏṛauwá*, and so throughout the singular.

[2] घोड़क *ghoṛak*, घोड़ा के *ghoṛá kĕ*, and घोड़ा केर *ghoṛá ker*, do not change for gender; घोड़ा केरा *ghoṛá kerá* and घोड़ा केरी *ghoṛá kerí* have only been noted near Patna City, and there are comparatively rare; केरा *kerá* is used before any masculine noun, without restriction of case; केरी *kerí* is only used before feminine nouns. So also in the plural.

Plural.

Nom.	घोड़न [1] *ghoṛan*,	'horses.'
Acc.	घोड़न *ghoṛan*, घोड़न के *ghoṛan ke*,	'horses.'
Instr.	घोड़न से, सेँ, सतेँ *ghoṛan se, sẽ, satí*,	'by horses.'

[1] Or घोड़वन *ghŏṛ'wan* or घोड़ौवन *ghŏṛauwan*, and so throughout the plural.

---

* See General Introduction, § 12. † See General Introduction, §§ 12, 38, and ff.

Dat.	घोड़न के, or ला, लेल, खातिर, लागी *ghoṛan ke*, or *lá, lel, khátir, lági,*	'to' *or* 'for horses.'
Abl.	घोड़न से, सँ, सतीँ *ghoṛan se, sẽ, satí,*	'from horses.'
Gen.	घोड़नक, घोड़न के, or घोड़न केर, केरा, केरी *ghoṛanak, ghoṛan kĕ,* or *ghoṛan ker, kerá, kerí,*[1]	'of horses.'
Loc.	घोड़न मे, मँ, मोँ *ghoṛan me, mẽ, mõ,*	'in horses.'
Voc.	ऐ घोड़न *ai ghoṛan !*	'O horses !'

See note [2] to singular.

§ 5. (b) Masculine Nouns ending in Silent Consonants.

Example of the declension of a masculine noun ending in a silent consonant:—

घर *ghar*, 'a house.'

Short form, { Weak, घर *ghar*. Strong, घरा *ghará*. } Long form,* घरऽवा *ghar'wá*. Redundant form,* घरौवा *gharauwá*.

Singular.

Nom.	घर [1] *ghar,*	'a house.'
Acc.	घर, घर के *ghar, ghar ke,* or घरे के *gharĕ ke,*	'a house.'
Instr.	घरेँ *gharẽ,* घर से or घरे से, *ghar se* or *gharĕ se, &c.,*	'by a house.'
Dat.	घर के, लेल, or घरे के, लेल *ghar ke, lel,* or *gharĕ ke, lel, &c.,*	'to' *or* 'for a house.'
Abl.	घर से or घरे से *ghar se* or *gharĕ se, &c.,*	'from a house.'
Gen.	घरक *gharak,* घर के *ghar kĕ, &c.,* घरेक *gharĕk,* घरे के *gharĕ kĕ, &c.,*	'of a house.'
Loc.	घरे *ghare,* घर मेँ *ghar mẽ,* or घरे मेँ *gharĕ mẽ, &c.,*	'in a house.'
Voc.	ऐ घर *ai ghar !*	'O house !'

[1] Or घरा *ghará*, घरऽवा *ghar'wá*, घरौवा *gharauwá*, and so throughout the singular.

* See General Introduction, §§ 12, 38, and ff.

Plural.

Nom.	घरन [1] *gharan,*	'houses.'
Acc.	घरन *gharan* or घरन के *gharan ke,*	'houses.'
Instr.	घरन से *gharan se, &c.,*	'by houses.'
Dat.	घरन के *gharan ke, &c.,*	'to' *or* 'for houses.'
Abl.	घरन से *gharan se, &c.,*	'from houses.'
Gen.	घरनक, घरन कें, *gharanak, gharan kĕ, &c.,*	'of houses.'
Loc.	घरन मेँ *gharan mẽ, &c.,*	'in houses.'
Voc.	ऐ घरन *ai gharan !*	'O houses!'

[1] Or घर्‌वन *ghar'wan,* घरौवन *gharauwan,* and so throughout the plural.

§ 6. It is not necessary to decline further any nouns in full, as the above examples suffice. All nouns ending in vowels are declined like घोड़ा *ghoṛá,* and all those ending in silent consonants like घर *ghar.* The final syllables of all long and redundant forms may optionally be nasalized by the addition of *anunásik:* thus घोड़्वा *ghŏṛ'wá* or घोड़्वाँ *ghŏṛ'wā̃;* घरौवा *gharauwá* or घरौवाँ *gharauwā̃;* मलिया *maliyá* or मलियाँ *maliyā̃.*

Note, however, that—

(1) All nouns ending in vowels have the oblique form the same as the direct form: as nom. घोड़ा *ghoṛá,* acc. घोड़ा के *ghoṛáke.*

(2) All *masculine* nouns ending in a silent consonant may take ए *ĕ* in the oblique form singular: as nom. घर *ghar,* acc. घर के *ghar ke* or घरे के *gharĕ ke.* Occasionally, also, in the case of these nouns we find an instrumental in ऐँ *ē* and a locative in ए *e*: thus हम बलेँ ले जाएब *ham balē le jáĕb,* 'I shall take away by force,' where बलेँ *balē* is the instrumental of बल *bal,* 'force;' घाटे *ghát̤e,* 'at a landing stage,' locative of घाट *ghát̤,* 'a landing stage:' so also घरे घरे *ghare ghare,* 'in every house,' 'from house to house.'

(3) All nouns ending in a long vowel shorten it in the genitive in क *k,* but preserve it long in the other forms of the genitive: thus घोड़क *ghoṛak,* but घोड़ा के *ghoṛá kĕ,* घोड़ा केर *ghoṛá ker, &c.*

An example of each of the more common forms of nouns follows :—

§ 7. (c) Masculine Tatsamas * in आ *á*.

राजा *rájá*, 'a king.'

Short form, राजा *rájá*. Long form,* रजःवा *raj'wá*. Redundant form,* रजौवा *rajauwá*.

Gen. sing. राजक *rájak*, राजा के *rájá kĕ*, *&c*.
Nom. plur. राजन, *rájan*, *&c*.

§ 8. (d) Masculine Nouns in ई *í*.

माली *málí*, 'a gardener.'

Short form, माली *málí*. Long form,* मलिया *maliyá*. Redundant form,* मलियवा *maliyawá*.

Gen. sing. मालिक *málik*, माली के *málí kĕ*, *&c*.
Nom. plur. मालिन *málin*, *&c*.

§ 9. (e) Masculine Nouns in ऊ *ú*.

नाऊ *náú*, 'a barber.'†

Short form, नाऊ *náú*. Long form,‡ नउआ *naüá* or नौआ *nauá*. Redundant form,‡ नउअवा *naüawá* or नौअवा *nauawá*.

Gen. sing. नाउक *náük*, नाऊ के *náú kĕ*, *&c*.
Nom. plur. नाउन *náün*, *&c*.

---

* See General Introduction, §§ 12, 38, and ff., 34 and 36.

† Kellogg in his Hindí Grammar incorrectly gives आँसू *ású* as an example of a feminine noun in ऊ. It is masculine. आँसू *ású* is not used in Bihárí, लोर *lor* being the word for 'a tear.'

‡ See General Introduction, §§ 12, 38, and ff., and 34 to 36.

§ 10. (f) Feminine Nouns in ई *í*.

पोथी *pothí*, 'a book.'

Short form, पोथी *pothí*. Long form, * पोथिया *pŏthiyá*. Redundant form, पोथियवा *pŏthiyawá*.

Gen. sing. पोथिक *pothik* or पोथी के *pothí kĕ*, *&c.*
Nom. plur. पोथिन *pothin*, *&c.*

§ 11. (g) Feminine Nouns ending in a Silent Consonant.

बात *bát*, 'a word.'

Short form, बात *bát*. Long form, * बतिया *batiyá*. Redundant form, * बतियवा *batiyawá*.

Acc. sing. बात के *bát ke*.
Gen. sing. बातक *bátak* or बात के *bát kĕ*, *&c.*
Nom. plur. बातन *bátan*, *&c.*

§ 12. Periphrastic Plural.

With reference to the above plural forms, it must be noted that every noun can also form a periphrastic plural by the addition of a word signifying plurality, such as सब *sab*, 'all;' or, in the case of *rational* beings, such as लोग *log*, 'people.' Example: घर सब *ghar sab* instead of घरन *gharan*, and माली लोग केर *málí log ker* for मलियन केर *maliyan ker*. Sometimes even this plural affix is omitted, so that a plural noun appears under a singular form. An example occurs in the ninth of the following sentences, where बेटा *beṭá* is used for बेटा सब *beṭá sab*. This is the regular rule when a numeral adjective precedes, as in Nos. 6 and 7 of the following sentences. Sometimes these plural affixes are added pleonastically to a word already in the usual form, *e.g.* पोथियन सब *pöthiyan sab* for पोथियन *pŏthiyan*.

---

* See General Introduction, §§ 12, 38, and ff., and 34 and 36.

§ 13. Genitival Affixes.

The following examples have been specially designed to exhibit the use of the genitival affixes. Each sentence is given as spoken (*a*) in Patna and (*b*) in Gayá :—

1. (*a*) ई राजा केर मट्ठ हइ.
Ī rájá ker maṭṭh haï.
(*b*) ई रज॰वा के मंदिर हइ.
Ī raj'wá kĕ mandir haï.
'This is the king's temple.'

2. (*a*) हम कन्स के नौँड़ी ही.
Ham Kans kĕ nãuṛí hí.
(*b*) हम कन्स के लौँड़ी हिअइ.
Ham Kans kĕ lãuṛí hiaï.
'I am the maid-servant of King Kans.'

3. (*a*) मध॰मच्छियन के झूँड़ उड़ गेलइ.
Madh'machchhiyan kĕ jhũṛ uṛ gĕlaï.
(*b*) मधुमखियन के थोक॰वा उड़ गेल.
Madhumakhiyan kĕ thŏk'wá uṛ gel.
'A swarm of bees flew away.'

4. (*a*) छली के मारे के कुच्छो दोस न॰ हइ.
Chhalí kĕ márĕ kĕ kuchchhŏ dos na haï.
(*b*) कप॰टी के मार॰लक कुछु दोख नइ.
Kap'ṭí kĕ már'lak kuchhu dokh naï.
'There is no sin in slaying a deceiver.'

5. (*a*) मथुरा केरी जन्नी सब कंद॰ते चल गेल॰थीन.
Mathurá kerí janní sab kand'tĕ chal gĕl'thín.
(*b*) मथुरा के मेह॰ररुअन (nom. plur. of मेह॰ररुआ, long form of मेह॰रारू) काँद॰ते चल गेल॰थीन.
Mathurá kĕ mĕh'raruan (nom. plur. of *mĕh'raruá,* long form of *mĕh'rárú*) *kãd'tĕ chal gĕl'thín.*
'The women of Mathurá departed weeping.'

6.	(*a*) अनेक प्रकारक बात सुनल गेलइ. *Anek prakárak bát sunal gĕlaï.*	'Matters of many kinds were heard.'
	(*b*) बहुत तरह के बात सुनल गेल. *Bahut tarah kĕ bát sunal gel.*	
7.	(*a*) स्फटिक के चार फाटक टूट गेलइ. *Sphaṭik kĕ chár pháṭak ṭúṭ gĕlaï.*	'Four gates of crystal broke.'
	(*b*) उजर पत्थर के चार गो फाटक टूट गेल. *Ujar patthar kĕ chár go pháṭak ṭúṭ gel.*	
8.	(*a*) देस देस के राजा सब अएलन्थिन. *Des des kĕ rájá sab aĕl'thin.*	'Kings of all countries came.'
	(*b*) मुलुक मुलुक के राजा ऐलन. *Muluk muluk kĕ rájá ailan.*	
9.	(*a*) ऊ सब माली के बेटा हहीँ. *U' sab máli kĕ beṭá hahí.*	'They are the sons of the gardener.'
	(*b*) उनऽकन्ही माली के बेटा हथिन. *Un'kanhi máli kĕ beṭá hathin.*	
10.	(*a*) हम राजा के गाँव मेँ अइलूँ. *Ham rájá kĕ gãw mẽ aïlű.*	'I came into the king's villages.'
	(*b*) हम राजा के गौँवन मेँ ऐली. *Ham rájá kĕ gaũwan mẽ aili.*	
11.	(*a*) पंडितन के घर मेँ अनेक पुस्तक रहऽ हईं. *Panḍitan kĕ ghar mẽ anek pustak raha haí.*	'There are many books in *panḍits'* houses.'
	(*b*) पंडितन के घर मेँ ढेर पोथी हइन. *Panḍitan kĕ ghar mẽ ḍher pothi haïn.*	

8. देस देस के राजा ऐलन.
Des des kĕ rájá ailan.
'Kings of all countries came.'

9. उन्हनीका माली के बेटा हवन सठ.
Unh'niká máli kĕ betá hawan sa.
'They are the sons of the gardener.'

10. हम राजा का गाँवन[1] पर ऐलीं.
Ham rájá ká gấwan[1] par ailĩ.
'I came into the king's villages.'

11. पंडितन[2] का घरे ढेर पोथी बाटे.
Paṇḍitan[2] ká ghare ḍher pothī báṭe.
'There are many books in *paṇḍits'* houses.'

[1] In Sáṛan and Champáran, optionally गाँव'सऽ *gấw'sa.*
[2] In Sáran and Champáran, optionally पंडित'सऽ *paṇḍit'sa.*

§ 13a. Definitive Terminations.

The termination ओ *o* is added to a word to give the sense of 'also:' as घरो में देखऽ *gharo mẽ dekha,* 'look in the house also.'

In Sáran and Sháhábád the long form of a noun in वा *wá* or वेँ *wẽ* (besides being used non-honorifically) is sometimes used to express definiteness: as घोड़वेँ कैलस बजाती *ghŏṛ'wẽ kailas bajátí,* '*the* horse did badzátí;' घोड़वन देखले तोबड़ा, जनले दानेँ भरल बा *ghŏṛ'wan dĕkh'le tŏb'ṛá, jan'le danẽ bharal bá,* '*the* horses saw the grain bag, and knew that it was filled with grain.' In Sháhábád the above sentence would be written घोड़वा तोबड़ा देखले सठ, जनले सठ दानेँ भरल बा *ghŏr'wá tŏb'ṛa dĕkh'le sa, jan'le sa danẽ bharul bá.*

CHAPTER II.

ADJECTIVES.

§ 14. Gender.

See General Introduction, § 42 and ff. In Ázamgaṛh and Banáras adjectives ending in आ *á* are inflected in the oblique cases of the singular and in the nominative plural, as in Hindí. Examples are—

बड़े बटा कै घर *baṛe beṭá kaĭ ghar*, 'the house of the elder son.'

पाँच अच्छे अच्छे बरद *păch achchhe achchhe barad*, 'five good bullocks.' As in the latter example, the adjective is generally repeated to express plurality.

§ 15. Numeral Adjectives.

The cardinals are nearly the same as those in High Hindí. The following are the ones that present points of difference :—

1 = एगो *ego.*
2 = दूइ or दू *dúi* or *dú.*
3 = तीनि *tíni.*
4 = चारि *chári.*
6 = छौ *chhau.*
11 = इगारह *igárah.*
16 = सोरह *sorah.*
19 = उनइस *unaïs.*
21 = एकइस *ĕkaïs.*
22 = बाइस *báis.*
23 = तेइस *teis.*
24 = चौबिस *chaubis.*
26 = छब्बिस *chhabbis.*
27 = सताइस *satáis.*
28 = अठाइस *aṭháis.*
29 = उनंतिस *un'tis.*
31 = एकंतिस *ĕk'tis.*
32 = बत्तिस *battis.*
33 = तैंतिस *tẽtis.*
34 = चौंतिस *chãũtis.*
35 = पैंतिस *pãĭtis.*
36 = छत्तिस *chhattis.*
37 = सैंतिस *sãĭttis*; and so on to 48, inclusive, each number including a short इ *i* in the last syllable.
60 = साठि *sáṭhi.*
61 = एकसठि *ĕk'saṭhi.*
62 = बासठि *básaṭhi*; and so on to 68, each word having a final short इ *i.*
92 = बाँवे *bắwe.*

93 = तिरॉवे *tirȁwe.*
94 = चौरॉवे *chaürȁwe.*
95 = पँचॉवे *pȁchȁwe.*
96 = छिआँवे *chhiȁwe.*
97 = सतॉवे *satȁwe.*
98 = अँठॉवे *ȁṭhȁwe.*
99 = निनॉवे *ninȁwe.*

The word गो *go* or ठो *ṭho* may be added to the end of any cardinal number except एगो *ego.*

§ 16. Ordinals.

The ordinals up to 'sixth' are as follows: —

1*st* = पहिल *pahil* or पहिलका *pahil'ká ; obl.* पहिला *pahilá.**
2*nd* = दूसर *dúsar* or दुसरका *dusar'ká ; obl.* दुसरा *dus'rá.**
3*rd* = तीसर *tísar* or तिसरका *tisar'ká ; obl.* तिसरा *tis'rá.**
4*th* = चौठ *chauṭh,* चौथ *chauth,* चौथा *chauthá.*
5*th* = पचवाँ *pach'wȁ* or पचाँ *pachȁ.*
6*th* = छट्ठाँ *chhaṭṭhȁ* or छठाँ *chhaṭhȁ.*

The ordinals above 'sixth' are all formed by adding आँ *ȁ* or वाँ *wȁ* to the cardinals, after shortening a long vowel in a final syllable: as दसाँ *dasȁ* or दसवाँ *das'wȁ,* 'tenth;' पचसवाँ *pachas'wȁ,* 'fiftieth.' The feminines are in अइँ *aȉ :* as सतइँ *sataȉ,* 'seventh;' नवइँ *nawaȉ,* 'ninth.'

§ 17. Fractional Numbers.

These are—

$\frac{1}{4}$ = पा *pá,* पाव *páw,* पौवा *pauwá,* or पउवा *paüwá.*
$\frac{1}{3}$ = तिसरी *tis'rí.*
$\frac{1}{2}$ = आध *ádh,* आधा *ádhá,* अधिया *adhiyá,* or खाँड़ा *khȁṛá.*
$\frac{3}{4}$ = पौन *paun* or पौना *pauná.*
$-\frac{1}{4}$ = पौना *pauná* or पवन्ने *pawanne.*
$1\frac{1}{4}$ or $+\frac{1}{4}$ = सावा *sáwá,* सवा *sawá,* सवाई *sawáí,* or सवइया *sawaïyá.*
$1\frac{1}{2}$ = डेढ़ *ḍeṛh.*
$2\frac{1}{2}$ = आढ़ा *áṛhá,* अढ़ाई *aṛhái,* अढ़इया *aṛhaïyá.*
$+\frac{1}{2}$ = साढ़े *sáṛhe.*

---

* The first three ordinals follow pronominal genitives in the formation of oblique forms. See *post,* § 34.

§ 18. Multiplicatives.

Multiplicatives, such as the English 'twice' and 'thrice,' are not found in Bhojpúrí. The Bihárí idiom is illustrated in such phrases as दू सते चौदह *dú sate chaudah*, 'two seven's, fourteen;' छौ तीयाँ अठारह *chhau tíyã aṭhárah*, 'six three's, eighteen,' which correspond to the English idioms 'seven times two' and 'three times six.' Numbers thus used are called multiplicatives, and differ in some respects from the cardinals. The following are the multiplicative numbers up to 10, including fractions :—

× 1, का *ká*, एक्का *ĕkká*, or एकाई *ĕkáí*.

× $1\frac{1}{4}$, सवा *sawá*.

× $1\frac{1}{2}$, डेढ़ा *deṛhá*, डेढ़े *deṛhe*, डेढ़ो *deṛho*, or डेवढ़ *dewaṛh*.

× 2, दूना *dúná*, दूनी *dúní*, दुगुनी *duguní*.

× $2\frac{1}{2}$, अढ़ाँ *aṛhấ*, अढ़ाई *aṛháí*, अढ़इया *aṛhaïyá*, अढ़ैया *aṛhaiyá*.

× 3, तियाँ *tiyấ*, तियाई *tiyáí*, तिरिका *tiriká*.

× $3\frac{1}{2}$, हूँठा *hū́ṭhá*, अँगूठा *ãgúṭhá*, or अँगूँढ़ा *ãgū́ṛhá*.

× 4, चौक *chauk*, चौका *chauká*, चौके *chauke*.

× $4\frac{1}{2}$, धमूचा *dhamúchá*, धँगूचा *dhãgúchá*.

× 5, पाच *pách*, पचा *pachá*, पचे *pache*.

× $5\frac{1}{2}$, पहूँचा *pahū́chá*.

× 6, छक *chhak*, छका *chhaká*, or छकें *chhake*.

× $6\frac{1}{2}$, बिछिया *bichhiyá*.

× 7, सात *sát* or सते *sate*.

× $7\frac{1}{2}$, चलौसा *chalausá*.

× 8, आठ *áṭh*, आठे *áṭhe*, or अढ़े *aṛhe*.

× 9, नवाँ *nawá*, नवाँई *nawấí*, or नउका *naüká*.

× 10, दहाँ *dahấ*, दहाँई *dahấí*, or दस्का *das'ká*.

§ 19. Definite Cardinals.

These are as follows:—

एगो *ego*, 'the one;'

दूनू *dúnú* or दूनो *dúno*, 'the two,' 'both;'

तीनो *tíno*, 'the three;'

चारो *cháro*, 'the four;' and so on,

adding ओ *o* to the numerals, after omitting a final short vowel.

§ 20. Indefinite Cardinals.

The termination अन *an* added to the numbers 'one hundred,' 'one thousand,' and so on, always denotes an indefinite number of these aggregates. In this idiom सँकड़ा *sãk'ṛá* is always substituted for सौ *sau*, 'one hundred.' Examples are सँकड़न फेड़ *sãk'ṛan pheṛ*, 'hundreds of trees;' हजारन *hajáran*, 'thousands;' लाखन *lákhan*, 'tens of thousands.' To other numbers the syllable हाँ *hã* may be added with a like result; thus पचसहाँ *pachas'hã*, 'fifties.'

§ 21. Collective Numerals.

These—viz. जोड़ा *joṛá*, 'a pair,' गंडा *gaṇḍá*, 'a four,'—are the sam as in High Hindí, except सँकड़ा *sãk'ṛá*, 'a hundred.'

CHAPTER III.

PRONOUNS.

§ 22. The following tables show the declensional forms of the principal pronouns and pronominal forms.

The declension of pronouns presents some important points of difference from that of nouns, which must be carefully noticed.

While nouns frequently remain unchanged before post-positions, pronouns, with few exceptions, change to some other form, called the *oblique* or *inflected base.*

The accusative singular of pronouns is, with one or two exceptions, never the same as the nominative. The only exceptions are रवाँ *rawā̃*, 'your Honour;' का *ká*, 'what?' केऊ *kĕú*, 'anyone,' 'some one;' and कुच्छो *kuchchhŏ*, 'anything,' 'some thing.' In circumstances corresponding to those in which the accusative of a noun takes the nominative form, the accusative of a pronoun takes the oblique form without any post-position.

The genitive form of pronouns ending in र *r* is also to be noticed. The genitive forms in र *r* and रे *rĕ* are direct genitives, while those in रा *rá* are oblique. I have noted also in poetry a rare feminine genitive in रि: thus मोरि बिनन्ती *mori bin'ti*, 'my petition.' As these feminine forms are very rare, I have not given them in the paradigms.

Pronouns have the same form, whether referring to masculine or feminine nouns. With the exception of the pronouns of the second person, they all want the vocative case.

§ 23. Pronouns of the First Person and of the Second Person Non-Honorific.

These pronouns have each two forms, a shorter and a longer.

हम *ham*, 'I.'

Singular.

	Shorter form.	*Longer form.*
Nom.	मैं *mẽ.*	हम *ham.*[1]
Acc.	मोरा[2] *morá* or मोरा के *morá ke.*	हमरा[2] *ham'rá* or हमरा के *ham'rá ke.*
Instr.	मोरा सँ *morá sẽ.*	हमरा सँ *ham'rá sẽ.*
Dat.	मोरा ला *morá lá.*	हमरा ला *ham'rá lá.*
Abl.	मोरा सँ *morá sẽ.*	हमरा सँ *ham'rá sẽ.*
Gen.	मोर or मोरे; मोरा[3], *mor* or *morĕ*; *morá.*[3]	हमार or हमरे; हमरा[3], *hamár* or *ham'rĕ*; *ham'rá.*[3]
Loc.	मोरा मेँ *morá mẽ.*	हमरा मेँ *ham'rá mẽ.*
Voc.	*Wanting.*	*Wanting.*

[1] In Sáran also हमे *hame.* In Western Bhojpúrí (see Introduction) the nominative is मैं *mãi* or मों *mõ*; हम *ham* or हमें *hamẽ.*

[2] The oblique base singular has a form मोरे *more,* हमरे *ham're,* meaning 'even me;' and another form मोरो *moro,* हमरो *ham'ro,* meaning 'me also.'

There is an old oblique base singular, मोहि *mŏhi,* or (contracted) मो, which I have met in poetry. It is not, however, so far as I am aware, used nowadays in conversation. In Western Bhojpúrí the oblique bases are मो *mo,* मों *mõ,* मोरा *morá* or मोरे *more,* and हमरा *ham'rá* or हमरे *ham're.*

[3] मोर *mor* and मोरे *morĕ,* हमार *ham'ár* and हमरे *ham'rĕ,* are direct genitives; मोरा *morá* and हमरा *ham'rá* are oblique genitives. In Western Bhojpúrí the oblique genitives are मोरे *more,* हमरे *ham're.*

Plural.

	Shorter form.	*Longer form.*
Nom.	हमनीका[1] *hamaniká.*	हमरन[2] *ham'ran.*
Acc.	हमनी (के) *hamaní (ke).*	हमरन (के) *ham'ran (ke).*
Instr.	हमनी सँ *hamaní sẽ.*	हमरन सँ *ham'ran sẽ.*
Dat.	हमनी ला *hamaní lá.*	हमरन ला *ham'ran lá.*
Abl.	हमनी सँ *hamaní sẽ.*	हमरन सँ *ham'ran sẽ.*

[1] Or हमन *haman,* हमन्ह *hamanh,* हमनिन्ह *ham'ninh,* हमइन (-न्ह) *hamaïn (-nh),* or हम लोग *ham log,* which forms can all be used throughout the plural. In Western Bhojpúrí the forms are हम्मन *hamman,* हमहन *ham'han,* or हमने *hamane.*

[2] Or हमरन्ह *ham'ranh,* or (in North Muzaffarpúr) हमरहिन (-न्ह) *hamar'hin (-nh),* all of which can be used throughout the plural.

Gen.	हमनी के ; का,[1] *hamaní kĕ ; ká.*[1]	हमःरन के ; का,[1] *ham'ran kĕ ; ká.*
Loc.	हमनी मेँ *hamaní mẽ.*	हमःरन मेँ *ham'ran mẽ.*
Voc.	*Wanting.*	*Wanting.*

[1] के *kĕ* direct ; का *ká* oblique.

तोँ *tō* or तूँ *tũ*, 'thou.'

Singular.

	Shorter form.	*Longer form.*
Nom.	तूँ or तेँ[1] *tũ* or *tẽ.*[1]	तूँ or तेँ[1] *tũ* or *tẽ.*[1]
Acc.	तोरा,[2] तोरा के *torá*[2] or *torá ke.*	तोह्ःरा[2] or तोह्ःरा के *tŏh'rá*[2] or *tŏh'rá ke.*
Instr.	तोरा सेँ *torá sẽ.*	तोह्ःरा सेँ *tŏh'rá sẽ.*
Dat.	तोरा ला *torá lá.*	तोह्ःरा ला *tŏh'ra lá.*
Abl.	तोरा सेँ *torá sẽ.*	तोह्ःरा सेँ *tŏh'rá sẽ.*
Gen.	तोर or तोरे ; तोरा[3] *tor* or *torĕ ; torá.*[3]	तोहार *or* तोह्ःरे ; तोह्ःरा[3] *tŏhár* or *tŏh'rĕ ; tŏh'rá.*[3]
Loc.	तोरा मेँ *torá mẽ.*	तोह्ःरा मेँ *tŏh'rá mẽ.*
Voc.	हे तूँ *he tũ* or हे तेँ *he tẽ.*	हे तोँ *he tō* or हे तूँ *he tũ.*

[1] In Western Bhojpúrí the nominative is तैँ *taĩ* or तुह *tuh.*

[2] The oblique base singular has a form तोरे *tore,* तोह्ःरे *tŏh're,* meaning 'even thee,' and another form तोरो *toro,* तोह्ःरो *tŏh'ro,* meaning 'thee also.'

There is an old oblique base singular तोहि *tŏhi,* or (contracted) तो *to,* which I have met in poetry. It is not, however, so far as I am aware, used nowadays in conversation. In Western Bhojpúrí the oblique bases are तूह, *tũh,* तो *to,* तोरा *torá* or तोरे *tore* and तुह्ःरा *tuh'rá,* तुह्ःरे *tuh're.*

[3] तोर *tor* and तोरे *torĕ,* तोहार *tŏhár* and तोह्ःरे *tŏh'rĕ,* are direct genitives. तोरा *torá* and तोह्ःरा *tŏh'rá* are oblique genitives. In Western Bhojpúrí the oblique genitives are तोरे *tore* and तुह्ःरे *tuh're.*

Plural.

	Shorter form.	*Longer form.*
Nom.	तोहनीका[1] *tŏhaniká.*	तोह्ःरन[2] *tŏh'ran.*
Acc.	तोहनी (के) *tŏhani (ke).*	तोह्ःरन (के) *tŏh'ran (ke).*

[1] Or तुन्हन *tunhan,* तुन्हन्ह *tunhanh,* तोह्ःनिन (-न्ह) *tŏh'nin (-nh),* or तूँ लोग *tũ log,* which forms can all be used throughout the plural. In Western Bhojpúrí the forms are तूँहन *tũhan* or तुहने *tuhane.*

[2] Or तोह्ःरन्ह *tŏha'ranh,* तोरन (-न्ह) *toran (-nh),* or (in North Muzaffarpúr) तोह्ःर-हिन (-न्ह) *tŏhar'hin (-nh),* all of which can be used throughout the plural. In Western Bhojpúrí the form is तुह्ःरन *tuh'ran.*

Instr.	तोहनी सँ *tŏhaní sē.*	तोहःरन सँ *tŏhran sē.*
Dat.	तोहनी ला *tŏhaní lá.*	तोहःरन ला *tŏh'ran lá.*
Abl.	तोहनी सँ *tŏhaní sē.*	तोहःरन सँ *tŏh'ran sē.*
Gen.	तोहनी के ; का,[1] *tŏhaní kĕ ; ká.*[1]	तोहःरन के ; का,[1] *tŏh'ran kĕ ; ká.*[1]
Loc.	तोहनी मेँ *tŏhaní mē.*	तोहःरनी मेँ *tŏh'raní mē.*
Voc.	हे तूँ लोग *he tú log.*	हे तूँ लोग *he tú log.*

[1] के *kĕ* direct ; का *ká* oblique.

§ 24. Pronoun of the Second Person Honorific.

रौवाँ *rauwā̃* or रवाँ *rawā̃*, or रौरा *raurá* or रउरा *raürá*, or अपःने *ap'nĕ* or अपःनि *ap'ni.*

This pronoun is declined quite regularly according to the rules for the declension of nouns, except in the genitive singular, which is रौवाँ के, का, *rauwā̃ kĕ, ká*, or राउर *ráur* ; also रौरे *raurĕ* ; (obl.) -रा -*rá* ; or रउरे *raürĕ* ; (obl.) -रा -*rá* ; also अपःने के, *ap'nĕ kĕ &c.* In Western Bhojpúrí the oblique genitive is रौरे *raure.* A direct fem., रउरि *raüri* is met in poetry.

The nominative plural is रौवन (-न्ह) *rauwan (-nh) or* रौरन (-न्ह) *rauran (-nh).* The vocative singular is ए रवोँ *raĭ.*

Reflexive Pronoun.

अपःने *ap'nĕ*, 'self.'

Nom. sing. अपःने *ap'nĕ.*
Obl. sing. अपःना *ap'ná.*
Gen. sing. आपन *ápan*, अप्पन *appan*, or अपःने *ap'nĕ* ; (obl.)-ना -*ná.*
Nom. plur. अपःनन (-न्ह) *ap'nan* (-*nh*).

The rest is quite regular.

In North Muzaffarpúr there is found a genitive plural आपुस के (का), *ápus kĕ (ká).* In Western Bhojpúrí the nominative is आप *áp*, आपु *ápu*, अपुए *apue*, अपःना *ap'ná*, or अपःने *ap'nĕ*, and the oblique form आपन *ápan*, अपःना *ap'ná*, or अपःने *ap'ne.*

§ 25. Demonstrative Pronouns.

These are (1) the proximate demonstrative ई *í*, 'this,' and (2) the remote demonstrative ऊ *ú*, 'that.'

These pronouns have each two declensions—a *non-honorific*, when special respect is not intended; and an *honorific*, when special respect is intended. The honorific declension is really an old plural.

Like the personal pronouns, they have each two forms for each eclension, a shorter and a longer.

ई *í*, 'this.'

NON-HONORIFIC.

Singular.

	Shorter form.	*Longer form.*
Nom.	ई *í*, or emphatic ईहे *íhĕ*.	ई *í*,[1] or emphatic ईहे *íhĕ*.
Acc.	एह[1] (के) *ĕh*[1] (*ke*).	एकरा (के) *ĕk'rá* (*ke*).
Instr.	एह सेँ *ĕh sẽ*.	एकरा सेँ *ĕk'rá sẽ*.
Dat.	एह ला *ĕh lá*.	एकरा ला *ĕk'rá lá*.
Abl.	एह सेँ *ĕh sẽ*.	एकरा सेँ *ĕk'rá sẽ*.
Gen.	एह के; का, *&c.*, *ĕh kĕ ; ká, &c.*	एकर *ekar*, एकरे ; -रा, *ĕk'rĕ ; -rá*.
Loc.	एह मेँ, *ĕh mẽ*.	एकरा मेँ *ĕk'rá mẽ*.

[1] Or एहि *ĕhi* or ए *e*, and so throughout the singular.

Plural.

	Shorter form.	*Longer form.*
Nom.	इन्ह सभन्का or इन्हन्का *inh*[1] *sabh'ká* or *inh'ká*.	एकन्रन *ĕk'ran*.[2]
Acc.	इन्ह (के) *inh* (*ke*).	एकन्रन (के) *ĕk'ran* (*ke*).
Instr.	इन्ह सेँ *inh sẽ*.	एकन्रन सेँ *ĕk'ran sẽ*.
Dat.	इन्ह ला *inh lá*.	एकन्रन ला *ĕk'ran lá*.
Abl.	इन्ह सेँ *inh sẽ*.	एकन्रन सेँ *ĕk'ran sẽ*.
Gen.	इन्ह के; का, *&c.*, *inh kĕ ; ká, &c.*	एकन्रन के; का, *&c.*, *ĕk'ran kĕ ; ká, &c.*
Loc.	इन्ह मेँ *inh mẽ*.	एकन्रन मेँ, *ĕk'ran mẽ*.

[1] Or इन्हन (न्ह) *inhan* (*nh*) or इन्हन्नी *inh'ní*, and so throughout the plural.

[2] Or एकन्नी *ĕk'ní*, and so throughout the plural.

HONORIFIC.

Singular.

	Shorter form.	*Longer form.*
Nom.	इहाँ *ihā́.*	इहाँ *ihā́.*
Acc.	ईहाँ[1] (के) *ihā́*[1] (*ke*).	इन्हन्का (के) *inh'ká* (*ke*).
Instr.	इहाँ सँ *ihā́ sẽ.*	इन्हन्का सँ *inh'ká sẽ.*
Dat.	इहाँ ला *ihā́ lá.*	इन्हन्का ला *inh'ká lá.*
Abl.	इहाँ सँ *ihā́ sẽ.*	इन्हन्का सँ *inh'ká sẽ.*
Gen.	इहाँ के ; का, *&c.*, *ihā́ kĕ ; ká, &c.*	इन्हन्कर (-करे ; -करा), *inh'kar,* (*-karĕ ; -kará.*)
Loc.	इहाँ मेँ *ihā́ mẽ.*	इन्हन्का मेँ *inh'ká mẽ.*

[1] Or इन (-न्ह) *in* (*-nh*), and so throughout the singular in the oblique cases.

Plural.

Nom.	इहाँ[1] सभन्का or इहाँका *ihā́*[1] *sabh'ká* or *ihā́ká.*	*Wanting.*
Acc.	इहाँ सभ (के) *ihā́ sabh* (*ke*).	
Instr.	इहाँ सभ सँ *ihā́ sabh sẽ.*	
Dat.	इहाँ सभ ला *ihā́ sabh lá.*	
Abl.	इहाँ सभ सँ *ihā́ sabh sẽ.*	
Gen.	इहाँ सभ के ; का *ihā́ sabh kĕ ; ká.*	
Loc.	इहाँ सभ मेँ *ihā́ sabh mẽ.*	

[1] Or इहन *ihan*, and so throughout the plural.

The word एथी *ĕthi* is used to signify 'this' when the name of a thing cannot be readily remembered,—something like the English 'what do you call it.'

In Sáran and Western Bhojpúrí the words एह *ĕh*, एकन्रा *ĕk'rá*, and एकर *ekar*, are often spelt ह *he*, हेकन्रा *hĕk'rá*, and हेकर *hekar* respectively. The nominative singular is frequently written हई *hai*.

In North Muzaffarpúr a variation of the oblique plural of the longer form non-honorific is एकरन्हिन *ĕkar'hin*.

The syllable का *ká* can be added to any form of the nominative plural.

In Western Bhojpúrí oblique forms ending in रा *rá* are written with रे *re:* thus एकरे *ĕk're* इन्हकरे *inh'kare,* instead of एकरा *ĕk'rá,* इन्हकरा *inh'kará.* Instead of इन्ह *inh,* इन्हका *inh'ká, &c.,* it often has हिन्ह *hinh,* हिन्हका *hinh'ká, &c.* It also has a non-honorific form इत्तू *itthú* or इतुआ *ithuá,* which is declined regularly like a substantive,—plural, इतुअन *ithuan.* This form refers only to things, and not to persons, and is sometimes spelt with an initial ह *h:* thus हित्तू *hitthú,* हितुआ *hithuá,* हितुअन *hithuan.*

ऊ *u,* 'that.'

The close analogy between the declension of this pronoun and that of ई *í,* 'this,' will be manifest from the following paradigm:—

NON-HONORIFIC.

Singular.

	Shorter form.	*Longer form.*
Nom.	ऊ or ओ *ú* or *o.*	ऊ or ओ *ú* or *o.*
Acc.	ओह[1] (के) *ŏh*[1] *(ke).*	ओकरा (के) *ŏk'rá (ke).*
Instr.	ओह सेँ *ŏh sē.*	ओकरा सेँ *ŏk'rá sē.*
Dat.	ओह ला *ŏh lá.*	ओकरा ला *ŏk'rá lá.*
Abl.	ओह सेँ *ŏh sē.*	ओकरा सेँ *ŏk'rá sē.*
Gen.	ओह के; का, &c., *ŏh kĕ; ká, &c.*	ओकर *okar,* ओकरे; -रा, *ŏk'rĕ; -rá.*
Loc.	ओह मेँ *ŏh mē.*	ओकरा मेँ *ŏk'rá mē.*

[1] Or ओहि *ŏhi* or ओ *o,* and so throughout the singular.

Plural.

Nom.	उन्ह[1] सभ का or उन्ह का *unh*[1] *sabh ká* or *unh'ká.*	ओकरन *ŏk'ran.*[2]
Acc.	उन्ह (के) *unh (ke).*	ओकरन (के) *ŏk'ran (ke).*
Instr.	उन्ह सेँ *unh sē.*	ओकरन सेँ *ŏk'ran sē.*

[1] Or उन्हन (-न्ह) *unhăn (-nh)* or उन्हनी *unh'ní,* and so throughout the plural.
[2] Or ओकनी *ŏk'ní,* and so throughout the plural.

Dat.	उन्ह ला *unh lá.*	ओक॰रन ला *ŏk'ran lá.*
Abl.	उन्ह सेँ *unh sẽ.*	ओक॰रन सेँ *ŏk'ran sẽ.*
Gen.	उन्ह के ; का, *&c., unh kĕ ; ká, &c.*	ओक॰रन के ; का *ŏk'ran kĕ ; ká.*
Loc.	उन्ह म *unh mẽ.*	ओक॰रन मेँ *ŏk'ran mẽ.*

HONORIFIC.

Singular.

	Shorter form.	*Longer form.*
Nom.	उहाँ *uhẚ.*	उन्हाँ *uhẚ.*
Acc.	उहाँ[1] (के) *uhẚ*[1] *(ke).*	उन्ह॰का (के) *unh'ká (ke).*
Instr.	उहाँ सेँ *uhẚ sẽ.*	उन्ह॰का सेँ *unh'ká sẽ.*
Dat.	उहाँ ला *uhẚ lá.*	उन्ह॰का ला *unh'ká lá.*
Abl.	उहाँ सेँ *uhẚ sẽ.*	उन्ह॰का सेँ *unh'ká sẽ.*
Gen.	उहाँ के ; का, *uhẚ kĕ ; ká.*	उन्ह॰कर (-करे ; -करा) *unh'kar (-karĕ ; -kará).*
Loc.	उहाँ मेँ *uhẚ mẽ.*	उन्ह॰का मेँ *unh'ká mẽ.*

[1] Or उन (-न्ह) *un (-nh)*, and so throughout the singular in the oblique cases.

Plural.

Nom.	उहाँ[1] सभ॰का or उहाँका *uhẚ sabh'ká* or *uhẚká.*	*Wanting.*
Acc.	उहाँ सभ (के) *uhẚ sabh (kĕ).*	
Instr.	उहाँ सभ सेँ *uhẚ sabh sẽ.*	
Dat.	उहाँ सभ ला *uhẚ sabh lá.*	
Abl.	उहाँ सभ सेँ *uhẚ sabh sẽ.*	
Gen.	उहाँ सभ के ; का, *uhẚ sabh kĕ ; ká.*	
Loc.	उहाँ सभ मेँ *uhẚ sabh mẽ.*	

[1] Or उहन *uhan*, and so throughout the plural.

Other forms of the nominative singular current in Sáran are हउ *haú*, हेउ *hĕú*, हउए *haüe*, हेउहे *hĕuhe*, and ऊहे *úhe.*

In Western Bhojpúrí the words ओह *ŏh*, ओक॰रा *ŏk'rá*, and ओकर *okar*, are often spelt हो *ho*, होक॰रे *hŏk're*, and होकर *hokar*. The nominative singular is frequently written हउ *haú*.

In North Muzaffarpúr a variation of the oblique plural of the longer form non-honorific is ओकरन्हिन *ŏkar'hin.* The syllable का *ká* can be added to any form of the nominative plural.

In Western Bhojpúrí oblique forms ending in रा *rá* are written with रे *re:* thus ओकरे *ŏk're,* उन्हन्करे *unh'kare,* instead of ओकरा *ŏk'rá,* उन्हन्करा *unh'kará.* Instead of उन्ह *unh,* उन्हन्का *unh'ká, &c.,* it often has हुन्ह *hunh,* हुन्हन्का *hunh'ká, &c.* It also has a non-honorific form ओत्थू *ŏtthú* or ओथुआ *ŏthuá,* which is declined regularly like a substantive,—plural ओथुअन *ŏthuan.* This form refers only to things, and not to persons, and is sometimes spelt with an initial ह *h:* thus होत्थू *hŏtthú,* होथुआ *hŏthuá,* होथुअन *hŏthuan.*

NOTE.—In the above two demonstrative pronouns the shorter form may be used either adjectivally or substantivally, but the longer form can only be used as a substantive, and never as an adjective.

§ 26. Correlative Pronouns.

These are (1) the relative pronoun जे *je,* 'who;' (2) the correlative pronoun से *se,* 'that;' and (3) the interrogative pronoun के *ke,* 'who?'

The close analogy between their forms will best be shown by printing them in proximity to each other. Like the personal and demonstrative pronouns, they have each a non-honorific and an honorific declension, each of which has a shorter and a longer form.

It is not necessary to give their declension in full, as, with the exception noted below, it is exactly on the same lines as that of the demonstrative pronouns. I shall therefore give only the nominative, genitive, and general oblique forms of the non-honorific declension for each number. They have no honorific short form corresponding to इहाँ *ihā̃* or उहाँ *uhā̃.* Taking जे *je* as an example, its honorific nominative singular is जिन्ह *jinh* or जिन *jin,* its oblique shorter form is जिन्ह *jinh* or जिन *jin,* and its oblique longer form जिन्हन्का *jinh'ká.* The honorific forms of the other correlative pronouns are formed exactly similarly; and as, like the honorific forms of ई *í* and ऊ *ú,* they are based on the shorter forms of the non-honorific plural, and can easily be formed by analogy therefrom, I shall not give them here, but shall confine myself to the non-honorific forms.

In Western Bhojpúrí, as usual, oblique forms ending in रा *rá* are spelt with रे *re* : thus जेकऱे *jĕk're*, तेकऱे *tĕk're*, केकऱे *kĕk're*, *&c.*, instead of जेकऱा *jĕk'rá*, तेकऱा *tĕk'rá*, केकऱा *kĕk'rá*, *&c.* In the shorter forms singular it has an optional neuter oblique form जाहे *jáhĕ*, ताहे *táhĕ*, or काहे *káhĕ*, used for things only; and in the longer form it has also an oblique form जौने *jaune*, instead of जौना *jauná*, with a plural जौनन *jaunan*, जौन्हन *jaunhan*, जौनने *jăun'ne*, or जौन्हने *jăunh'ne*. Corresponding to इत्थू *itthú*, ओत्थू *ŏtthú*, *&c.*, there are neuter forms जित्थू *jitthú* or जिथुआ *jithuá*,—plural जिथुअन *jithuan*; तित्थू *titthú* or सित्थू *sitthú*, or तिथुआ *tithuá* or सिथुआ *sithuá*,—plural तिथुअन *tithuan* or सिथुअन *sithuan*; and कित्थू *kitthú* or किथुआ *kithuá*,—plural किथुअन *kithuan*, all of which refer to things only, and not to persons.

The Non-Honorific Correlative Pronouns.

Relative.

जे *je*, 'who.'

Singular.

	Shorter form.	*Longer form.*
Nom.	जे *je.*	जवन *jawan* or जौन *jaun.*
Gen.	जेह[1] के ; का, &c., *jĕh*[1] *kĕ ; ká, &c.*	जेकर *jekar* or जेक॰रे ; -रा,[1] *jĕk'rĕ ; -rá.*
Obl.	जेह, *jĕh.*	जेक॰रा *jĕk'rá* or जौना *jauná.*

[1] Or जेहि *jĕhi* or जे *je*, and so throughout the singular.

Plural.

Nom.	जे[1] *je.*[1]	जवन[2] *jawan*[2] or जौन *jaun.*
Gen.	जिन्ह[1] के ; का, &c., *jinh*[1] *kĕ ; ká, &c.*	जेक॰रन[2] के ; का, *jĕk'ran*[2] *kĕ ; ká.*
Obl.	जिन्ह[1] *jinh.*[1]	जेक॰रन[2] *jĕk'ran.*[2]

[1] Or जिन्हन (-न्ह) *jinhan* (-*nh*) or जिन्ह॰नी *jinh'ní*, and so throughout the plural.

[2] Or जेक॰नी *jĕk'ní* or जिन्ह॰करा (का) *jinh'kará* (*ká*), and so throughout all the cases of the plural, का *ká* being omitted in the oblique cases. In North Muzaffarpúr there is a variation, जौनन (-न्ह) *jaunan* (-*nh*) or जेकर॰हिन *jĕkar'hin*, in the oblique plural.

Correlative.

से *se*, 'that.'

Singular.

	Shorter form.	*Longer form.*
Nom.	से *se* or ते *te.*	तवन *tawan* or तौन *taun.*
Gen.	तेह[1] के ; का, &c., *tĕh*[1] *kĕ ; ká, &c.*	तेकर *tekar*, तेक॰रे ; -रा, *tĕk'rĕ ; -rá.*
Obl.	तेह *tĕh.*	तेक॰रा *tĕk'rá* or तौना *tauná.*

[1] Or तेहि *tĕhi* or ते *te*, and so throughout the singular.

Plural.

	Shorter form.	*Longer form.*
Nom.	से[1] *se.*	तवन[2] *tawan* [2] or तौन *taun.*
Gen.	तिन्ह[1] के; का, &c., *tinh*[1] *kĕ; ká, &c.*	तेकऽरन[2] के; का, *tĕk'ran kĕ; ká.*
Obl.	तिन्ह[1] *tinh.*[1]	तेकऽरन[2] *tĕk'ran.*[2]

[1] Or तिन्हन (-न्ह) *tinhan* (-*nh*) or तिन्हऽनी *tinh'ní*, and so throughout the plural.

[2] Or तेकऽनी *tĕk'ní* or तिन्हऽकारा (का) *tinh'kará (ká)*, and so throughout all the cases of the plural, का *ká* being omitted in the oblique cases. In North Muzaffarpúr there is a variation, तौनन(-न्ह) *taunan* (-*nh*) or तेकरऽहिन *tĕkar'hin*, in the oblique plural.

Interrogative.

के *ke*, 'who?'

Singular.

	Shorter form.	*Longer form.*
Nom.	के *ke.*	कवन *kawan* or कौन *kaun.*
Gen.	केह[1] के; का, *kĕh*[1] *kĕ; ká.*	केकर *kekar*, केकऽरे; -रा, *kĕk'rĕ; -rá.*
Obl.	केह *kĕh.*	केकऽरा *kĕk'rá* or कौना *kauná.*

[1] Or केंहि *kĕhi* or के *ke*, and so throughout the singular.

Plural.

Nom.	के[1] *ke.*[1]	कवन[2] *kawan*[2] or कौन *kaun.*
Gen.	किन्ह[1] के; का &c., *kinh*[1] *kĕ; ká, &c.*	केकऽरन[2] के; का, *kĕk'ran*[2] *kĕ; ká.*
Obl.	किन्ह[1] *kinh.*[1]	केकऽरन[2] *kĕk'ran.*[2]

[1] Or किन्हन (-न्ह) *kinhan* (-*nh*) or किन्हऽनी *kinh'ní*, and so throughout the plural.

[2] Or केकऽनी *kĕk'ní* or किन्हऽकारा (का) *kinh'kará (ká)*, and so throughout all cases of the plural, का *ká* being omitted in the oblique cases. In North Muzaffarpúr there is a variation, कौनन (-न्ह) *kaunan* (-*nh*) or केकरऽहिन *kĕkar'hin*, in the oblique plural.

NOTE.—In the above correlative pronouns the shorter form may be used either adjectivally or substantivally, but the longer form can only be used as substantive, and never as an adjective. The shorter forms जेह *jĕh*, तेह *tĕh*, and केह *kĕh*, are often written in poetry जाहि *jáhi*, ताहि *táhi*, and काहि *káhi* respectively. It should be noted that although the *á* in these three words is written long, it is invariably scanned as if it were short in poetry.

The syllable का *ká* can be added to any form of the nominative plural.

§ 27. Interrogative Pronoun.

SUBSTANTIVAL.

का *ká*, 'what?'

This pronoun is really a neuter form of के *ke*, and can only refer to inanimate things. It can only be used as a substantive. Its plural is the same as that of के *ke*.

Singular.

Nom. का *ká*. Also in Western Bhojpúrí कित्थू *kitthú* or किथुआ *kithuá*.

Obl. का *ká*, काहे *káhĕ*, or केथी *kĕthi*. Also in Western Bhojpúrí कित्थू *kitthú* or किथुआ *kithuá*.

Gen. का के, का, *ká kĕ*, *ká*, काहे के, का, *káhĕ kĕ*, *ká*, or केथी के, का, *kĕthi kĕ*, *ká*, &c. It has a common form of the instrumental केथिएँ *kĕthiẽ*, meaning, 'why?' 'how?' A North Muzaffarpúr variety of the oblique form is कथी *kathí*.

§ 28. Indefinite Pronoun.

केउ *kĕú*, 'anyone,' 'some one.'

When used as an adjective, this pronoun takes also the form कौनो *kauno*. It has a variety of forms, viz.—

Direct: केउ *kĕú*, केउ *keú*, केहू *kĕhú*, or कौनो *kauno*.

Oblique: केउ *kĕú*, केहू *kĕhú*, कौनो *kauno*, केकरो *kĕk'rŏ*, केथियो *kĕthiyŏ*, or कथियो *kathiyŏ*.

It is regularly declined in the singular except in the genitive, which is केकरो *kĕk'rŏ* (dir. and obl.)

It is not used in the plural.

§ 29. The indefinite pronoun कछु *kachhu*, कुच्छो *kuchchhŏ*, or कुछुवो *kuchhuwŏ*, or कुछुओ *kuchhuŏ*, or (in Sáran) किछु *kichhu*, 'anything,' 'something,' is declined regularly like a substantive: thus कुच्छो के *kuchchhŏ ke*, कुच्छो सेँ *kuchchhŏ sẽ*, &c.

A North Muzaffarpúr variety is किछियो *kichhiŏ*. A Western Bhojpúrí variety is किछ *kichh* or किछउ *kichhaú*.

§ 30. The indefinite pronoun सभ *sabh* or सब *sab*, 'all,' 'every one,' is declined regularly like a substantive. It is usually written सभ *sabh*. When plurality is to be emphasised, it has an oblique plural form सभन *sabhan*: thus सभ के *sabh kĕ*, 'of all,' *taken as a whole*; but सभन के *sabhan kĕ*, 'of all,' *taken severally*.

§ 31. The indefinite pronouns जेकेहू *jekĕhú*, 'whoever,' and जेकुच्छो *jekuchchhŏ*, 'whatever,' are compounds, and are declined regularly like their component parts: thus acc. sing. जेह केकरो के *jĕh kĕk'rŏ ke*, जेह कुच्छो के *jĕh kuchchhŏ kĕ*; instr. जेह केकरो सें *jĕh kĕk'rŏ sē*, &c.

The indefinite pronominal adjective कइक *kaïk* means 'many,' 'several.' It is also used as an interrogative, meaning 'how many?'

§ 32. Derivative Pronominal Forms.

The following table gives the more usual pronominal adjectives and adverbs in a succinct form.

		Pronoun.	Manner.	
			Pron. Adj.	Pron. Adv.
Demonstrative ...	Proximate ...	ई *í*, 'this' ...	अइसन *aïsan*, 'of this kind.'	अइसेँ *aïsẽ*, 'thus.'
	Remote ...	ऊ *ú*, 'that' ...	वइसन *waïsan*, 'of that kind.'	वइसेँ *waïsẽ*, 'in that way.'
Relative		जे *je*, 'who' ...	जइसन *jaïsan*, 'of what kind.'	जइसे *jaïsẽ*, 'how.'
Correlative		से *se*, 'that' ...	तइसन *taïsan*, 'of that kind.'	तइसेँ *taïsẽ*, 'so.'
Interrogative		के *ke*, 'who?'...	कइसन *kaïsan*, 'of what kind?'	कइसेँ *kaïsẽ*, 'how.'

Pron. adj. of Quantity.	Pron. adv. of Time.	Pron. adv. of Place.	Pron. adv. of Direction.
अतेक *atĕk*, **हतेक** *hatĕk*, **अत॰हत** *at'hat*, **हत॰हत** *hat'hat*, **अतिनाँ** *atinā̃*, or **हतिनाँ** *hatinā̃*, 'this much.'	**एह॰बेरा** *ĕh'bĕrá*, or **एह॰जून** *ĕh'jún*, 'now.'	**ईह॰वाँ** *īh'wā̃*, **एहिजा** *ĕhijá*, or **एठेन** *eṭhĕn*, 'here.' *Also Sáran* **हियाँ** *hiyā̃*.	**एने** *enĕ*, **हेने** *henĕ*, or **एहर** *ehar*, 'hither.'
ओतेक *ŏtĕk*, **होतेक** *hŏtĕk*, **ओत॰हत** *ŏt'hat*, **होत॰हत** *hŏt'hat*, **ओतिनाँ** *ŏtinā̃*, or **होतिनाँ** *hŏtinā̃*, 'that much.'	**ओह॰बेरा** *ŏh'bĕrá*, **ओह॰जून** *ŏh'jún*, 'then.'	**ऊँह॰वाँ** *ũh'wā̃*, **ओहिजा** *ŏhijá*, or **ओठेन** *oṭhĕn*, 'there.' *Also Sáran* **हुआँ** *huā̃*.	**ओने** *onĕ*, **होने** *honĕ*, or **ओहर** *ohar*, 'thither.'
जतेक *jatĕk*, **जत॰हत** *jat'hat*, or **जतिनाँ** *jatinā̃*, 'how much.'	**जेह॰बेरा** *jĕh'bĕrá*, or **जेह॰जून** *jĕh'jún*, 'when.'	**जाँह॰वाँ** *jā̃h'wā̃*, **जेहिजा** *jĕhijá*, or **जेठेन** *jeṭhĕn* 'where.'	**जेने** *jenĕ* or **जेहर** *jehar*, 'whither.'
ततेक *tatĕk*, **तत॰हत** *tat'hat*, or **ततिनाँ** *tatinā̃*, 'so much.'	**तेह॰बेरा** *tĕh'bĕrá*, or **तेह॰जून** *tĕh'jún*, 'then.'	**ताँह॰वाँ** *tā̃h'wā̃*, **तेहिजा** *tĕhijá*, or **तेठेन** *teṭhĕn*, 'there.'	**तेने** *tenĕ* or **तेहर** *tehar*, 'thither.'
कतेक *katĕk*, **कत॰हत** *kat'hat*, or **कतिनाँ** *katinā̃*, 'how much?'	**केह॰बेरा** *kĕh'bĕrá*, or **केह॰जून** *kĕh'jún*, 'when?'	**काँह॰वाँ** *kā̃h'wā̃*, **केहिजा** *kĕhijá*, or **केठेन** *keṭhĕn*, 'where?	**केने** *kenĕ* or **केहर** *kehar*, 'whither?'

§ 33. Adjectival Pronouns.

The following sentences are designed to show the use of the various pronouns, both adjectivally and substantivally. Note that the forms जौन *jaun*, तौन *taun*, and कौन *kaun* are only used as adjectives. This includes their variations in spelling, such as जवन *jawan*, *&c.*, and their oblique forms जौना *jauná*, *&c.*

(1) जे आइल रहे, से गइल, *je áil rahe, se gaïl:* 'he who had come, went.'

(2) जे जन आइल रहे, से जन गइल, *je jan áil rahe, se jan gaïl:* 'the man who had come, went.'

(3) जेकर खेत, तेकर धान, *jekar khet, tekar dhán:* 'he who owns the field, owns the paddy.'

(4) जे जन के खेत, ते जन के धान, *je jan kĕ khet, te jan kĕ dhán:* 'the man who owns the field, owns the paddy.'

(5) के रहे *ke rahe?* 'who was it?'

(6) ऊ कौन जात हऽ *ú kaun ját ha?* 'what caste is he?'

(7) केकर घोड़ा हऽ *kekar ghoṛá ha?* 'whose is the horse?'

(8) कौना जन के घोड़ा हऽ *kauná jan kĕ ghoṛá ha?* 'to what man does the horse belong?'

(9) का हऽ, *ká ha?* 'what is it?'

(10) कौन फेड़ (or पेड़) हऽ *kaun pheṛ* (or *peṛ*) *ha?* 'what tree is it?'

(11) केथी मेँ पानी ले आइलऽ हऽ *kĕthí mẽ pání le aïla ha?* 'in what have you brought the water?'

(12) कौना लोटा मेँ पानी ले आइलऽ हऽ *kauná loṭá mẽ pání le aïla ha?* 'in what *loṭa* have you brought the water?'

(13) केहू नाहीँ आइल *kĕhú náhí äil,* 'no one came.'

(14) कौनो लड़िका नाहीँ आइल *kauno laṛiká náhí äil,* 'no boy came.'

(15) ओ गाँव मेँ केकरो कुछुवो नइखे *o gā̃w mẽ kĕk'rŏ kuchhuwŏ naïkhe,* 'in that village no one has anything.'

(16) ओ गाँव का कौनो बनियाँ सेँ कुछुवो नाँ मिली *o gẫw ká kauno baniyẫ sẽ kuchhuwŏ nẫ milí*, 'in that village nothing will be got from any shopkeeper.'

(17) ऊ बीरो के केथियो मेँ धरे के* होई *ú bíro ke kĕthiyŏ mẽ dharĕ ke* hoí*, 'it will be (necessary) to put that medicine into something.'

(18) कइक आदिमी अइलन *kaïk adimí aïlan*, 'several men came.'

§ 34. The Pronominal Oblique Genitive.

The following are examples of pronominal genitives which end in र *r* or न *n*, and which have an oblique form ending in रा *rá* or ना *ná*. These oblique forms occur for all pronominal genitives ending in र *r*, and are used with nouns in any form except that of the nominative singular or plural :—

Direct Genitive.	Meaning.	Oblique form
मोर *mor.*	'My.'	मोरा *morá.*
हमार *hamár.*	'My.'	हमऽरा *ham'rá.*
तोर *tor.*	'Thy.'	तोरा *torá.*
तोहार *tohár.*	'Thy.'	तोहऽरा *tŏh'rá.*
आपन *ápan.*	'Own.'	अपऽना *ap'ná.*
एकर *ekar.*	'Of this.'	एकऽरा *ĕk'rá.*
ओकर *okar.*	'Of that,' 'his.'	ओकऽरा *ŏk'rá.*
जेकर *jekar.*	'Whose.'	जेकऽरा *jĕk'rá.*
तेकर *tekar.*	'His.'	तेकऽरा *tĕk'rá.*
केकर *kekar.*	'Whose?'	केकऽरा *kĕk'rá.*

* Dative of the verbal noun.

In Western Bhojpúrí all the above oblique forms end in ए *e;* thus मोर *more,* हमरे *ham're, &c.,* with a feminine in ई *í:* thus मोरी *morí,* हमरी *ham'rí.*

The following examples will show the use of the genitive in—(*a*) its direct form, (*b*) its oblique form.

a.—GENITIVES AGREEING WITH NOUNS IN THE NOMINATIVE FORM,
i.e. DIRECT GENITIVES.

ओकर मेहर सुन्दर बा *okar mehar sundar bá,* 'his wife is beautiful.'

केकर बेटा हठ *kekar beṭá ha?* 'whose son is he?'

हमार काम बिगड़ी *hamár kám big'ṛi,* 'my profession will be ruined.'

ओकर रोअल सुन के *okar roal sun kĕ,* 'on hearing her lamentations.'

ओकर अकरार लिखठ *okar ak'rár likha,* 'write a bond to that effect (*lit.* of that).

आपन रुपैया पइसा उड़ा के, भिखार हो गइले *ápan rupaiyá païsá uṛá kĕ bhikhár ho gaïle,* 'having wasted his substance he became poor.'

The following is Western Bhojpúrí:—ई घर मोर बा *í ghar mor bá,* 'this house is mine.'

b.—GENITIVES AGREEING WITH NOUNS NOT IN THE NOMINATIVE FORM,
i.e. OBLIQUE GENITIVES.

ऊ ओकरा फुलवारी में आइल *ú ŏk'rá phul'wárí mē áil,* 'he came into *his* (some one else's) garden.'

हमरा सिरकी में *ham'rá sir'kí mē,* 'in my hovel.'

तोहरा घर में *tŏh'rá ghar mē,* 'in your house.'

तोहरा हाथ से *tŏh'rá háth sē,* 'from thy hand.'

हमार दुआर ओकरा दुआर से बाँस भर पर बा *hamár duár ŏk'rá duár sē bā̃s bhar par bá,* 'my doorway is a rod distance from his.'

गिरहस्त अपना मन में कहलस *gir'hast ap'ná man mē kah'las,* 'the husbandman said in his heart.'

The following is Western Bhojpúrí :—

मोरे घर कै भीत *more ghar kaĩ bhít*, 'the wall of my house.'

मोरी बेटिया कै बिआह *morí bĕṭiyá kaĩ biáh*, 'the wedding of my little daughter.'

Sometimes, by the vulgar, the direct form is used instead of the oblique, but the oblique form is never used instead of the direct. Idiomatically these oblique forms are used to signify possession: thus, मोरा (*i.e.* मोरा पास) घोड़ा हौ? हाँ, मोरा (*i.e.* मोरा पास) बा *morá* (i.e. *morá pás*) *ghoṛá hau? hã́*, *morá* (i.e. *morá pás*) *bá*, 'have I a horse?—Yes, I have;' or, literally, 'is there a horse to me?—Yes, there is to me.'

DIVISION II.

CONJUGATION.

CHAPTER IV.

VERBS.

§ 35. It must be noted with respect to the following paradigms that colloquially the plural is commonly used in the place of the singular: thus तोँ बाटठ *tō báṭa*, 'thou art,' is commonly used instead of तेँ बाटस *ts báṭas*, which is the more correct form.

Note also that there is great laxity colloquially in regard to gender. The forms given for the feminine are only those which are specially confined to that gender; but instead of these, the masculine forms are often used colloquially. In the following paradigms when the masculine and feminine forms coincide, the latter are not given.

§ 36. To form a non-honorific plural the word सठ *sa* is attached to the ordinary plural. In one tense, the present conjunctive, it may be attached to the singular with the the same effect.

Besides the personal forms given, each tense has a special honorific form common to the second and third person in both numbers, which will in each instance be noted.

With regard to the shortening of antepenultimate vowels, see General Introduction, § 36.

§ 37. Conjugational System.

The conjugation of the verb √ देख *dekh*, 'see,' being given in full, it is not necessary to give here the details of conjugation at length.

§ 38. There are three moods—the Indicative, Conjunctive, and Imperative. These may again be divided into *simple tenses*—formed from the root direct, and *periphrastic tenses*—formed with the aid of auxiliary verbs added to the present or past participle, or to the conjugated preterite indicative.

§ 39. The *simple tenses* are as follows :—

INDICATIVE.	CONJUNCTIVE.	IMPERATIVE.
Present.	Present.	Present.
Preterite.	Preterite.	
Future.		

Of these, the present imperative is always the same as the present conjunctive.

§ 40. The *periphrastic tenses* are as follows :—

a) From the present participle, direct form—

Indicative—

Definite present	with auxiliary	present.
Imperfect	,,	preterite.
Durative future	,,	future.

Conjunctive—

Future	with auxiliary	present conjunctive.
Durative present	,,	preterite ,,

b) From the past participle : direct form in the neuter verb, oblique form in the active verb—

Indicative—

Future exact with auxiliary future.

Conjunctive—

Future with auxiliary present conjunctive.
Preterite „ preterite.

c) From the preterite indicative—

Indicative—

Perfect with auxiliary present.
Pluperfec „ preterite.

Concerning the use of the auxiliary in tenses formed from the past participle, see General Introduction, p. 13, cl. (4).

§ 41. The Simple Tenses.

The personal terminations are nearly the same for all tenses. They are added to a tense-stem, the formation of which will be described afterwards. They are exactly the same for the present conjunctive, the preterite indicative, and the preterite conjunctive.

The terminations of these three tenses are given in the following table. It will be observed that there are sometimes two or more forms of terminations for each person. They are all used with nearly equal frequency. They should be carefully committed to memory.

It must be noted that the termination अह *ah* or अ *a* of the 2nd plural masculine is pronounced with a peculiar drawl, something like the English word 'awe.' Thus, देखऽ *dekh*'awe.' So also is pronounced the penultimate अ *a* of the present indicative: thus देखलों *dekhalõ*, 'I see,' pronounced *dekh*'awe'*lõ*; देखलऽ *dekhala*, 'you see,' pronounced *dekh*'awe'*l*'awe.' Similarly is pronounced the √ अव *haw*, 'be.'

Table showing the Personal Terminations of the Present Conjunctive, the Preterite Indicative, and the Preterite Conjunctive.

Person.	Singular.		Plural.	
	Masculine.	Feminine.	Masculine.	Feminine.
1st	ओँ *ō*.*	यूँ *yū̃*.*	ईं *ī*.	यूँ *yū̃*.*
2nd	ए *e*.	ई *í*.‡	अह *ah*, अ *a*.	ऊ *ú*.
	अस *as*, एस *ĕs*.†	इस *is*.		
3rd	ए *e*.		अन *an*, एन *ĕn*.†	इन *in*.
	अस *as*.	असि *asi*.	ऐँ *aĩ*.‡	

* These terminations are rarely used at the present day, the plural masculine being used instead. They are, however, met with in poetry.

† These terminations एस *ĕs* and एन *ĕn* are peculiar to Sáran.

‡ This termination is peculiar to Western Bhojpúrí.

§ 42. These terminations are added to various tense-stems, and it is by these tense-stems that the tenses are distinguished. The formation of each tense-stem will be given separately under the heading of each tense, and the conjugation of each tense will now be described in the order in which they will subsequently be given in the conjugation of the model verb √देख *dekh*, 'see.'

§ 43 (a). The Present Indicative.

This tense is peculiar to Bhojpúrí, and its conjugation is formed by adding the following terminations to the root.

Terminations of the Present Indicative.

Person.	Singular.		Plural.	
	Masculine.	Feminine.	Masculine.	Feminine.
1st	अलों *alō.**†	अल्यूं *alyú.**	ईला *ílá*‡ or इले *ile.*	अल्यूं *'alyú.**
2nd	अले *ale.*	अलिसि *alisi.*	अलह *alah* or अलऽ *ala,* एलह *ĕlah* or एलऽ *ĕla.*	अलू *alú.*
3rd	अला *alá.* एला *ĕlá.*	अलि *ali.*	अले *ale* or अलन *alan,* एले *ĕle* or एलन *ĕlan.*‡	अलीं *alí,* अलिन *alin.*

* These terminations are rarely used at the present day, the plural masculine being used instead. They are, however, met with in poetry.

† Throughout, in Western Bhojpúrí, the terminations may be ऐलों *ăĩlŏ,* ऐले *ăĩle,* ऐला *ăĩlá, &c.,* instead of अलों *alŏ,* अले *ale,* अला *alá, &c.*

‡ In Western Bhojpúrí also ईलां *ílā́* or ऐलैं *ăĩlā̃* respectively.

Concerning the pronunciation of these terminations, see § 41.

§ 43 (b). The Preterite Indicative.

The stem of this tense is formed by adding अल *al* to the root. To this the terminations in § 41 are added. Thus √ देख *dekh,* 'see,' preterite stem देखल *dekhal,* to which the terminations are added: thus देखलों *dĕkh'lŏ,* 'I saw.' This tense has this peculiarity in the third person that neuter verbs may, and usually do—

(1) Drop the termination in the 3rd sing. masc.

(2) Take इ *i* in the 3rd sing fem.

(3) Take ई *í* in the 3rd plur fem.

Examples.

(1) गिरल *giral,* as well as गिरलस *gir'las,* 'he fell.'

(2) गिरलि *gir'li,* as well as गिरलसि *gir'lasi,* 'she fell.'

(3) गिरलीं *gir'lí,* as well as गिरलिन *gir'lin,* 'they (*fem.*) fell.'

In Sáran the following terminations may optionally be added to the root to form a preterite. They have not been noted by the author in the first person singular, nor in the feminine gender singular.

Terminations of the Preterite Indicative peculiar to Sáran.

Person.	Singular.	Plural.	
	Masculine.	Masculine.	Feminine.
1st	*Wanting.*	उई *uí.*	*Wanting.*
2nd	उए *ue.*	उअह *uah,* उअ *ua.*	उऊ *uú.*
3rd	उए *ue.*	उअन *uan.*	उइन *uin.*

These terminations are added to the root direct: thus देखुई *dĕkhuí*, *&c.*

§ 44. The Future Indicative.

This tense has two stems—one for the first and second persons, and the other for the third person. The first stem is formed by adding अब *ab* to the root; the second is the root itself.

The following are the terminations of this tense. All the following should be added to the root direct.

After certain vowels, *e.g.* ओ *o*, the stem terminations may be इब *ib* instead of अब *ab*.

Terminations of the Future.

Person.	Singular.		Plural.	
	Masculine.	Feminine.	Masculine.	Feminine.
1st	ऽबों *'bõ.** ऽबउ *'baü.*	ऽब्यूँ *'byú.**	अब *ab,* ऽबी *'bí.*†	इब *ib,* or ऽबी *'bí.*
2nd	ऽबे *'be.*	ऽबिस *'bis.*‡	ऽबह *'bah,* ऽबऽ *'ba.*	ऽबू *'bú.*
3rd	ई *í.*	ई *í.*	इहँ *ihẽ,* इहेन *ihĕn*§.	इहँ *ihẽ,* इहेन *ihĕn.*

* These terminations are rarely used at the present day, the plural masculine being used instead. They are, however, met with in poetry.

† In Western Bhojpúrí also ऽबाँ *'bā̃.*

‡ In Western Bhojpúrí also ऽबी *'bí*

§ In Western Bhojpúrí also इहाँ *ihā̃.*

§ 45. The Present Conjunctive and Imperative.

In this tense the terminations are added to the root itself. thus देखीं *dekhí*, 'let me see.' As already stated, the terminations are those given in § 41. Besides these, this tense may, in the second person singular masculine, either drop the termination altogether or take the following terminations :—

2nd sing. masc. असि *asi*, उए *ue*. Of these उए *ue* is confined to Sáran. In Western Bhojpúrí the termination is altogether dropped in this person.

In the third person singular masculine it may either drop the termination altogether, or take the following in addition to those given in § 41 :—

3rd sing. masc. अ *a*, ओ *o*, असु *asu*, असि *asi*, उए *ue*, ऐ *ai*. Of these उए *ue* and ऐ *ai* are peculiar to Sáran.

§ 46. The Preterite Conjunctive.

In this tense अत *at* or इत *it* is added to the root to form the stem. The personal terminations in § 41 are then added: thus देखःतीं *děkh'tí*, '(if) I had seen.'

This tense, whether in the case of active or of neuter verbs, follows the preterite of neuter verbs, in that in the third person it may—

(1) Drop the termination in the 3rd sing. masc.

(2) Take इ *i* in the 3rd sing. fem.

(3) Take ई *í* in the 3rd plur. fem.

CHAPTER V.

AUXILIARY VERBS.

§ 47. There are five auxiliary verbs in use :—(1) the ***defective auxiliary verb,*** (2) the ***weak complete auxiliary verb,*** (3) the ***strong complete auxiliary verb,*** (4) the ***defective negative auxiliary verb,*** and (5) the ***defective emphatic auxiliary verb.***

§ 48. The ***defective auxiliary verb*** uses up four roots in its conjugation, viz. the √ बाट *bát*, 'be ;' the √ हव *haw*,* 'be ;' √ रह *rah*, 'remain ;' and √ अछ *achh*, 'be.'

The ***defective negative auxiliary verb*** is formed from the √ नहिँख *nahīkh* or नइख *naïkh*. The form नहिँख *nahīkh* is more used in the North-Western Provinces, while the form नइख *naïkh* is usual in the districts to which this Grammar mainly refers.

The ***defective emphatic auxiliary verb*** is really a perfect of the defective auxiliary verb ; but as it has acquired a distinct meaning of its own, it will be treated of separately.

§ 49. The ***weak complete auxiliary verb*** is formed from the √ हो *ho*, 'become,' and is conjugated regularly throughout, except that its preterite is irregular. Its preterite is never used as an auxiliary, but only as a verb substantive.

The ***strong complete auxiliary verb*** is formed from the root होख *hokh*, 'become,' and is conjugated regularly throughout.

---

* In other dialects this root appears under the form अह्व *ahw*.

§ 50. Defective Auxiliary Verb.

√ बाट *báṭ*, √ हव *haw*, √ अछ *achh*, 'be, √ रह *rah*, 'remain.'

There are only two tenses—the present and the preterite. There is also a present participle; the rest is borrowed from the complete verb √ हो *ho*, 'become.'

The present has two forms—one based on the √ बाट *báṭ*, and the other based on the √ हव *haw*.

The preterite is formed from the √ रह *rah*, 'to remain,' and has two forms.

The present participle, formed from the √ अछ *achh*, अछइत *achhaït*, is used only in an absolute sense, as in the phrase तोहʼरा अछइत *tŏh'rá achhaït*, 'while you exist,' *i.e.* 'in your presence.'

§ 51 (*a*). Present: (FIRST FORM) '*I am,*' *&c.*

Person.	SINGULAR.		PLURAL.	
	Masculine.	Feminine.	Masculine.	Feminine.
1st	बाटों *báṭõ.**	बाट्यूँ *báṭyũ.**	बाटीं *báṭí* or बानीं *bání.*	बाट्यूँ *báṭyũ.**
2nd	बाटे *báṭe,* बाटस *báṭas.* बाट् *báṭ,* बटसि *baṭasi.* बटुए, बाटेस, *baṭue,*† *báṭẽs.*†	बाटी *báṭí.*‡ बाटिस *báṭis.*	बाटह *báṭah,* बाटऽ *báṭa.*	बाटू *báṭú.*
3rd	बा *bá,* बाय *báy.*‡ बाटे *báṭe,* बाटस *báṭas.* बाटऽ *báṭa* बाटो *báṭo.* बटसु, बटसि, *baṭasu, baṭasi.* बटुए बाटै *baṭue,*† *báṭai.*†	बटसि *baṭasi.*	बाटन *báṭan,* बाटेन *báṭẽn.*† बाटैं *báṭaĩ.*‡	बाटिन *báṭin.*

* These forms are rarely used at the present day, the plural masculine being used instead. They, however, occur in poetry.

† These forms are peculiar to Sáran.

‡ These forms are Western Bhojpúrí.

NOTE.—ड़ *ṛ* or र *r* may be substituted for ट *ṭ* throughout: thus बाड़ीं *báṛí* or बारीं *bárí*, &c. This is usually done in Sháhábád and Champáraṇ.

The honorific form for the second and third persons is बानी *báni*, बानीं *báni*, बाटी *báti*, or बाटीं *báti*.

North Muzaffarpúr variations are—

1st masc. sing. बाड़ूँ *báṛū̃*. 3rd ditto बाड़ैक *báṛaik* or बाड़ौक *báṛauk*.

3rd masc. plur. बाड़थ *báṛath*.

In the plural masculine the following Maithilí forms are also used:—

(1) छी *chhi*; (2) छठ *chha*; (3) छथ *chhath*.

§ 51 (*b*). Present: (SECOND FORM) '*I am,*' &c.

Person.	SINGULAR.		PLURAL.	
	Masculine.	Feminine.	Masculine.	Feminine.
1st	हवों *hawõ*.*	हव्यूँ *hawyũ*.*	हवीं *hawí*. हईं *haí*, हैं *hãĩ*.†	हव्यूँ *hawyā̃*.*
2nd	हवे *hawe*, &c. हवस *hawas*, &c.	हौई *haui*.‡ हविस *hawis*. हइस *haïs*.	हवह *hawah*, हवठ *hawa*.	हऊ *haú*.
3rd	हवे *hawe*, &c. हवस *hawas*, &c. हठ *ha*, है *hai*,† हौ [*hau*.‡ हैक *haik*.§	हवसि *hawasi*.	हवन *hawan*, &c. हौएँ *hauã̃*.‡*	हविन *hawin*. हौईं *hauí*.‡ हई *hai*.‡

* These forms are rarely used at the present day, the plural masculine being used instead. They, however, occur in poetry.

† Peculiar to North Muzaffarpúr.

‡ These forms are Western Bhojpúrí.

§ Only met in poetry.

NOTE.—There are many optional forms, which may be formed after the analogy of the first form.

The honorific form for the second and third persons is हवीँ *hawí* or हवी *hawi*.

The pronunciation of this √ हव *haw* is very peculiar. It is pronounced with a long drawl, something like the English word 'awe:' thus हवीँ *hawí* is pronounced something like *h'* awe *'wí*. Natives have no means of representing this sound, which occurs also in all second persons plural and in the present indicative (see § 41). Sometimes (especially in Western Bhojpúrí) they represent it by औ *au*. Thus they occasionally write the √ हव *haw* as हौ *hau*, and conjugate the present as follows:—हौओँ *hauô*, हौए *haue*, हौअस *hauäs*, हौए *haue*, &c., substituting everywhere हौ *hau* for हव *haw*.

§ 52. (*a*) Preterite: (FIRST FORM) '*I was*,' &c.

Person.	SINGULAR.		PLURAL.	
	Masculine.	Feminine.	Masculine.	Feminine.
1st	रह॰लोँ* *rah'lõ.**	रह॰ल्यूँ *rah'lyũ.**	रह॰लीँ *rah'lí.* रहुईँ *rahuí.*†	रह॰ल्यूँ *rah'lyũ.**
2nd	रह॰ले *rah'le*, रह॰लस *rah'las.* रह॰लेँस *rah'lĕs.*† रहुए *rahue.*†	रह॰ली *rah'li.*‡ रह॰लिस *rah'lis.*	रह॰लह *rah'lah*, रह॰ल० *rah'la.* रहुअह *rahuah*,† रहुअ, *rahua.*†	रह॰लू *rah'lú.* रहुऊ *rahuú.*†
3rd	रहल *rahal*, रह॰ले *rah'le.* रह॰लस, *rah'las.* रहुए *rahue.*†	रह॰लि *rah'li.* रह॰लसि *rah'lasi.*	रह॰लन *rah'lan.* रह॰लैँ *rah'lãi.*‡ रह॰लेँन *rah'lĕn.*† रहुअन *rahuan.*†	रह॰ली *rah'li.* रह॰लिन *rah'lin.* रहुइन *rahuin.*†

* These forms are rarely used at the present day, the plural masculine being used instead. They, however, occur in poetry.

† These forms are peculiar to Sáran.

‡ These forms are Western Bhojpúrí.

(*b*) The second form is formed from the first by omitting the letter ल *l* : thus, रहीं ***rahí***, रहे *rahe*, रहस *rahas*, रहिस *rahis*, *&c.*

North Muzaffarpúr varieties are—

Form 1—

1st plur. fem. रहऽलिऐक *rah'liaik.* 2nd ditto रहऽलुक *rah'luk.*
3rd plur. masc. रहऽलाह *rah'láh.*

Similarly form 2.

§ 53.—The Weak Complete Auxiliary Verb.

√ हो *ho*, '*be*,' '*become*.'

INDICATIVE MOOD.

(a)—Preterite : *'I became.'*

NOTE.—This tense is never used as an auxiliary, रहलीं *rah'li* or रहीं *rahí* (see above) being used instead.

Person.	SINGULAR.		PLURAL.	
	Masculine.	Feminine.	Masculine.	Feminine.
1st	भइलौं *bhaïlō.**	भइल्यूँ *bhaïlyú.**	भइलीं *bhaïlí.*†	भइल्यूँ *bhaïlyú.**
2nd	भइले *bhaïle.*	भइली *bhaïlí.*§		
2nd	भइलस, भइलेस,‡ *bhaïlas, bhaïlĕs.*‡	भइलिस *bhaïlis.*	भइलह or भइलऽ, *bhaïlah* or *bhaïla.*	भइलू *bhaïlú.*
3rd	भइल, भइले, *bhaïl, bhaïle.*	भइलि *bhaïli.*		भइली *bhaïlí.*
3rd	भइलस *bhaïlas.*	भइलसि *bhaïlasi.*	भइलन, भइलेन,‡ भइलें,§ *bhaïlan, bhaïlĕn,*‡ *bhaïlaĩ.*§	भइलिन *bhaïlin.*

* These forms are rarely used at the present day, the plural masculine being used instead. They, however, occur in poetry.

† Or भैलीं *bhailí*, and so on throughout.

‡ Peculiar to Sáran.

§ These forms are Western Bhojpúrí.

North Muzaffarpúr variations are—

The stem form is भेल *bhel* or भैल *bhail* throughout.

1st plur. fem. भेलिऐक *bhĕliaik.* 2nd ditto भेलहुक *bhĕlahuk.*

3rd plur. masc. भेलाह *bheláh.*

Honorific form for second and third persons : भइलीं *bhaïlí* or भइली *bhaïlí.*

§ 54. (b)—Future : '*I shall be,*' '*I shall become,*' &c.

Person.	Singular.		Plural.	
	Masculine.	Feminine.	Masculine.	Feminine.
1st	होइबों* *hoïbō.* होइबउ* *hŏïbaŭ.**	होइब्यूं **hoïbyū̃.*	होइब *hoïb*† or होइबी *hoïbí.*	होइब्यूं* *hoïbyū̃.*
2nd	होइबे *hoïbe.*	होइबी *hoïbí.*‡ होइबिस *hoïbis.*	होइबह *hoïbah* or होइबऽ *hoïba.*	होइबू *hoïbú.*
3rd	होई *hoi.*		होइहें *hoïhĕ* or होइहेन *hoïhĕn.* होइहैं *hoïhaĩ.*‡	

* These terminations are rarely used at the present day, the plural masculine being used instead. They, however, occur in poetry.

† Or होब *hob*, and so on throughout. In Chumpáran the word is spelt होअब *hoëb* throughout.

‡ These forms are Western Bhojpúrí.

North Muzaffarpúr variations, borrowed from Maithilí, are—

3rd sing. masc. होअत *hoat* or होअतैन *hŏatain.*

1st plur. masc. होइबैन *hŏïbain*, होइबैक *hŏïbaik.* 3rd ditto होअताह *hoatáh.*

Honorific form for second and third persons : होइब *hoïb* or होइबी *hoïbí.*

CONJUNCTIVE MOOD.

§ 55. (*c*)—Present : '(*If*) *I be*,' *&c.*

Person.	SINGULAR.		PLURAL.	
	Masculine.	Feminine.	Masculine.	Feminine.
1st	होओँ *hoõ.**	होयूँ *hoyũ.**	होईँ *hoī̃.*†	होयूँ *hoyũ.**
2nd	हो, होए, *ho*, *hoe*. होअस, होअसि, *hoas*, *hoasi*.	होई *hoī.* ‡ होइस *hoïs*.	होअह, होअ, *hoah*, *hoa*.	होऊ *hoū*.
3rd	होअ, होए, होओ, *hoa*, *hoe*, *hoö*. होअस, होअसु, होअसि, *hoas*, *hoasu*, *hoasi*.	होअसि *hoasi*.	होअन *hoan*, होऐँ *hoaĩ*. ‡	होइन *hoïn*.

* These forms are rarely used, the plural masculine being used instead. They, however, occur in poetry.

† Or होवीँ *howī̃*, and so on throughout.

‡ These forms are Western Bhojpúrí.

Honorific forms for first and second persons : होईँ *hoī̃* and होई *hoī*.

§ 56. (*d*)—Preterite : '(*If*) *I had been*,' *&c.*

Person.	Singular.		Plural.	
	Masculine.	Feminine.	Masculine.	Feminine.
1st	होइतों* *hoïtõ.*	होइत्यूँ* *hoïtyū̃.*	होइतीं† *hoïtī̃.*	होइत्यूँ* *hoïtyū̃.*
2nd	होइत *hoïte.*	होइती *hoïti.* ‡		
	होइतस *hoïtas.*	होइतिस *hoïtis.*	होइतह or होइतऽ, *hoïtah* or *hoïta.*	होइतू *hoïtū.*
3rd	होइत, होइते, *hoït*, *hoïte.*	होइति *hoïti.*		होइती *hoïtī.*
	होइतस *hoïtas.*	होइतसि *hoïtasi.*	होइतन, होइतैं, *hoïtan*, *hoïtaĩ.*‡	होइतिन *hoïtin.*

* These forms are rarely used at the present day, the plural masculine being used instead. They, however, occur in poetry.

† Or होतीं *hotī̃*, and so on throughout.

‡ These forms are Western Bhojpúrí.

Honorific form for first and second persons : होइतीं *hoïtī̃* or होइती *hoïtī.*

IMPERATIVE MOOD.

§ 57. (*f*)—Present Tense.—Same as the Present Conjunctive.

The periphrastic tenses are quite regular, and need not be given.

§ 58a.—Present Participle, '*being*.'

Singular and Plural.

Masc.	Fem.
होत* *hot*.	होति *hoti*.

Past Participle, '*been*.'

भइल *bhaïl*.	भइलि *bhaïli*.

Infinitive, '*to be*.'

होअब *hoab* or होइब *hoib*. Western Bhojpúrí obl. होबे *hobaï* or भैबे *bhaibaï*.

§ 58b.—The Strong Complete Auxiliary Verb.

√ होख *hokh*, 'be,' 'become.'

This verb is conjugated regularly throughout exactly like the verb √ देख *dekh*, except that, being intransitive, its third person singular preterite is होखल *hokhal* or होखलस *hŏkh'las*, fem. होखलि *hŏkh'li* or होखलसि *hŏkh'lasi*. Its conjugation is therefore not given here.

§ 58c.—The Defective Negative Auxiliary Verb.

√ नइख *naïkh* or नहिँख *nahĩkh*, 'be not.'

This verb exists only in the present tense of the three moods.

---

* होइत *hoit* or होअत *hoat* may be written for होत *hot* throughout.

INDICATIVE MOOD.

(a) Present : '*I am not,*' &c.

Person.	Singular. Masculine.	Singular. Feminine.	Plural. Masculine.	Plural. Feminine.
1st	नइखों *naïkhõ.**	नइख्यूँ *naïkhyû.**	नइखीं *naïkhî.*†	नइखूँ * *naïkhû.**
2nd	नइख, नइखे, नइखुए, *naïkh, naïkhe, naïkhue.*	नइखी *naïkhi.*§	नइखह, नइखठ, *naïkhah, naïkha.*	नइखु *naïkhú.*
	नइखस, नइखसि, *naïkhas, naïkhasi.*	नइखिस *naïkhis.*		
3rd	नइख, बइखे, नइखुए,‡ *naïkh, naïkhe, naïkhue,* नइखो, *naïkho.*			
	नइखस, मइखसि, *naïkhas, naïkhasi.* नइखसु, *naïkhasu.*	नइखसि *naïkhasi.*	नइखन, मइखैं, *naïkhan, naïkhãi.*§	नइखिन *naïkhin.*

* These forms are rarely used at the present day, the plural masculine being used instead. They, however, occur in poetry.

† Or नेखीं *naïkhî* or नहिँखीं *nahîkhî*, and so throughout.

‡ Peculiar to Sáran.

§ These forms are Western Bhojpúrì.

A North Muzaffarpúr variation of the stem is नहिख *nahikh.*

(*b*)—**Present Conjunctive and Imperative.**—Like the Present Indicative.

Honorific form for second and third persons : नइखीं *naïkhî* or नइखी *naïkhi.*

§ 58d. The Defective Emphatic Auxiliary Verb.

This verb only exists in the present of the three moods.

It is not here conjugated with all its optional forms, as these can be obtained by comparison with the conjugation of बाटीं *báṭí*.

(*a*)—**Present** : '*I am indeed,*' *&c.*

Person.	SINGULAR.		PLURAL.	
	Masculine.	Feminine.	Masculine.	Feminine.
1st	बड़्ले बाटों,* *baṛ'lĕ báṭō.*	बड़्ले बाट्यूँ,* *baṛ'lĕ báṭyū́.*	बड़्ले बाटीं,† *baṛ'lĕ báṭí.*	बड़्ले बाट्यूँ,* *baṛ'lĕ báṭyū́.*
2nd	बड़्ले बाटे, *baṛ'lĕ báṭe.*	बड़्ले बाटिस, *baṛ'lĕ bátis.*	बड़्ले बाटऽ, *baṛ'lĕ báṭa.*	बड़्ले बाटू, *baṛ'lĕ báṭú.*
3rd	बड़्ले बाटस, *baṛ'lĕ bátas.*	बड़्ले बटसि, *baṛ'lĕ baṭasi.*	बड़्ले बाटन, *baṛ'lĕ báṭan.*	बड़्ले बाटिन, *baṛ'lĕ bátin.*

* These forms are rare.

† Or बाड़ीं *báṛí* or बारो *bárí, &c.*

(*b*)—**Present Conjunctive and Imperative.**—Like the present indicative.

CHAPTER VI.

THE REGULAR ACTIVE VERB.

§ 59. There is only one conjugation of active verbs, if we except a few irregular verbs to be noted further on. The conjugation of neuter verbs differs from that of active verbs only in the past tenses of the indicative mood, and these will be treated of in a future page. Verbs whose roots end in vowels also exhibit slight variations, which will be explained at the proper place. For the sake of uniformity the tenses are given in the same order, and under the same names, as these in Dr. Hœrnle's Grammar.

Throughout the verb it must be remembered that the first person singular (masculine and feminine) and the first person plural feminine are rarely used, the plural masculine being used instead. They, however, occur in poetry, and are therefore given, but are enclosed in brackets, so that the learner may be warned against their use.

§ 60. √देख *dekh*, 'see.'

Infinitive: देखब *dekhab.*

Present Participle: देखित *dekhit* or देखत *dekhat.*

Past Participle: देखल *dekhal.*

Complete Past Participle: देखल भइल *dekhal bhaïl.*

(A)—Simple Tenses.

INDICATIVE MOOD.

§ 61a. (*a*)—Present: '*I see*,' '*I shall see*,' *&c*.

NOTE.—This tense is frequently used with future signification.

Person.	SINGULAR.		PLURAL.	
	Masculine.	Feminine.	Masculine	Feminine.
1st	(देखलों *dekhalō̃*.)*	(देखल्यूँ *dekhalyū̃*.)	देखीला or देखीले, *dekhílá*. or *dekhíle*.	(देखल्यूँ *dekhalyū̃*.)
2nd	देखले or देखेले, *dekhale* or *dekhĕle*.	देखलिसि *dekhalisi*,	देखलह or देखलऽ, *dekhalah* or *dekhala*. देखेलह or देखेलऽ, *dekhĕlah* or *dekhĕla*.	देखलू *dekhalú*.
3rd	देखला or देखेला, *dekhalá* or *dekhĕlá*.	देखलि *dekhali*.	देखले or देखलन, *dekhale* or *dekhalan*. देखेले or देखेलन, *dekhĕle* or *dekhĕlan*.	देखली *dekhalí*. देखलिन *dekhalin*.

* Or Western Bhojpúrí देखइलों *dekhaïlō̃*, and so throughout. The first plural masculine is, however, देखीलां *dekhílā̃*, and the third plural देखइलैं *dekhaïlaĩ*.

NOTE.—In this tense the vowel of the root always remains long, and is never shortened when antepenultimate.

Throughout the plural may be used for the singular in an honorific sense. This is always the case in the first person. In addition to the special feminine forms given above, masculine forms may be used in a feminine sense.

The forms देखीला *dekhílá* and देखीले *dekhíle* are used in the second and third persons in an honorific sense.

To form a non-honorific plural in the second and third persons, the word सऽ *sa* may be suffixed to any plural form: thus देखलऽ सऽ *dekhala sa*, 'you see,' देखले सऽ, *dekhale sa*, 'they see.'

Concerning the pronunciation of this tense, see § 41.

§ 61b. (*b*)—Preterite: '*I saw*,' *&c.*

Person.	Singular.		Plural.	
	Masculine.	Feminine.	Masculine.	Feminine.
1st	(देखलों *dĕkh'lõ.*)	(देखल्यूँ) (*dĕkh'lyũ.*)	देखलीं *dĕkh'lĩ.* देखुईं *dĕkhuĩ.**	(देखल्यूँ *dĕkh'lyũ.*)
2nd	देखले, देखलस, *dĕkh'le, dĕkh'las.* देखलेस, देखुए, *dĕkh'lĕs,* dĕkhue.**	देखली *dĕkh'lí.*† देखलिस *dĕkh'lis.*	देखलह, देखलऽ *dĕkh'lah, dĕkh'la.* देखुअह, देखुअ, *dĕkhuah,* dĕkhua.**	देखलू, *dĕkh'lú.*
3rd	देखले *dĕkh'le.* देखलस *dĕkh'las.* देखुए *dĕkhue.**	देखलसि *dĕkh'lasi.*	देखलन, *dĕkh'lan.* देखलैं *dĕkh'laĩ.*† देखलेन, देखुअन, *dĕkh'lĕn,* dĕkhuan.**	देखलिन, *dĕkhalin.*

* Forms peculiar to Sáran.

† Forms peculiar to Western Bhojpúrí.

NOTE.—Throughout the plural may be used for the singular in an honorific sense. This is always the case with the first person. In addition to the special feminine forms given above, masculine forms may be used in a feminine sense.

The form देखलीं *dĕkh'lĩ* or देखली *dĕkh'lí* is used in the second and third persons in an honorific sense.

To form a non-honorific plural the word सऽ *sa* may be suffixed to any plural forms: thus देखलऽ सऽ *dĕkh'la sa*, 'you saw;' देखलन सऽ *dĕkh'lan sa*, 'they saw.'

Sáran has some peculiar forms in the first and second persons plural of this tense which must be noted here.

1st person : हम देख॰लियइन *ham dĕkh'liyaïn.*—Only used when the object of the verb is in the third person and special respect is shown to the object: as हम राजा के देख॰लियइन *ham rájá ke dĕkh'liyaïn*, 'I saw his Majesty the King.'

हम देख॰लियवऽ *ham dĕkh'liyawa.*—Only used when the object of the verb is in the second person and special respect is shown to the object: as हम रउरा के देख॰लियवऽ *ham raürá ke dĕkh'liyawa*, 'I saw your Honour.'

2nd person : तूँ देख॰लहुस *tú dĕkh'lahus.*—Only used when contempt is shown to the object in the third person: as तूँ मलिया के देख॰लहुस *tú maliyá ke dĕkh'lahus*, 'you saw the gardener,' where the gardener is spoken of contemptuously.

तूँ देख॰लहुन *tú dĕkh'lahun.*—Only used when respect is shown to the object in the third person: as तूँ राजा के देख॰लहुन *tú rájá ke dĕkh'lahun*, 'you saw his Majesty.'

The following forms, adopted from Maithilí, obtain in North Muzaffarpúr :—

1st sing. masc.	देखल	*dekhal.*
3rd do. do.	देख॰लक	*dĕkh'lak.*
1st plur. fem.	देख॰लिऐक	*dĕkh'liaik.*
2nd do. do.	देख॰लहक	*dĕkh'lahak.*
3rd do. masc.	देखल॰थिन	*dĕkhal'thin.*

§ 62. (c)—Future: '*I shall see*,' *&c.*

Person.	Singular.		Plural.	
	Masculine.	Feminine.	Masculine.	Feminine.
1st	(देखब्वों *děkh'bõ*.) (देखब्बउ *děkh'baü*.)	(देखब्यु) (*děkh'byü*.)	देखब, देखब्बी, *dekhab, děkh'bí*. देखबैं *děkh'baĩ*.†	देखिब, देखब्बी, *dekhib, děkh'bí*.
2nd	देखबे *děkh'be*.	देखबी *děkh'bí*.† देखबिस *děkh'bis*.	देखबह, देखबठ, *děkh'bah, děkh'ba*.	देखबू *děkh'bú*.
3rd	देखी *dekhí*. देखीत *dekhít*.*		देखिहें, देखिहेन, *děkhihẽ, děkhi'hěn*. देखिहें *děkhihaĩ*.†	

* Peculiar to Champáran.
† Peculiar to Western Bhojpúrí.

Note.—Throughout the plural may be used instead of the singular in an honorific sense. This is always the case in the first person. In addition to the special feminine forms given above, masculine forms may be used in a feminine sense.

The form देखब *dekhab* or देखबी *děkh'bí* is used in the second and third persons in an honorific sense.

To form a non-honorific plural, the word सठ *sa* may be suffixed to any plural form: thus देखबठ सठ *děkh'ba sa*, 'you will see;' देखिहें सठ *děkhihẽ sa*, 'they will see.'

The following forms, borrowed from Maithilí, are in use in North Muzaffarpúr:—

3rd sing. masc. देखत *dekhat*, देखतैन *děkh'tain*.

1st pl. do. देखबैक *děkh'baik*, देखबैन *děkh'bain*.

CONJUNCTIVE (CONDITIONAL) MOOD.

§ 63. (*d*)—Present : '(*If*) *I see*;' rarely '*I see*,' or '*I shall see*,' &c.

Person.	Singular.		Plural.	
	Masculine.	Feminine.	Masculine.	Feminine.
1st	(देखोँ *dekhõ*.)	(देखूँ *dekhyũ*.)	देखीँ *dekhí*.	(देखूँ *dekhyũ*.)
2nd	देखे, देख, *dekhe, dekh*. देखस, देखसि, *dekhas, dekhasi*. देखुए,* देखेँस,* *dĕkhue,* dekhĕs.**	देखी *dekhí*.† देखिस *dekhis*.	देखह, देखऽ, *dekhah, dekha*.	देखू *dekhú*.
3rd	देखे, देखस, *dekhe, dekhas*. देखऽ, देखो, *dekha, dekho*. देखसु, देखसि, *dĕkhasu, dĕkhasi*. देखुए,* देखै,*† *dĕkhue,* dekhai.*†*	देखसि *dĕkhasi*.	देखन *dekhan*. देखेँन *dekhĕn*.* देखैँ *dekhaĩ*.†	देखिन *dekhin*.

* These forms are peculiar to Sáran.

† These forms are peculiar to Western Bhojpúrí.

NOTE.—Throughout the plural may be used instead of the singular in an honorific sense. This is always the case in the first person. In addition to the special feminine forms given above, masculine forms may be used in a feminine sense.

The form देखीँ *dekhí* or देखी *dekhí* is used in the second and third persons in an honorific sense.

To form a non-honorific plural, the word सठ *sa* may be suffixed to a plural form, or sometimes even to a singular one : thus देखे सठ *dekhe sa* or देखन सठ *dekhan sa*, '(if) they see.'

The following forms, borrowed from the Maithilí, are in use in North Muzaffarpúr :—

1st sing. masc. देखूँ *dekhū̃.*
3rd do. do. देखइक *dĕkhaïk*, देखउक *dĕkhaük.*
3rd pl. do. देखथ *dekhath.*

§ 64. (*e*)—Preterite : '(*If*) *I had seen*,' &c.

Person.	Singular. Masculine.	Singular. Feminine.	Plural. Masculine.	Plural. Feminine.
1st	(देख॰तोँ *dĕkh'tõ.*)	(देख॰त्यूँ *dĕkh'tyū̃.*)	देख॰तीँ* *dĕkh'tī̃.**	(देख॰त्यूँ *dĕkh'tyū̃.*)
2nd	देख॰ते *dĕkh'te.*	देख॰ती *dĕkh'tí.*‡	देख॰तह, देख॰तऽ, *dĕkh'tah, dĕkh'ta.*	देख॰तू *dĕkh'tú.*
	देख॰तस *dĕkh'tas.*	देख॰तिस *dĕkh'tis.*		
	देख॰तेस *dĕkh'tĕs.*†			
3rd			देख॰तन *dĕkh'tan.*	देख॰तिन *dĕkh'tin.*
	देखत, देख॰ते *dekhat, dĕkh'te.*	देख॰ति *dĕkh'ti.*		देख॰ती *dĕkh'tí.*
	देख॰तस *dĕkh'tas.*	देख॰तसि *dĕkh'tasi.*	देख॰तेन *dĕkh'tĕn.*† देख॰तैँ *dĕkh'taĩ.*‡	

* Or देखितीँ *dĕkhitī̃*, and so throughout.

† These forms are peculiar to Sáran.

‡ These forms are peculiar to Western Bhojpúrí.

NOTE.—Throughout the plural may be used for the singular in an honorific sense. This is always the case in the first person. In addition to the special feminine forms given above, masculine forms may be used in a feminine sense.

The form देखन्तीं *dĕkh'tí* (देखितीं *dĕkhití*) or देखन्ती *dĕkh'tí* (देखिती *dĕkhiti*) is used in the second and third persons in an honorific sense.

To form a non-honorific plural the word सᴑ *sa* may be suffixed to any plural form : thus देखन्तᴑ सᴑ *dĕkh'ta sa*, '(if) you had seen ;' देखन्तन सᴑ *dĕkh'tan sa*, '(if) they had seen.'

The following forms, borrowed from Maithilí, are in use in North Muzaffarpúr :—

3rd sing. masc. देखइत *dĕkhaït* or देखैत *dĕkhait.*

3rd pl. do. देखितथ *dĕkhitath.*

IMPERATIVE MOOD.

§ 65. (*f.*)—**Present.**—Same as Present Conjunctive.

Precative Forms.

Person.	Singular.		Plural.	
	Masculine.	Feminine.	Masculine.	Feminine.
1st	*Wanting.*	*Wanting.*	*Wanting.*	*Wanting.*
2nd	देखिहे, देखु, देखन्बे, *dĕkhihe, dekhú, dĕkh'be.*	*Wanting.*	देखिहᴑ, देखिहौ, देखीं, *dĕkhiha, dĕkhihau, dekhí,* or देखन्बᴑ *dĕkh'ba.*	*Wanting.*
3rd	*Wanting.*	*Wanting.*	*Wanting.*	*Wanting.*

The form देखिहᴑ *dĕkhiha* is also used as a future indicative, meaning 'you will see.'

(B)—Periphrastic Tenses.

§ 66. In the following paradigms the optional and dialectic forms of the auxiliary verb will not all be given, as taking up too much valuable space.

The footnote, too, regarding the 1st. person singular, which has been added to each of the radical and participial tenses, will be omitted to save space.

INDICATIVE MOOD.

§ 67. (*g*)—Definite Present: '*I am seeing,*' *&c.*

Person.	Singular. Masculine.	Singular. Feminine.	Plural. Masculine.	Plural. Feminine.
1st	(देखत बाटों) (*dekhat báṭŏ.*)	(देखत बाट्यूँ) (*dekhat báṭyū̆.*)	देखत* बानीं† *dekhat bánī.*	(देखत बाट्यूँ) (*dekhat báṭyū̆.*)
2nd	देखत बाटस, *dekhat báṭas.*	देखत बाटिस *dekhat báṭis.*	देखत बाटठ *dekhat báṭa.*	देखत बाटू *dekhat báṭú*
3rd	देखत बाटे or बा, *dekhat báṭe* or *bá.*	देखत बटसि *dekhat baṭasi.*	देखत बाटन *dekhat báṭan.*	देखत बाटिन, *dekhat báṭin.*

* Or देखइत *dĕkhaït,* and so throughout. This form is most used north of the Ganges; North Muzaffarpúr uses देखइत *dĕkhaït* or देखैत *dĕkhait.*

† Or बाटीं *báṭī*, बाड़ीं *báṛī*, *&c.*, especially in Champáran. Also हवीं *hawī*, and so throughout: thus देखत हवीं *dekhat hawī.*

NOTE.—North Muzaffarpúr in the plural also has for auxiliary छी *chhí,* छठ *chha,* छथ *chhath.* See paradigm of auxiliary verb.

§ 68 (*h*). Frequently the initial ब *b* of बाट *báṭ* or बाड़ *báṛ* is omitted, which gives rise to the following variety of this tense:—

Person.	Singular.		Plural.	
	Masculine.	Feminine.	Masculine.	Feminine.
1st	देखन्तारों *dĕkh'tárõ.*)	(देखन्तार्यूँ) (*dĕkh'táryũ.*)	देखन्तानीं or देखन्तारीं, *dĕkh'tání* or *dĕkh'tárí.*	(देखन्तार्यूँ *dĕkh'táryũ.*)
2nd	देखन्तारस *dĕkh'táras.*	देखन्तारिस *dĕkh'táris.*	देखन्तारऽ *dĕk'tára.*	देखन्तारू *dĕkh'tárú.*
3rd	देखन्तारे or देखन्ता, *dĕkh'táre* or *dĕkh'tá.*	देखन्तारसि,* *dĕkh'tárasi.*	देखन्तारन *dĕkh'táran.*	देखन्तारिन *dĕkh'tárin.*

* Sáran here also uses a form देखतिया *dĕkhatiyá.*

§ 69 (*i*)—Imperfect: '*I was seeing,*' *&c.*

Person.	Singular.		Plural.	
	Masculine.	Feminine.	Masculine.	Feminine.
1st	(देखत रह्लों) (*dekhat rah'lõ.*)	(देखत रह्ल्यूँ) (*dekhat rah'lyũ.*)	देखत रह्लीं* (हँ) *dekhat rah'lí (hã.)*	(देखत रह्ल्यूँ) (*dekhat rah'lyũ.*)
2nd	देखत रह्लस (हऽ) *dekhat rah'las (ha.)*	देखत रह्लिस (हऽ) *dekhat rah'lis (ha.)*	देखत रह्लऽ (हऽ) *dekhat rah'la (ha.)*	देखत रह्लू (हऽ) *dakhat rah'lú (ha.)*
3rd	देखत रहल (हऽ) *dekhat rahal (ha.)*	देखत रह्लि (हऽ) *dekhat rah'li (ha.)*	देखत रह्लन (हँ) *dekhat rah'lan (hã.)*	देखत रह्लिन (हँ) *dekhat rahalin (hã.)*

* Or रहीं *rahí*, and so throughout.

In Sáran हँ *hã* or हउ *ha* can be inserted optionally, as indicated in parenthesis. In North Muzaffarpúr the participle is written देखइत *dĕkhaït* or देखैत *dĕkhait.*

§ 70. (*j*)—**Durative Future**: '*I shall be reading,*' *&c.*

Person.	Singular.		Plural.	
	Masculine.	Feminine.	Masculine.	Feminine.
1st	(देखत होबों) (*dekhat hobõ.*)	(देखत होब्यूँ) (*dekhat hobyũ.*)	देखत होब* *dekhat hob.**	(देखत होब्यूँ) (*dekhat hobyũ.*)
2nd	देखत होबे *dekhat hobe.*	देखत होबिस *dekhat hobis.*	देखत होबऽ *dekhat hoba.*	देखत होबू *dekhat hobú.*
3rd	देखत होई *dekhat hoí.*		देखत होइहें *dekhat hoïhẽ.*	

* Or होइब *hoib*, and so throughout the first and second persons.

In North Muzaffarpúr the participle is written देखइत *dĕkhaït* or देखैत *dĕkhait.*

§ 71. (*k*)—**Perfect**: '*I have seen,*' *&c.*

Person.	Singular.		Plural.	
	Masculine.	Feminine.	Masculine.	Feminine.
1st	(देखऽलों हा†) (*dĕkh'lõ há.*†)	(देखऽल्यूँ हा†) (*dĕkh'lyũ há.*†)	देखऽलीं हाँ *dĕkh'lĩ hã.**	(देखऽल्यूँ हा *dĕkh'lyũ há.**)
2nd	देखऽले हा† *dĕkh'le há.*† देखऽलस हा† *dĕkh'las há.*†	देखऽलिस हा† *dĕkh'lis há.*†	देखऽलऽ हा *dĕkh'la há.*†	देखऽलू हा *dĕkh'lú há.*†
3rd	देखऽलस हा† *dĕkh'las há.*†	देखऽलसि हा† *dĕkh'lasi há.*†	देखऽलन हाँ *dĕkh'lan hã.**	देखऽलिन हाँ *dĕkh'lin hã.**

* Or हँ *hã* or हैं *haĩ*.

† Or हउ *ha* or हवस *hawas*.

The various dialectic forms of the preterite are also used in this tense.

In addition to the above, the following form also obtains in Champáran. It is also the form current in Western Bhojpúrí :—

Person.	Singular.		Plural.	
	Masculine.	Feminine.	Masculine.	Feminine.
1st	(देख॰ले बाड़ों) (*děkh'lě báṛõ.*)	(देख॰ले बाड़्यूँ) (*děkh'lě báṛyũ.*)	देख॰ले बानीं *děkh'lě bání.**	(देख॰ले बाड़्यूँ) (*děkh'lě báṛyũ.*)
2nd	देख॰ले बाड़स *děkh'lě báṛas.*	देख॰ले बाड़िस *děkh'lě báṛis.*	देख॰ले बाड़॰ *děkh'lě báṛa.*	देख॰ले बाड़ू *děkh'lě báṛú.*
3rd	देख॰ले बा *děkh'lě bá.*	देख॰ले बड़सि *děkh'lě baṛasí.*	देख॰ले बाड़न *děkh'lě báṛan.*	देख॰ले बाड़िन *děkh'lě báṛin.*

* Or बाड़ीं *báṛí, &c.*; also हवीं *hawí*, and so throughout : thus देखले हवीं *děkhalě hawí.*

§ 72. (*l*)—Pluperfect : '*I had seen,*' &c.

Person.	Singular.		Plural.	
	Masculine.	Feminine.	Masculine.	Feminine.
1st	(देख॰ले रह॰लों) (*děkh'lě rah'lõ.*)	(देख॰ले रह॰ल्यूँ) (*děkh'lě rah'lyũ.*)	देख॰ले रह॰लीं (हँ)* *děkh'lě rah'lí (hã.)**	(देख॰ले रह॰ल्यूँ) (*děkh'lě rah'lyũ.*)
2nd	देख॰ले रह॰लस (ह॰) *děkh'lě rah'las (ha.)*	देख॰ले रह॰लिस (ह॰) *děkh'lě rah'lis (ha.)*	देख॰ले रह॰ल॰ (ह॰) *děkh'lě rah'la (ha.)*	देख॰ले रह॰लू (ह॰) *děkh'lě rah'lú (ha.)*
3rd	देख॰ले रहल (ह॰) *dekh'lě rahal (ha.)*	देख॰ले रह॰लि (ह॰) *děkh'lě rah'li (ha.)*	देख॰ले रह॰लन (हँ) *děkh'lě rah'lan (hã.)*	देख॰ले रह॰लिन (हँ) *děkh'lě rah'lin (hã.)*

* Or रहीं *rahí*, and so throughout.

In Sáran हँ *hã* or हऽ *ha* can be added optionally, as indicated in parenthesis. Also in Sáran there is a special optional form of the auxiliary verb. See the paradigm thereof.

§ 73. (*m*)—Future Exact: '*I shall have seen,*' '*I may have seen,*' &c.

Person.	Singular.		Plural.	
	Masculine.	Feminine.	Masculine.	Feminine.
1st	(देखऽले होबों) (*dĕkh'lĕ hobõ.*)	(देखऽले होब्यूँ) (*dĕkh'lĕ hobyũ.*)	देखऽले होब *dĕkh'lĕ hob.**	(देखऽले होब्यूँ) (*dĕkh'lĕ hobyũ.*)
2nd	देखऽले होबे *dĕkh'lĕ hobe.*	देखऽले होबिस *dĕkh'lĕ hobis.*	देखऽले होबऽ *dĕkh'lĕ hoba.*	देखऽले होबू *dĕkh'lĕ hobú.*
3rd	देखऽले होई *dĕkh'lĕ hoí.*		देखऽले होइहें *dĕkh'lĕ hoihē.*	

* होइब *hoïb* or any other form of the future of the complete auxiliary verb may be used instead throughout.

Conjunctive (Conditional) Mood.

§ 74. (*n.*)—Future Conditional: '*(If) I be seeing,*' &c.

Person.	Singular.		Plural.	
	Masculine.	Feminine.	Masculine.	Feminine.
1st	(देखत होओं) (*dekhat hoõ.*)	(देखत होयूँ) (*dekhat hoyũ.*)	देखत होईं *dekhat hoí.**	(देखत होयूँ) (*dekhat hoyũ.*)
2nd	देखत होअस *dekhat hoäs.*	देखत होइस *dekhat hoïs.*	देखत होअ *dekhat hoä.*	देखत होऊ *dekhat hoú.*
3rd	देखत होअस *dekhat hoäs.*	देखत होअसि *dekhat hoäsi.*	देखत होअन *dekhat hoän.*	देखत होइन *dekhat hoïn.*

* होखीं *hokhī*, and so throughout.

§ 75. (*o*)—Durative Present Conditional: '*(If) I were seeing,*' *&c.*

Person.	Singular.		Plural.	
	Masculine.	Feminine.	Masculine.	Feminine.
1st	(देखत होतों) (*dekhat hotō.*)	(देखत होत्यूँ) (*dekhat hotyū́.*)	देखत होतीं *dekhat hotī́.*	देखत होत्यूँ *dekhat hotyū́.*
2nd	देखत होतस *dekhat hotas.*	देखत होतिस *dekhat hotis.*	देखत होत॰ *dekhat hota.*	देखत होतू *dekhat hotú.*
3rd	देखत होतस *dekhat hotas.*	देखत होतसि *dekhat hŏtasi.*	देखत होतन *dekhat hotan.*	देखत होतिन *dekhat hotin.*

§ 76. (*p*)—Future Exact Conditional: '*(If) I have seen,*' *&c.*

Person.	Singular.		Plural.	
	Masculine.	Feminine.	Masculine.	Feminine.
1st	(देखऽले होओं) (*dĕkh'lĕ hoō.*)	(देखऽले होयूँ) (*dĕkh'lĕ hoyū́.*)	देखऽले होईं *dĕkh'lĕ hoī́.**	(देखऽले होयूँ) (*dĕkh'lĕ hoyū́.*)
2nd	देखऽले होअस *dĕkh'lĕ hoäs.*	देखऽले होइस *dĕkh'lĕ hoïs.*	देखऽले होअ *dĕkh'lĕ hoa.*	देखऽले होऊ *dĕkh'lĕ hoú.*
3rd	देखऽले होअस *dĕkh'lĕ hoäs.*	देखऽले होअसि *dĕkh'lĕ hoäsi.*	देखऽले होअन *dĕkh'lĕ hoän.*	देखले होइन *dĕkh'lĕ hoïn.*

* Or होखीं *hokhī́*, and so throughout.

§ 77. (q)—Preterite Conditional: *'(If) I had seen,' &c.*

Person.	Singular.		Plural.	
	Masculine.	Feminine.	Masculine.	Feminine.
1st	(देख॰ले होतोँ) (*dĕkh'lĕ hotō.*)	(देख॰ले होत्यूँ) (*dĕkh'lĕ hotyū̃.*)	देख॰ले होतीँ *dĕkh'lĕ hotī́.*	(देख॰ले होत्यूँ) (*dĕkh'lĕ hotyū̃.*)
2nd	देख॰ले होतस *dĕkh'lĕ hotas.*	देख॰ले होतिस *dĕkh'lĕ hotis.*	देख॰ले होतऽ *dĕkh'lĕ hota.*	देख॰ले होतू *dĕkh'lĕ hotụ́.*
3rd	देख॰ले होतस *dĕkh'lĕ hotas.*	देख॰ले होतसि *dĕkh'lĕ hŏtasi.*	देख॰ले होतन *dĕkh'lĕ hotan.*	देख॰ले होतिन *dĕkh'lĕ hotin.*

§ 78. Participles.

Adjectival.

	Masculine.	Feminine.	Oblique.
Present, 'seeing'	देखत *dekhat.*	देख॰ति *dĕkh'ti.*	देख॰ते *dĕkh'tĕ.*
	देखित *dekhit.*	देखिति *dĕkhiti.*	देखिते *dĕkhitĕ.*
	देखइत *dĕkhaït.**	देखइति *dĕkhaïti.*	देखइते *dĕkhaïtĕ.*

* This last form is most used north of the Ganges.

	Masculine.	Feminine.	Oblique.
Past, 'seen'	*a)* देखल *dekhal.*	देख॰लि *dekh'li.*	देख॰ले *dĕkh'lĕ.*
	b) देखल भेल *dekhal bheḷ.*	देखल भेलि *dekhal bheli.*	

Conjunctive.

'Having seen' . . . . देख के *dekh kĕ* or (in poetry) देखि के *dekhi kĕ.*

§ 79. Infinitives or Verbal Nouns, '*to see,*' '*the act of seeing.*'

Nominative.	Oblique.
देख * *dekh.**	देखे *dekhĕ.* (W. Bh. देखै *dekhaĭ.*)
देखल *dekhal.*	देखला *dĕkh'lá.* (W. Bh. देखले *dĕkh'le.*)
देखब *dekhab.*	*Wanting.*†

* This form of the verbal noun is always the same as the root. In poetry it sometimes takes the form देखि *dekhi.*

† In Western Bhojpúrí there is an oblique form देखबै *dĕkh'baĭ.*

§ 80. Noun of Agency, '*one who sees.*'

देखवैया *dĕkh'waiyá.*

देखनहारा *dĕkh'nahárá* or देखनिहारा *dĕkh'nihárá.*

CHAPTER VII.

THE REGULAR NEUTER VERB.

§ 81. This verb differs from the active verb only in the formation of the third person of certain of its past tenses [see § 43 (*b*)]. The three more usual past tenses are here given; the conjugation of the rest of the verb can be learnt from the conjugation of the √ देख *dekh.*

NOTE that in Champáran throughout the periphrastic tenses of the neuter verb, in which the past participle occurs, the past participle takes the direct form गिरल *giral,* not the oblique form गिरले *gir'lĕ,* which might be expected: thus हम गिरल होब *ham giral hob,* 'I shall have fallen,' and not हम गिरले होब *ham gir'lĕ hob,* 'I shall have fallen,' which would be the form elsewhere.

§ 82. √ गिर *gir,* 'fall.'

PAST PARTICIPLE: Masc. गिरल *giral.* Fem. गिरलि *gir'li,* '*fallen.*' Obl. गिरले *gir'lĕ.*

INDICATIVE MOOD.

§ 83. (*b*)—Preterite '*I fell,*' *&c.*

Person.	SINGULAR.		PLURAL.	
	Masculine.	Feminine.	Masculine.	Feminine.
1st	(गिर॰लौँ *gir'lō.*)	(गिर॰ल्यूँ) (*gir'lyū̃.*)	गिर॰लीँ, गिरुईँ,* *gir'lī̃, giruī̃.**	(गिर॰ल्यूँ *gir'lyū̃.*)
2nd	गिर॰ले, गिरुए,* *gir'le, girue.**	गिर॰ली*gir'lí.*†	गिर॰लह or गिर॰लऽ, *gir'lah* or *gir'la.*	
2nd	गिर॰लस, गिर॰लेस,* *gir'las, gir'lĕs.**	गिर॰लिस *gir'lis.*	गिरुअह,* गिरुअ,* *giruah,* girua.**	गिर॰लू, गिरुऊ,* *gir'lú, giruú.**
3rd	गिरल *giral.*			
3rd	गिर॰ले, गिरुए,* *gir'lĕ, girue.**	गिर॰लि *gir'li.*		गिर॰ली *gir'lí.*
3rd	गिर॰लस *gir'las.*	गिर॰लसि *gir'lasi.*	गिर॰लन, गिर॰लेन,* *gir'lan, gir'lĕn,** गिरुअन, *giruan.** गिर॰लैँ *gir'lāĩ.*†	गिर॰लिन, गिरुइन,* *gir'lin, giruïn.**

* Forms peculiar to Sáran.

† Forms peculiar to Western Bhojpúrí.

NOTE.—Throughout the plural may be used for the singular in an honorific sense. This is always the case in the first person. In addition to the special feminine forms given above, masculine forms may be used in a feminine sense.

The form गिर॰लीँ *gir'lī̃* or गिर॰ली *gir'lí* is used in the second and third persons in an honorific sense.

To form a non-honorific plural the word सऽ *sa* may be suffixed to any plural form: thus गिर॰लऽ सऽ *gir'la sa*, 'you fell;' गिर॰लन सऽ *gir'lan sa*, 'they fell.'

The following forms, borrowed from Maithilí, are used in North Muzaffarpúr :—

1st plur. fem. गिर॰लिऐक *gir'liaik.*
2nd do. do. गिर॰लुक *gir'luk.*
3rd plur. masc. गिर॰लाह *gir'láh.*

§ 84. (*j*)—Perfect: '*I have fallen,*' &c.

Person.	Singular.		Plural.	
	Masculine.	Feminine.	Masculine.	Feminine.
1st	(गिरऽलों हा) (*gir'lõ há.*)	(गिरऽल्यूँ हा) (*gir'lyũ há.*)	गिरऽलीं हाँ *gir'lĩ hã.**	(गिरऽल्यूँ हा *gir'lyũ há.*)
2nd	गिरऽले हा *gir'le há.*†		गिरऽलऽ हा *gir'la há.*†	गिरऽलू हा *gir'lú há.*†
	गिरऽलऽ हा † *girl'as há.*†	गिरऽलिस हा † *gir'lis há.*†		•
3rd	गिरल हा *giral há.*†	गिरऽलि हा † *gir'li há.*†	गिरऽले हाँ *gir'le hã.**	गिरऽली हाँ *gir'lĩ hã.**
			गिरऽलन हाँ *gir'lan hã.**	गिरऽलिन हाँ *gir'lin hã.*
	गिरऽलस हा † *gir'las há* †	गिरऽलसि हा † *gir'lasi há.*†		

* Or हँ *hã* or हैं *haĩ*. † Or हऽ *ha* or हवे *hawe*.

Other dialectic varieties as in the preterite.

In addition to the above the following form also obtains in Champáran and Sháhábád. It differs from the above somewhat in signification, meaning 'I *am* fallen,' rather than 'I *have* fallen':—

Person.	Singular.		Plural.	
	Masculine.	Feminine.	Masculine.	Feminine.
1st	(गिरल बाड़ों) (*giral báṛõ.*)	(गिरल बाड़्यूँ) (*giral báṛyũ.*)	गिरल बानीं *giral bánĩ.**	गिरल बाड़्यूँ *giral báṛyũ.*
2nd	गिरल बाड़स *giral báṛas.*	गिरल बाड़िस *giral báṛis.*	गिरल बाड़ऽ *giral báṛa.*	गिरल बाड़ू *giral báṛú.*
3rd	गिरल बा *giral bá.*	गिरल बड़सि *giral baṛasi.*	गिरल बाड़न *giral báṛan.*	गिरल बाड़िन *giral báṛin.*

* Or बाड़ीं *báṛĩ* or बारी *bári*, and so throughout; also हवीं *hawĩ*, and so throughout: thus गिरल हवीं *giral hawĩ*.

§ 85. (*k*)—Pluperfect: '*I had fallen,*' &c.

Person.	Singular.		Plural.	
	Masculine.	Feminine.	Masculine.	Feminine.
1st	(गिर॰ले रह॰लों) (*gir'lĕ rah'lõ.*)	(गिर॰ले रह॰ल्यूँ) (*gir'lĕ rah'lyũ.*)	गिर॰ले* रह॰लीं† *gir'lĕ** *rah'lĩ.*†	(गिर॰ले रह॰ल्यूँ) (*gir'lĕ rah'lyũ.*)
2nd	गिर॰ले रह॰लस *gir'lĕ rah'las.*	गिर॰ले रह॰लिस *gir'lĕ rah'lis.*	गिर॰ले रह॰लऽ *gir'lĕ rah'la.*	गिर॰ले रह॰लू *gir'lĕ rah'lŭ.*
3rd	गिर॰ले { रहल *rahal.* / रह॰लस *rah''as.* }	गिर॰ले { रह॰लि *rah'li.* / रह॰लसि *rah'lasi.* }	गिर॰ले { रह॰ले *rah'le.* / रह॰लन *rah'lan.* }	गिर॰ले { रह॰लीं *rah'lĩ.* / रह॰लिन *rah'lin.* }

* In Champáran the form गिरल *giral* is used throughout instead of गिर॰ले *gir'lĕ*.

† Or रहीं *rahĩ*, and so throughout.

For dialectic varieties of the auxiliary verb, see its paradigm.

CHAPTER VIII.

VOCALIC ROOTS.

§ 86. Many verbs have roots ending in vowels, and the junction of the root with the termination frequently causes some slight apparent irregularity.

For this reason the following examples are given of the conjugation of verbs having roots ending in vowels. They are here conjugated in the masculine gender, and through the four more difficult radical and participial tenses. From these the periphrastic tenses can easily be formed. It has not been thought necessary to give the conjugation in full for each person, or to give the majority of the dialectic variations.

With regard to the shortening of the root vowel, see General Introduction, § 36.

§ 87. Example of a verb whose root ends in आ *á* :—

The conjugation of these verbs should be carefully studied, as a large class of active and causal verbs follows it.

In the preterite indicative these verbs insert a junction vowel between the root and the ल *l* of the termination: thus ख* + इ + लौँ *kha* + *i* + *lí*, 'I ate,' where इ *i* is the junction vowel; and प* + उ + लौँ *pa* + *u* + *lí*, 'I got,' where उ *u* is the junction vowel. As will be subsequently seen, the some peculiarity exists in other tenses besides the preterite.

The following rules show when इ *i* and when उ *u* is the junction vowel :—

1) All active (including causal) verbs take उ *u*.: thus पउलौँ* *paülí*, 'I got;' चढ़उलौँ *chaṛhaülí*, 'I caused to ascend.'

Exception.—The root √ खा *khá*,* 'eat,' always takes इ *i*: thus खइलौँ *khaïlí*, 'I ate.'

* With regard to the shortening of the root vowel, see General Introduction, § 36.

2) All neuter verbs take इ *i*: thus अघइलीं *aghaïlĩ*, 'I was satiated;' अइलूँ *aïlũ*, 'I came.'

Exception.—The √ गा *gá*, 'sing,' always takes उ *u*: thus गउलीं *gaülĩ*, 'I sang.'

It is usual to add the letter व *w* to the end of all roots which take उ *u* in order to distinguish them from those which take the letter इ *i*: thus, √ पाव *páw*, √ गाव *gáw*, *&c.*, which take उ *u*; but √ अघा *aghá*, आ *á*, &c., which take इ *i*.

All verbs which take a उ *u* in the preterite indicative insert a व *w* in the past participle; but all verbs which take इ *i*, insert an इ *i* in the past participle and in that form of the 3rd singular preterite which is the same as the past participle.

§ 88. The following examples will make the above remarks clear. It must be observed that the √ आ *á*, 'come,' irregularly takes उ *u* as its junction vowel in the present indicative, the present participle, and the preterite conditional. In the other tenses it regularly takes इ *i*. It should also be noted that all verbs, without exception, take इ *i* in the future indicative.

Pres. Ind.		Present Participle.	1st Plur. Pret. Cond.
1st Plural.	2nd Plural (as model of other persons).		
पाइला *páĭlá.*	पावेलऽ *páwĕla.*	पावत *páwat.*	पउतीं *paütĭ.*
बजाइला *bajáĭlá.*	बजावेलऽ *bajáwĕla.*	बजावत *bajáwat.*	बजउतीं *bajaütĭ.*
चढ़ाइला *chaṛháĭlá.*	चढ़ावेलऽ *chaṛháwĕla.*	चढ़ावत *chaṛháwat.*	चढ़उतीं *chaṛhaütĭ.*
गाइला *gáĭlá.*	गावेलऽ *gáwĕla.*	गावत *gáwat.*	गउतीं *gaütĭ.*
खाइला *kháĭlá.*	खालऽ *khála.*	खाइत *kháit* or खात [*khát.*	खइतीं *khaïtĭ* or खातीं [*khátĭ.*
अघाइला *agháĭlá.*	अघालऽ *aghála.*	अघाइत *agháit* or अघात [*aghát.*	अघइतीं *aghaïtĭ* or [अघातीं *aghátĭ.*
घबड़ाइला *ghab'ṛáĭlá.*	ड़ालऽ *ghab'ṛála.*	घबड़ाइत *ghab'ṛáit* or घबड़ात *ghab'ṛát.*	घबड़इतीं *ghab'ṛaïtĭ* or [घबड़ातीं *ghab'ṛátĭ.*
हड़बड़ाइला *haṛ'baṛáĭlá.*	हड़बड़ालऽ *haṛ'baṛála.*	हड़बड़ाइत *haṛ'baṛáit* or हड़बड़ात *haṛ'baṛát.*	हड़बड़इतीं *haṛ'baṛaïtĭ* or हड़बड़ातीं *haṛ'baṛátĭ.*
आँइला *áĭlá.*	आवेलऽ *áwĕla.*	आवत *áwat.*	अ तीं *aütĭ.*

खैलीं *khailĭ*, अघैलीं *aghailĭ*. See General Introduction, § 35.

The easiest way of remembering these changes is to note the form of the past participle of each verb; and then, as explained in General Introduction, § 37, the व *wa* is weakened in certain cases to उ *u*.

Some people (especially in Sáran and Champáran) write ए *ĕ* instead of इ *i* : thus अएलीं *aĕlī* instead of अइलीं *aïlī*.

§ 89. √ पा *pá*, 'get.'

INFINITIVE (1ST FORM): पा *pá*; obl. पाए *páĕ*, पावे *páwĕ*.

" (2ND FORM): पावल *páwal*; obl. पौला *paulá*.* (See General Introduction, § 37.)

" (3RD FORM): पाअब *páab*, पाइब *páib*; obl. पाबै *pábaĭ*, पैबै *paibaĭ*, 'to get.'

PRES. PART. पाइत *páit*, पाबित *páwit* or पावत *páwat*.†

* But from √ खा *khá*, खायल *kháyal*, obl. खैला *khailá*, and so also in other verbs whose junction vowel is इ *i*.

† But from √ खा *khá*, खाइत *kháit* or खात *khát*, and so also in other verbs whose junction vowel is इ *i*, except √ आ *á*, 'come,' which makes आवित *áwit* or आवत *áwat*.

INDICATIVE MOOD.

Person.	PRETERITE. (See remarks above.)		FUTURE.	
	Singular.	Plural.	Singular.	Plural.
1st	(पउलौं or पौलौं) (*paülõ*, *paulõ*.)	पउलीं or पौलीं *paülí*, *paulí*.	(पइबौं or पैबौं) (*païbô* or *paibô*.)	पाइब or पायब* *páib* or *páyab*.
2nd	पउले or पौले, *paüle*, *paule*.	पउलऽ or पौलऽ *paüla*, *paula*.	पइबे *païbe* or पैबे *paibe*.	पइबऽ or पैबऽ *païba*, *paiba*.
3rd	पउलस or पौलस *paülas* or *paulas*.	पउलन or पौलन *paülan*, *paulan*.	पाई *pái*.*	पइहें or पैहें *païhẽ* or *paihẽ*.

* In Champáran also पाएब *paĕb*, पाईत *páít*.

Pres. 2nd sing. पावेले *páwĕle*, but from √ खा *khá*, खाले *khále* or खाइले *kháïle*.
3rd do. पावेला *páwĕlá* . . . . खाला *khálá* or खाइला *kháïlá*.
1st pl. पाईला *páïlá* . . . . खाईला *kháïlá*.
2nd do. पावेलऽ *páwĕla* . . . . खालऽ *khála* or खाइलऽ *kháïla*.
3rd do. पावेले *páwĕle* . . . . खाले *khále* or खाइले *kháïle*.

It will be seen that verbs which take इ *i* as the junction vowel drop the syllable वे *wĕ* in this tense. The only exception is the √ आ *á*, 'come,' which makes आवेले *áwĕle*, आवेला *áwĕlá*, &c.

CONDITIONAL MOOD.

Person.	Present.		Preterite.	
	Singular.	Plural.	Singular.	Plural.
1st	(पाओं *páõ*.*)	पाईं *páí*.	(पउतों *paütõ*.)	पउतीं *paütí*.†
2nd	पावे *páwe*.	पावऽ *páwa*.	पउते *paüte*.	पउतऽ *paüta*.
3rd	पावस *páwas*.	पावन *páwan*.*	पाइत *páït* or पावत *páwat*.‡	पउतन *paütan*.

* North Muzaffarpúr पाऊँ *páũ*, पावथ *páwath*.

† पौत *paut*, 'पइत *paït*, पैत *pait*, or पवित *pawit*' may be substituted for पउत *paüt* throughout. But from √ खा *khá*, खइतीं *khaïtí* or खातीं *khátí*, and so on throughout for all verbs whose junction vowel is इ *i*, except the √ आ *á*, 'come.'

‡ North Múzaffarpúr पवैत *pawait*.

It will be seen that verbs whose junction vowel is इ *i* omit व *w* in the present indicative, the present participle, and the preterite conditional. In these forms also they optionally insert इ *i*. The only exception is the √ आ *á*, 'come,' which retains the व *w* in these cases, though it takes इ *i* and not उ *u* in the past participle and tenses formed therefrom. In short, the √ आ *á* is conjugated like a verb whose junction vowel is उ *u* in the present indicative, the present participle, and its derived forms, but like a verb whose junction vowel is इ *i* in the past participle and its derived forms.

§ 90. **Example of a verb whose root ends in ई í:—**

√ पी *pí*, 'drink.'

INFINITIVE: पीअल *píal*, 'to drink.'

PRES. PART. पीहित *píhit* or पीअत *píat*.

INDICATIVE MOOD.

Person.	PRETERITE.		FUTURE.	
	Singular.	Plural.	Singular.	Plural.
1st	(पीअलौँ *pialõ*.)	पीअलीँ *piali*.	(पीअबौँ *piabõ*.)	पीअब् *píab*.
2nd	पीअले *piale*.	पीअलऽ *piala*.	पीअबे *piabe*.	पीअबऽ *píaba*.
3rd	पीअलस or पीलस *píalas*, *pílas*.	पीअलन or पीलन *píalan*, *pilan*.	पीही *píhi*.*	पीहेँ *píhẽ*.

* In Champáran also पीहीत *píhít*.

Pres. 1st pl. पीईला *píílá*.
2nd sing. पीअले *piale*.

CONDITIONAL MOOD.

Person.	PRETERITE.		PRETERITE.	
	Singular.	Plural.	Singular.	Plural.
1st	(पीऔँ *píõ*.*)	पीहीँ, पीईँ, पीँ *píhí*, *píí*, *pí*.	(पिहितौँ or पीअतौँ) (*pihitõ* or *piatõ*.)	पिहितीँ or पीअतीँ *pihití* or *piatí*.
2nd	पीए or पी *píe* or *pí*.	पीअ or पीहऽ *pía* or *píha*.	पिहिते or पीअते *pihite* or *piate*.	पिहितऽ or पीअतऽ *pihita* or *piata*.
3rd	पीअस *pías*.	पीअन *pían*.*	पीहित or पीअत *píhit* or *piat*.*	पिहितन, पीअतन, पीतन *pihitan*, *piatan*, *pítan*.

* North Muzaffarpúr पीऐँ *píẽ*, पीअथ *piath*. † North Muzaffarpúr पिऐत *piait*.

§ 91. Example of a verb whose root ends in ऊ *ú*:—

√ चू *chú*, 'drip.'

INFINITIVE: चूअल *chúal*, 'to drip.'

PRES. PART. चूइत *chúit* or चूअत *chúat*.

INDICATIVE MOOD.

Person.	PRETERITE.		FUTURE.	
	Singular.	Plural.	Singular.	Plural.
1st	(चूलों *chúlõ*.)	चूलीं *chúlí*.*	(चूबों *chúbõ*.)	चूअब *chúab*.
2nd	चूले *chúle*.	चूलऽ *chúla*.	चूबे *chúbe*.†	चूबऽ *chúba*.
3rd	चूअल *chúal*.	चूलन *chúlan*.	चूई *chúí*.‡	चूइहें *chúihẽ*.

* Or चूअलीं *chúalí*, and so throughout.
† Or चूअबे *chúabe*; so also in the plural.
‡ Or in Champáran चूईत *chúít*.

Pres. 1st pl. चूईला *chúílá*.
2nd sing. चूअले *chúale*.

CONDITIONAL MOOD.

Person.	PRETERITE.		FUTURE.	
	Singular.	Plural.	Singular.	Plural.
1st	(चूओं *chúõ*.)*	चूईं *chúí*.	(चूअतों *chúatõ*.)	चूअतीं *chúatí*.†
2nd	चूए *chúe* or चू *chú*.	चूअ *chúa*.	चूअते *chúate*, चूते *chúte*.	चूअतऽ *chúata*, चूतऽ *chúta*.
3rd	चूअस *chúas*.	चूअन *chúan*.*	चूइत *chúit*, चूअत *chúat*.	चूअतन *chúatan*.

* North Muzaffarpúr चूऊँ *chúú*, चूअथ *chúath*. † Or चूइतीं *chúití*, and so on throughout.

§ 92. Example of a verb whose root ends in ओ *o*:—

√ रो *ro*, 'weep.'

INFINITIVE: रोअल *roal*, 'to weep.'

PRES. PART. रोइत *roït*, रोअत *roät*.

INDICATIVE MOOD.

Person.	Preterite.		Future.	
	Singular.	Plural.	Singular.	Plural.
1st	(रोलौं *rolõ*.)	रोलीं *rolí*.*	(रोबौं *robõ*.)	रोअब *roäb*.§
2nd	रोले *role*.	रोलऽ *rola*.	रोअबे *roabe*, रोबे *robe*.	रोअबऽ, रोबऽ, *roaba*, *roba*.
3rd	रोअल *roal*.†	रोलन *rolan*.	रोई *roí*.‡	रोइहें *roïhẽ*.

* Or रोअलीं *roalí̃* or रोवलीं *rowalí̃*, and so throughout.

† North Muzaffarpúr रोएल *roĕl*.

‡ In Champáran also रोईत *roít*.

§ Or रोइब *roïb*, and so throughout.

CONDITIONAL MOOD.

Person.	Present.		Preterite.	
	Singular.	Plural.	Singular.	Plural.
1st	(रोओं *roõ*.)*	रोईं *roí*.	रोइतौं *roïtõ*.	रोइतीं *roïtí*.†
2nd	रोवे *rowe*, रोए *roe*, रो *ro*.	रोअ *roa*, रोवऽ *rowa*.	रोइते *roïte*.	रोइतऽ *roïta*.
3rd	रोअस *roas*, रोवस *rowas*.	रोअन *roan*, रोवन *rowan*.*	रोइत *roït*.‡	रोइतन *roïtan*.

* North Muzaffarpúr रोऊँ *roũ*, रोअथ *roath*.

† Or रोअतीं *roatí̃* or रोतीं *rotí̃*, and so on throughout.

‡ North Muzaffarpúr रोऐत *rŏait*.

For further examples of verbs of this class, see conjugation of √ हो *ho*, § 53 & ff.

Pres. 1st pl. रोईला *roílá*.

2nd sing. रोअले *roale*.

CHAPTER IX.

IRREGULAR VERBS.

§ 93. The following verbs are irregular only in their preterite tense indicative :— √ कर *kar*, 'do ;' √ धर *dhar*, 'seize' or 'place ;' √ हो *ho*, 'become ;' and √ जा *já*, 'go.' Their conjugation is therefore given in that tense only.

The conjugation of √ हो *ho* has been already given in § 53 and ff., and is not given here.

The verbs √ मर *mar*, 'die,' √ दे *de*, 'give,' and √ ले *le*, 'take,' are more or less irregular in all the tenses, especially the preterite indicative and present conditional. The verbs √ मर *mar* and √ दे *de* are therefore given conjugated throughout the radical and participial tenses. The verb √ ले *le* is conjugated precisely like the verb √ दे *de*.

OBSERVE that the present indicative of all these verbs is quite regular : thus 1st pl. करीला *karílá*, 'I do,' जाईला *jáílá*, 'I go,' देईला *deílá*, 'I give,' &c. 3rd sing. करेला *karělá*, 'he does,' जाला *jálá*, 'he goes,' आवेला *áwělá*, 'he comes.' Two contracted forms are, however, of common occurrence, viz. देला *delá*, 'he gives,' लेला *lelá*, 'he takes.' Similarly 2nd sing. देले *dele*, लेले *lele*, and so on.

§ 94. √ कर *kar*, 'do.' √ धर *dhar*, 'place,' 'seize.'

INFINITIVE : करल *karal* or कइल *kaïl*, 'to do ;' धरल *dharal* or धइल *dhaïl*, 'to place,' 'to seize.'

INDICATIVE MOOD.

Person.	√ कर *kar*, PRETERITE.		√ धर *dhar*, PRETERITE.	
	Singular.	Plural.	Singular.	Plural.
1st	(कइलौं *kaïlõ*.)	कइलीं *kaïlí*.*	(धइलौं *dhaïlõ*.)	धइलीं *dhaïlí*.*
2nd	कइले *kaïle*.	कइलऽ *kaïla*.	धइले *dhaïle*.	धइलऽ *dhaïla*.
3rd	कइलस *kaïlas*.	कइलन *kaïlan*.	धइलस *dhaïlas*.	धइलन *dhaïlan*.

* Or कैलीं *kailí*, धैलीं *dhailí*, and so on throughout all forms.

1st pres. ind. करीला *karílá*, धरीला *dharílá*.

§ 95. √ मर *mar*, 'die.'

Infinitives: (1) मर *mar*; obl. मरे *marĕ*, मुए *muĕ*.
(2) मरल *maral*, मुअल *mual*; obl. मरल्ला *mar'lá*, मुअला *mualá*.

Indicative Mood.

Person.	Preterite.		Future.	
	Singular.	Plural.	Singular.	Plural.
1st	(मुअलों *mualõ*.)	मुअलीं *mualī*.	(मरब्बों *mar'bõ*.)	मरब *marab*.
2nd	मुअंले *muale*.	मुअलऽ *muala*.	मरब्बे *mar'be*.	मरब्बऽ *mar'ba*.
3rd.	मुअल *mual*.	मुअलन *mualan*.	मरी *marī*.	मरिहैं *marihẽ*.

Pres. ind. मरीला *marílá*, &c.

Conditional Mood.

Person.	Present.		Preterite.	
	Singular.	Plural.	Singular.	Plural.
1st	(मुओं *muõ* or मरों *marõ*.)	मुईं *muī* or मरीं *marī*.	(मुअतों *muatõ* or मरत्तों *mar'tõ*.)	मुअतीं *muatī** or मरत्तीं *mar'tī*.†
2nd	मू *mú*, मुए *mue*, or मरे *mare*.	मुअ *mua* or मरऽ *mara*.	मुइते *muite* or मरत्ते *mar'te*.	मुअतऽ *muata* or मरत्तऽ *mar'ta*.
3rd	मुअस *muas* or मरस *maras*.	मुअन *muan* or मरन *maran*.	मुअत *muat* or मरत *marat*.	मुअतन *muatan* or मरत्तन *mar'tan*.

* Or मुइतीं *muitī*, and so throughout.
† Or मरितीं *maritī*, and so throughout.

§ 96. √ जा *já*, 'go.'

This root is conjugated like √ खा *khá* in all tenses but the preterite indicative, which is therefore here given. (See § 87 and ff.) With it is given the same tense of √ आ *á*, 'come,' for the sake of comparison. (Cf. § 89.)

	√ आ *á*, 'come'	√ जा *já*, 'go'
INFINITIVE No. 1 ...	आ *á* or आवि *áwi*.	जा *já* or जाइ *jái*.
No. 2 ...	आइल *áïl*; obl. ऐला *ailá*.	जाइल *jáil*; obl. जैला *jailá* or जाला *jálá*. गाइल *gáil*; obl. गैला *gailá*.
No. 3 ...		(√ जा *jā*) जाइब *jáib*; Western Bhojpúrí obl. गैबै *gaibaĭ*.
PRES. PART. ...	आवित *áwit* or आवत *áwat*.	जाइत *jáït* or जात *ját*.

Person.	√ आ *á*, PRETERITE INDICATIVE.		√ जा *já*, PRETERITE INDICATIVE.	
	Singular.	Plural.	Singular.	Plural.
1st	(अइलों *aïlõ*.)	अइलीं *aïlí*.*	(गइलों *gaïlõ*.)	गइलीं *gaïlí*.†
2nd	अइले *aïle*.	अइलऽ *aïla*.	गइले *gaïle*.	गइलऽ *gaïla*.
3rd	आइल *áïl*.	अइलन *aïlan*.	गइल *gaïl*.	गइलन *gaïlan*.

* Or ऐलीं *ailí*, and so on throughout, except in third singular, which makes only आइल *áïl*.

† Or गैलीं *gailí*, and so throughout. North Muzaffarpúr has गेलीं *gelí*, &c.

PRESENT INDICATIVE.

Person.	√ आ *á*. (See § 89.)		√ जा *já*.	
	Singular.	Plural.	Singular.	Plural.
1st	(आवेलों *áwělõ*.)	आइला *áílá*.	(जालों *jálõ*.)	जाइला *jáílá*.
2nd	आवेले *áwěle*.	आवेलऽ *áwěla*.	जाले *jále* or जाइले *jáïle*.	जालऽ *jála*.
3rd	आवेला *áwělá*.	आवेले *áwěle*.	जाला *jálá*.	जाले *jále*.

§ 97. √ दे de, 'give.

INFINITIVE: देल del (Western Bhojpúri दीहल díhal), 'to give.'
OBL. FORM OF 1ST VARIETY OF INFINITIVE: देवे dewaĭ or देऍ deaĭ.

INDICATIVE MOOD.

Present: हम दे ही ham de hí, &c.

Person.	PRETERITE.		FUTURE.	
	Singular.	Plural.	Singular.	Plural.
1st	(देलों delõ.)	देलीं delí.*	(देबों debõ.)	देब deb, देहब dehab.
2nd	देले dele.	देलऽ dela.	देबे debe, देह्बे dĕh'be.	देबऽ deba, देह्बऽ dĕh'ba.
3rd	देलस delas.	देलन delan.	दी dí, दीही díhi.	दीहें díhẽ.

* Or दिह्लीं dih'lí, and so on throughout.

Pres. ind. 1st pl. देईला deílá.
2nd sing. देले dele, pl. देलऽ dela.
3rd sing. देला delá, pl. देले dele.

CONDITIONAL MOOD.

Person.	PRESENT.		PRETERITE.	
	Singular.	Plural.	Singular.	Plural.
1st	(देओं deõ.*)	दीं dí, दिहीं dihí.	(देतों detõ.)	देती detí. §
2nd	दे de.	दऽ da.	देते dete.	देतऽ deta or दीतऽ díta.
3rd	देओ deo, देस des, दे de.†	देन den.‡	देत det or दीत dít.	देतन detan.

* North Muzaffarpúr दिऊँ diũ.
† North Muzaffarpúr देइक deik, देउक deuk.
‡ North Muzaffarpúr देथ deth.
§ Or दिह्तीं dih'tí, दिहितीं dihití, or दितीं dití, and so on throughout.

Similarly is conjugated the √ ले le, 'take,' the letter ल l being substituted for the letter द d throughout.

CHAPTER X.

THE PASSIVE VERB.

§ 98. The passive verb is formed by conjugating the verbal noun ending in ल *l* with the verb √ जा *já*, 'go:' thus देखल जाइल *dekhal jáil*, 'to be seen.' This verbal noun is not altered for gender, number, person, or tense, only the verb जाइल *jáil* being conjugated. Thus—

Indicative Present Masculine.

Singular.	Plural.
1. देखल जालों *dekhal jálõ.*	1. देखल जाइला *dekhal jáilá.*
2. देखल जाइले *dekhal jáile.*	2. देखल जाला *dekhal jála.*
3. देखल जाला *dekhal jálá.*	3. देखल जाले *dekhal jále.*

§ 99. This verbal noun in ल *l* must be carefully distinguished from the past participle having the same termination. The former even in irregular verbs is sometimes quite regular, while the latter is in them almost always irregular. Thus we have verbal nouns such as करल *karal*, मरल *maral*, जाइल *jáïl*, besides past participles like कइल *kaïl*, मुअल *mual*, and गइल *gaïl*. The only exceptions are देल *del* and लेल *lel*, for which see the conjugation of the former verb in § 97. At the same time it must be remembered that the verbal noun can always also take the form of the past participle as well as its proper form: so that we may have कइल *kaïl*, मुअल *mual*, verbal nouns, as well as करल *karal* and मरल *maral*. An example of an irregular passive verb is जाइल जाला *jáil jálá* (impersonal), 'it is gone'—*itum est*; but, used in the sense of a potential, 'it can go.' When neuter verbs are used in the passive voice,' they are always used in an impersonal potential sense. Thus हमरा से चलल नाँ जाला *ham'rá se chalal ná jálá*, 'by me it cannot be gone,' 'I cannot go.' Compare below, § 101.

§ 100. Another common form of the passive is made by adding to the direct form of the first variety of the verbal noun (which is the same in form as the root) the verb पड़ल *paṛal*, 'to fall;' the whole then forms an intensive compound. (See § 114.) Examples of this form are—

किछु किछु जान पड़ैला *kichhu kichhu ján paṛĕlá*, 'a little is evident,' *i.e.* 'it is slightly apparent.'

एकरा सँ ई बूझ पड़ैला *ĕk'rá sẽ í bújh paṛĕlá*, 'from this, this is understood.'

किछु उमड़ल ना देख पड़ैला *kichhu um'ṛal ná dekh paṛĕlá*, 'it is not seen to be at-all increased in size.'

§ 101. The Potential Passive Voice.

This voice is formed by adding आ *á* to the root: thus √ देख *dekh*, potential passive देखा *dekhá*. देखा *dekhá* is then conjugated exactly like any intransitive verb in आ *á*, as explained in § 88. It thus differs from the causal verb (see § 103), which adds आव *áw* to the root. The potential passive is conjugated quite regularly, the following being its principal parts, with which the corresponding causal forms are given for the sake of comparison.

	POTENTIAL PASSIVE.	CAUSAL.
Root	देखा *dekhá*.	देखाव *dĕkháw*.
Infinitive, 2nd form ...	देखायल *dĕkháyal*; obl. देखैला *dĕkhailá*.	देखावल *dĕkháwal*; obl. देखौला *dĕkhaulá*.
Pres. part. ...	देखाइत *dĕkháït*.	देखावत *dĕkháwat*.
Past part. ...	देखाइल *dĕkháïl*.	देखावल *dĕkháwal*.
1st pl. pret. ind. ...	देखइलीं *dĕkhaïlī́*.	देखउलीं *dĕkhaülī́*.
2nd sing. pret. ind. ...	देखइले *dĕkhaïle*.	देखउले *dĕkhaüle*.
2nd pl. pret. ind. ...	देखइलऽ *dĕkhaïla*.	देखउलऽ *dĕkhaüla*.
3rd sing. pret. ind. ...	देखाइस *dĕkháïl*.	देखउलस *dĕkhaülas*.
3rd pl. pret. ind ...	देखइलन *dĕkhaïlan*.	देखउलन *dĕkhaülan*.
2nd pl. pres. ind. ...	देखालऽ *dĕkhála*.	देखावेलऽ *dĕkháwĕla*.
3rd pl. pres. ind. ...	देखाले *dĕkhále*.	देखावेले *dĕkháwĕle*

It will be observed that the potential passive verb shortens its antepenultimate, as occurs in the case of causals. (See § 104.)

There is a tendency, which amounts almost to a rule, to drop the junction vowel of all verbs which take इ *i* in the conjugation of the tenses not derived from the past participle of the potential passive. Thus we get the following forms :—

	Usual forms, dropping the junction vowel.	Regular forms, according to § 89.
Infinitive, 3rd form	देखाब *dĕkháb.*	देखाइब *dĕkháïb.*
1st pl. fut. ...	देखाब *dĕkháb.*	देखाइब *dĕkháïb.*
2nd pl. fut. ...	देखाबऽ *dĕkhába.*	देखइबऽ *dĕkhaïba.*
1st pl. pret. conj. ...	देखातीं *dĕkhátī.*	देखइतीं *dĕkhaïtī.*
3rd pret. conj. and pres. part.	देखात *dĕkhát.*	देखाइत *dĕkháït.*

The potential passive has a peculiar force, intimating, not that a thing *is* done, but that it *can be* done. Thus ई पोथी पढ़ाला *ī pothī paṛhálá*, 'this book *can be* read,' but ई पोथी पढ़ल जाला *ī pothí paṛhal jálá*, 'this book is being read.'

§ 102. The Periphrastic Passive Voice.

A very common kind of passive voice is formed by placing the verb √ आ *á* after the first or shortest form of a verbal noun in the locative case: thus देखे में आइल *dekhĕ mĕ áil*, 'the coming into seeing,' *i.e.* 'to be seen.' The person by whom the action is done is put in the oblique genitive form of the noun or pronoun when there is one: thus तूँ हमरा देखे में ऐलऽ

tū ham'rá dekhĕ mē aila, 'you came into my seeing,' 'you were seen by me.' The following example shows a verb in this voice conjugated in the present indicative masculine:—

Singular.	Plural.
1. (मैं देखे में आवेलों *mē dekhĕ mē áwĕlō*,) ('I am seen.')	1 हमनीका देखे में आइला *hamaniká dekhĕ mē áilá*, 'we are seen.'
2. तूं देखे में आवेले *tū dekhĕ mē áwĕle*, 'thou art seen.'	2. तोहनीका देखे में आवेलऽ *tŏhaniká dekhĕ mē áwĕla*, 'you are seen.'
3. ऊ देखे में अविला *ú dekhĕ mē áwĕlá*, 'he is seen.'	3. उहाँका देखे में आवेले *uhā̆ká dekhĕ mē áwĕle*, 'they are seen.'

EXAMPLE.—हमनी का तोहरा देखे में आइला *hamaní ká tŏh'rá dekhĕ mē áilá*, 'we are seen by you,' 'you see us.' This form of the passive is especially used in the language of politeness.

CHAPTER XI.

CAUSAL VERBS.

§ 103. A causal verb is formed by adding आव *áw* to the root of the simple verb, and a double causal by adding वाव *wáw*. The stems thus formed are conjugated exactly like verbs whose roots end in आव *áw*. (See § 87.) The long vowel of आव *áw* and वाव *wáw* is, as usual, liable to be shortened in the antepenultimate of all tenses except the present indicative (see General Introduction, § 36); and if the व *wa* is followed by the neutral vowel, it becomes उ *u* (see General Introduction, § 37), which with a preceding अ *a* (see General Introduction, § 35) may be written औ *au*.

Thus, taking the simple verb √ उठ *uṭh*, 'rise,' the first plural present indicative of its causal would be regularly उठावीला *uṭháwílá*, and the first plural preterite उठवल्लीँ *uṭhaw'lí*, which, as व *wa* is followed by the neutral vowel, becomes उठउल्लीँ *uṭhaülí*, and finally उठौलीँ *uṭhaulí*.

Similarly, for the double causal the forms would be उठ॰वावीला *uṭh'wáwílá* and उठ॰वउलीँ *uṭh'waülí* or उठ॰वौलीँ *uṭh'waulí*.

The following are examples of the regular formation of causals and double causals:—

Simple Verb.	Causal.	Double Causal.
√ उठ *uṭh*, 'rise.'	उठाव *uṭháw*, 'raise.'	उठ॰वाव *uṭh'wáw*, 'cause to raise.'
√ कट *kaṭ*, 'be cut.'	कटाव *kaṭáw*, 'cut.'	कट॰वाव *kaṭ'wáw*, 'cause to cut.'
√ छिप *chhip*, 'be hidden.'	छिपाव *chhipáw*, 'hide.'	छिप॰वाव *chhip'wáw*, 'cause to hide.'
√ मिल *mil*, 'meet.'	मिलाव *miláw*, 'mix.'	मिल॰वाव *mil'wáw*, 'cause to mix'
√ सुन *sun*, 'hear.'	सुनाव *sunáw*, 'tell.'	सुन॰वाव *sun'wáw*, 'cause to tell.'

§ 104. If the simple root contains a long vowel it is shortened, viz. आ *á* to अ *a*, ई *í* to इ *i*, ऊ *ú* to उ *u*, ए *e* to ऍ *ĕ*, ओ *o* to ऒ *ŏ*, ऐ *ai* to ऐ *aĭ*, and औ *au* to औ *aŭ*.

Similarly, if a root ends in a double consonant, it is made single : thus—

Simple Verb.	Causal.	Double Causal.
√ पाक *pák*, 'be cooked.'	पकाव *pakáw*, 'cook.'	पकवाव *pak'wáw*, 'cause to cook.'
√ जाग *jág*, 'be awake.'	जगाव *jagáw*, 'awaken.'	जगवाव *jag'wáw*, 'cause to awake.'
√ धाव *dháw*, 'run.'	धवाव *dhawáw* 'cause to run.	
√ ढाँक * *ḍhā̃k*, 'cover.	ढँकाव *ḍhãkáw* 'cause to cover.'	
√ जीत *jít*, 'conquer.'	जिताव *jitáw*, 'cause to conquer.'	जितवाव *jit'wáw*, 'cause to cause to conquer.'
√ सीख *síkh*, 'learn.'	सिखाव *sikháw*, 'teach.'	सिखवाव *sikh'wáw*, 'cause to teach.'
√ पी *pí*, 'drink.'	पिआव *piáw*, 'cause to drink.'	पिअवाव *piawáw*, 'cause to cause to drink.'
√ भींग * *bhíg*, 'be wet.'	भिँगाव *bhĩgáw*, 'moisten.'	
√ घूम *ghúm*, 'be turned.'	घुमाव *ghumáw*, 'turn.'	घुमवाव *ghum'wáw*, 'cause to turn.'
√ सूत *sút*, 'sleep.'	सुताव *sutáw*, 'put to sleep.'	सुतवाव *sut'wáw*, 'cause to put to sleep.'
√ बूड़ *búṛ*, 'sink.'	बुड़ाव *buṛáw*, 'immerse.'	

* Regarding *anunásik*, see General Introduction, § 28.

Simple Verb.	Causal.	Double Causal.
डूब *ḍúb*, 'sink.'	डुबाव *ḍubáw*, 'immerse.'	
टोप *ṭop*, 'be covered.'	टोपाव *ṭŏpáw*, 'cover.'	
देख *dekh*, 'see.'	देखाव *dĕkháw*, 'show.'	देखवाव *dĕkh'wáw*, 'cause to show.'
बैस *bais*, 'sit.'	बैसाव *baïsáw*, 'seat.'	बैसवाव *baïs'wáw*, 'cause to sit.'
पैंर *paũr*, 'swim.'	पैंराव *paũráw*, 'cause to swim.'	
धौड़ *dhauṛ*, 'run.'	धौड़ाव *dhaŭṛáw*, 'cause to run.'	
लुक्क *lukk*, 'be hidden.'	लुकाव *lukáw*, 'hide.'	लुकवाव *luk'wáw*, 'cause to hide.'

Note in connection with the above :—

Simple Verb.	Causal.
कह *kah*, 'say.'	कहलाव *kah'láw* or कहाव *kaháw*.
खा *khá*, 'eat.'	खिआव *khiáw* or खिलाव *khiláw*.

§ 105. Some primitive neuter verbs, having a monosyllabic root enclosing a short vowel, form the first causal by simply lengthening that vowel. The double causal is formed in the usual way, *e.g.*—

Simple Verb.	Causal.
कट *kaṭ*, 'be cut.'	काट *káṭ*, 'cut.'
बंध *bandh*, 'be tied.'	बाँध * *bãdh*, 'tie.'
लद *lad*, 'be loaded.'	लाद *lád*, 'load.'
घिंच *ghiṅch*, 'be dragged.'	घींच * *ghích*, 'drag.'

§ 106. Sometimes a cognate diphthong is substituted for the long vowel, *e.g.*—

खुल *khul*, 'be open.'	खोल *khol*, 'open.'
घुल *ghul*. 'melt.' (*Neut.*)	घोल *ghol*, 'melt.' (*Act.*)

* When the vowel is lengthened, *anuswár* becomes *anunásik*. (See General Introduction, § 28.)

§ 107. The verb √ निकस *nikas*, 'come out,' makes its causal निकास *nikás*, 'take out,' on the analogy of the above. So also √ पसर *pasar*, 'be scattered,' makes पसार *pasár*, 'scatter,' 'extend;' √ ससर *sasar*, 'slip,' ससार *sasár*, 'cause to slip;' √ उपर *upar*, 'be rooted up,' उपार *upár*, 'root up;' and √ उखर *ukhar*, 'be rooted up,' उखार *ukhár*, 'root up.'

§ 108. (*e*) The following are irregular :—

Simple Verb.	Causal.	Double Causal.
√ अट *aṭ*, 'be stopped.'	आड़ *áṛ*, 'stop.'	अड़ाव *aṛáw*.
√ फट *phaṭ* or फाट *pháṭ* ['be torn.'	फाड़ *pháṛ* or फार *phár* ['tear.'	फड़ाव *phaṛáw* or फड़वाव [*phaṛ'wáw*. फराव *pharáw* or फरवाव [*phar'wáw*.
√ छुट *chhuṭ*, 'be sepa- [rated.'	छोड़ *chhoṛ* or छाड़ *chháṛ*, ['separate.'	छोड़ाव *chhŏṛáw*.
√ जुट *juṭ*, 'be joined.'	जोड़ *joṛ*, 'join.'	जोड़ाव *jŏṛáw*.
√ फूट *phúṭ*, 'be burst.'	फोड़ *phoṛ* or फोर *phor*, ['burst.'	फोड़ाव *phŏṛáw* or फोड़वाव [*phŏṛ'wáw*. फोराव *phoráw* or फोरवाव [*phŏr'wáw*.
√ टूट *ṭúṭ*, 'be broken.'	तूर *túr*, तूड़ *túṛ*, टूड़ *ṭúṛ*, ['break.'	तुराव *turáw* or तुड़ाव [*tuṛáw*.
√ बिक्क *bikk*, 'be sold.'	बेँच *bĕch* or बिकाव *bikáw*, ['sell,'	
√ रह *rah*, 'remain.'	राख *rákh* or रक्ख *rakkh* ['place.'	
√ मर *mar*, 'die.'	मार *már* or मुआव *muáw*, ['kill.'	

CHAPTER XII.

COMPOUND VERBS.

§ 109. Compound verbs are either intensives, potentials, completives, frequentatives, desideratives, continuatives, staticals, inceptives, permissives, or acquisitives.

§ 110. Compound verbs may be classed as—(1) those formed with the verbal noun, and (2) those formed with the participles.

(1) Those formed with the verbal noun are—

a) Intensives.	*e*) Desideratives.
b) Potentials.	*f*) Inceptives.
c) Completives.	*g*) Permissives.
d) Frequentatives.	*h*) Acquisitives.

(2) Those formed with the participles—

a) Continuatives.	*b*) Staticals.

Class I.—Compounds formed with the Verbal Noun.*

§ 111. There are three varieties of the verbal noun—

a) In अ *a* (silent), oblique form, ए *ĕ*; as देख *dekh*, obl. देखे *dekhĕ*.†

b) In ल *l*, oblique form, ला *lá*; as देखल *dekhal*, obl. देखल्ला *dĕkh'lá*.†

c) In ब *b*, oblique form, wanting; as देखब *dekhab*, obl. wanting.†

The direct first form is always the same as the root.

Compound verbs are either formed with the direct form of the first or second variety of the verbal noun, or with the oblique form of the first variety.

---

* Much of the succeeding matter is based on Kellogg's Hindí Grammar.

† Western Bhojpúrì oblique,—देखैं *dekhāi*, देखन्ले *dĕkh'le*, and देखन्बैं *dĕkh'bāi*, respectively.

§ 112. In pure Bhojpúrí *Intensives, Potentials,* and *Completives,* are always formed with the direct form of the first variety; *Frequentatives* are always formed with the direct form of the second variety; and *Desideratives* are generally so. *Inceptives, Permissives,* and *Acquisitives,* are always formed with the oblique form of the first variety. In Western Bhojpúrí, the practice is different.

113. *Intensive* compounds intensify or otherwise modify the meaning of the verb whose root stands first in the compound. They are formed by adding to a verbal noun of the first variety in the direct form one of certain other verbs, which latter verb in conjunction with the verbal noun is then conjugated as usual. This second conjugated member does not, however, retain its separate character and significance, but only modifies, in accordance with the general idea which it embodies, the meaning of the unconjugated verbal noun to which it is annexed. Examples are—

फेँकल *phēkal*, 'to throw.'	फेँक देल *phēk del*, 'to throw away.'
टूरल *túral*, 'to break.'	टूर डालल *túr ḍálal*, 'to break in pieces.'
बनल *banal*, 'to be made.'	बन आइल *ban áil* or बन जाइल *ban jáil*, 'to be completed.'
खाइल *kháil*, 'to eat.'	खा जाइल *khá jáil*, 'to eat up.'
बोलल *bolal*, 'to speak.'	बोल उठल *bol uṭhal*, 'to speak suddenly.'
काटल *káṭal*, 'to cut.'	काट लेल *káṭ lel*, 'to cut for oneself.'
राखल *rákhal*, 'to place.'	राख लेल *rákh lel*, 'to lay by.'

§ 114. The auxiliary verbs usually employed to form intensives are—

देल *del*, 'to give,'	implying	*intensity.*
डालल *ḍálal*, 'to throw,'	,,	*violence.*
आइल *áil*, 'to come,' / जाइल *jáil*, 'to go,'	,,	*completion.*
पड़ल *paṛal* or परल *paral*, 'to fall,'	,,	*chance.*
उठल *uṭhal*, 'to rise,'	,,	*suddenness.*
लेल *lel*, 'to take,'	,,	*reflexiveness.*

पड़ल *paṛal* is also used in intensive compounds to form passives of transitive verbs. (See § 100.)

§ 115. *Potentials* are formed by adding to the same form of the verbal noun of any verb the verb सकल *sakal,* 'to be able,' which may then be conjugated throughout. Examples are—

बोल सकल *bol sakal,* 'to be able to speak.'

ऊ धौड़ सकला *ú dhauṛ sakalá,* 'he can run.'

हम जा सकब (or सकीला) *ham já sakab* (or *sakílá*), 'I shall be able to go.'

उन्हन्नीका आ सकन्लन *unh'níká á sak'lan,* 'they were able to come.'

हम नाहीं जा सकीं *ham náhí já sakí,* 'I cannot go.'

§ 116. *Completives* are formed by adding to the same form of the verbal noun of a verb the verb चुकल *chukal,* 'to be finished,' which may then be conjugated throughout. This compound denotes the *completion* of the act denoted by the primary member of the compound. Examples are—

ऊ खा चुकल *ú khá chukal,* 'he has done eating.'

जब ऊ खा चुकी *jab ú kha chukí,* 'when he shall have eaten.'

ऊ तऽ जा चुकल *ú ta já chukal,* 'he is indeed already gone.'

§ 117. *Frequentatives* are formed by affixing to the direct form of the second variety of the verbal noun of any verb the verb करल *karal,* 'to do.' which may then be used in any tense. Examples are—

आइल करऽ *áïl kara,* 'come often,' *lit.* 'do the act of coming.'

ऊ कहल करेला *ú kahal karělá,* 'he is in the habit of saying.'

हम सासन्तर पढ़ल करीला *ham sás'tar paṛhal karílá,* 'I am in the habit of reading the shástras.'

तूँ हमार बात मानल करऽ *tû hamár bát mánal kara,* 'always obey my words.'

तूँ काहे ऐसन कइल करलऽ *tû káhě aisan kaïl karala,* 'why do you always do so?'

ऊ जाइल करेला *ú jáil karělá,* 'he often goes.'

The Western Bhojpúrí idiom is illustrated by the phrases देखै करल *dekhaň karal,* देखल करल *dekhal karal,* or देखन्बै करल *děkh'baň karal,* 'to see frequently.'

§ 118. ***Desideratives*** are formed, like frequentatives, with the direct form of the verbal noun in ल *l*, substituting the verb चाहल *cháhal* for करल *karal* as the second or conjugated member. These denote primarily *desire* to do the action expressed of the principal member ; secondarily, the *immediate futurity* of that action. Examples are—

ऊ बोलल चाहत बा *ú bolal cháhat bá*, 'he wishes to speak.'

घड़ी बाजल चाहत बाटे *ghaṛí bájal cháhat báṭe*, 'the clock is on the point of striking.'

Sometimes the principal verb is put in the oblique form of the first variety of the verbal noun with or without the dative postposition के *ke* or ला *lá*. Examples are—

घड़ी बाजे चाहत रहे *ghaṛí bájĕ cháhat rahe*, 'the clock was about to strike.'

ऊ बोले के चाहला *ú bolĕ ke cháhalá*, 'he wishes to speak.'

ऊ मुए (or मरे) चाहऽता *ú muĕ* (or *marĕ*) *cháh'tá*, 'he is on the point of death.'

ऊ जाए के चाहऽता *ú jáĕ ke cháh'tá*, 'he wishes to go.'

भेजे ला चाहीला *bhejĕ lá cháhílá* , 'I wish to send.'

Generally the form with के *ke* or ला *lá* expresses desire, and the form without these postpositions immediate futurity.

The desiderative compound in the precative form with चाही *cháhí* is idiomatically used to express obligation or duty. Examples are—

ई पोथी के पढ़ल चाही *í pothí ke paṛhal cháhí*, '(one) ought to read this book.' (*Lit.* 'be good enough to wish to read.')

तोहरा उहाँ जाए के चाही *tŏh'rá uhá̃ jáĕ ke cháhí*, 'it is right for you (*i.e.* you ought) to go there.'

The Western Bhojpúrí idiom is illustrated by the phrases देखैं चाहल *dekhaĩ cháhal*, देखल चाहल *dekhal cháhal*, or देखनै चाहल *dĕkh'baĩ cháhal*, 'to wish to see.'

§ 119. *Inceptives* are formed by using the inflected form of the first variety of the verbal noun in construction with the verb लागल *lágal*, 'to be joined to,' 'to begin,' and denote the action of the verbal noun as *beginning*. Examples are—

कहे लागल *kahĕ lágal*, 'he began to say.'

मारे लागल *márĕ lágal*, 'he began to beat.'

बाघ खाए लागल *bágh kháĕ lágal*, 'the tiger began to eat.'

The Western Bhojpúrí idiom is illustrated by the phrases देखै लागल *dekhaĭ lágal* or देखब्बै लागल *dĕkh'baĭ lágal*, 'to begin to see.'

§ 120. *Permissives* are formed by combining the same form of the verbal noun with the verb देल *del*, 'to give,' and express *permission* to do the act denoted by the verbal noun. Examples are—

हमरा के जाए द० *ham'rá ke jáĕ da*, 'let me go.'

हमरा के बोले दीहीं *ham'rá ke bolĕ díhí*, 'be good enough to let me speak.'

ऊ ओकरा के खाए देलस *ú ŏk'rá ke kháĕ delas*, 'he allowed him to eat.'

The Western Bhojpúrí idiom is illustrated by the phrases देखै देल *dekhaĭ del* or देखब्बै देल *dĕkh'baĭ del*, 'to allow to see.'

§ 121. *Acquisitives* are the exact converse of the preceding, and are formed in the same way, substituting पावल *páwal*, 'to get,' for देल *del*. Examples are—

तूँ उहाँ जाए ना पइब० *tú uhā̃ jáĕ ná païba*, 'you will not obtain permission to go there.'

हम बैसे ना पौलीं *ham baisĕ ná paulí*, 'I was not allowed to sit.'

Class II.—Compounds formed with the Participles.

§ 122. *Continuatives* are formed by combining the present participle of any verb with the verbs जाइल *jáil*, 'to go,' or रहल *rahal*, 'to remain. The compound with जाइल *jáil* expresses *steady progression*, and with रहल *rahal* the *continuance* of a complete action. Examples—

ऊ लिखित जात बाटे *ú likhit ját báṭe*, 'he is going on writing.'

ऊ लरिकी पढ़त जात रहली स॰ *ú lariki paṛhat ját rah'li sa,* } 'those girls were going on reading.'

पानी बहत जात बाटे *páni bahat ját báṭe,* 'the water keeps flowing away.'

ऊ गावत रहले *ú gáwat rahale,* 'they continue singing.'

तोहनी काहे हँसत रहल *tõhaní káhĕ hãsat rahala,* 'why do you keep laughing?'

नदी के धार बहत रहेला *nadí kĕ dhár bahat rahĕlá,* 'the stream of the river keeps flowing on.'

The Western Bhojpúrí idiom is illustrated by the phrases देखै पावल *dekhaĭ páwal* or देखबै पावल *dĕkh'baĭ páwal,* 'to be allowed to see.'

Closely connected with the above is a common combination in which the past instead of the present participle takes the first place and a verb of motion the second place. Examples are—

एक बाघ पड़ल फिरत रहे *ĕk bágh paṛal phirat rahe,* 'a tiger was prowling about.'

लौँड़ी चलल जात रहे *lãũṛí chalal ját rahe,* 'a girl was going away.'

§ 123. *Staticals* denote motion in a state of doing anything. They are formed by combining a verb of motion with a present participle. Examples are—

ऊ रोअत आवत बा *ú roat áwat bá,* 'he comes weeping.'

एगो मेहरारू गावत आवत रहे *ego mĕh'rárú gáwat áwat rahe,* 'a woman came singing.'

DIVISION III.

INDECLINABLES.

§ 124. See General Introduction.

APPENDIX I.

THE following selections are in the Bhojpúrí dialect of Sáran. They were translated for me by Bisesar Parśád of Dahiáw, in that district. A translation will be found in the General Introduction.

SELECTIONS FROM THE BHOJPÚRÍ DIALECT.

CONVERSATION BETWEEN TWO VILLAGERS.

१ प्रश्न कहऽ भाई, कहवाँ सेँ आवेलऽ ?

उत्तर परोसे का गाँव सेँ आवत बानी ।

२ प्र. ओहिजा सेँ कब चलल रहीं ?

उ. सँवकेरे के चलल हवीं ।

३ प्र. काहे खातिर ऊहाँ गइल रहलीं हाँ ?

उ. उहवाँ हमार खेत बाटे, जहे देखे गइल रहलीं हाँ ।

४ प्र. ओह में का बोअल बा ?

उ. धानी रहर बोअल बाटे ।

५ प्र. कहऽ भाई, अबकी जजात के कइसन रङ्ग बा ?

उ. एह फसिल के का हाल पुछले बाड़ऽ ; बरखा बिना अनेर हो गइल ।

६ प्र. आज काल्ह रउरा भाई के नइखीं देखत ?

उ. हमार भाई आज काल्ह जिला में नोकर बाड़; एने का ओर बहुत कम आवेले ।

७ प्र. आज काल्ह अपन्ने का बड़की गाय के का हाल हवे ?

उ. ऊ आज काल्ह गाभिन बा, बाकी सेहन्ना नइखे मीलत, तेही* सेँ दूबरि बाटे ।

---

* Emphatic form of तेह सेँ.

८ प्र. कऽ महीना सँ गाभिन बा ?

उ. आठ महीना तऽ भइल, बाकी ओकर पेट ऊँच नइखे बुझात *।

९ प्र. कोँहनरवतिया कि अबन्ही ना ?

उ. हँ, तनी तनी बुझात बा।

१० प्र. ई एकर कऽ बियान भइल ? केतन्ना दूध करेले ?

उ. ई एकर अठएँ बियान हऽ। दू अढ़ाई सेर दूध एक जून करेले।

११ प्र. हमन्रा एगो बकन्री कीने के बा ; रवाँ गाँवे मीली ?

उ. हमन्रा गाँवे बकन्री तऽ बाड़ी सऽ, बाकी दामे बड़ कड़ा बा।

१२ प्र. अपन्ने के बकन्री का भइल ?

उ. हम चरे खातिर ओ के गाँवन्ही ढिलन्हे * रहीले।

१३ प्र. किछु दूध करेले ?

उ. लड़िकन के पीए भर हो जाला।

१४ प्र. अबन्रिक ऊखि बोअले बाडऽ की ना ?

उ. ऊखि तऽ बोअले बानी, बाकि ओह मेँ किछु जान नइखे।

१५ प्र. रवाँ हिआँ सेँ बरन्हा मोटि मील सकेला ?

उ. काहे ना ? पठउनी भइला पर ले लेब।

१६ प्र. रवाँ हिआँ कऽ गो मोटि चलेला ?

उ. तीन गो मोटि तऽ नधन्ले बानी।

१७ प्र. राउर आम के बगइचा किछु फरेला की ना ?

उ. एह बेरी तऽ बदन्री सेँ फोड़नि मेँ मधुआ लागि गइल; नाही तऽ बड़े फरत रहल हा।

१८ प्र. थोरिका थांम हमन्रो के अचार खातिर पेठा देब ?

उ. जब रवाँ मन मेँ आवे, तबे आ के तुरन्वा लीहीँ।

१९ प्र. राउर लड़िका किछु पढ़ेले की ना ?

---

* Potential passive pres. part. with negative auxiliary, forming the periphrastic present.

† From √ होब.

उ. हँ कुछ कोसौँ जाले; बहुत तऽ चिन्हले बाड़े, बाकि आज काल्ह पढ़ाइ बढ़ल्ताड़े।

१० प्र. इस्कोल मेँ काहे ना भेजौँ ?

उ किछु सीख लेहु, तऽ भेज देब।

११ प्र हमहूँ अपना लड़िका के इस्कोल मेँ भेजे के चाहताड़ौँ ?

उ. बेस; तऽ हमरा लड़िका का संङ्गे ओकरो के भेज दौँ।

FABLES.

पहिल बात।

मुरगा आउर मोती के दाना।

एगो मुरगा गोबर का ढेरी के बैँगुर सेँ उटकोरत रहे। एके बेर एगो बड़ि बुक के मोती निकल आइल। मुरगा कहलस, अहा, एकर सूरत सकल आउर जोत कैसन बा, परखिया एकरा के पाइत, खुसी सेँ फूल जाइत। बाकि हमार भूख एकरा सेँ ना जाई। हाए, एगो चाउर के दाना हमरा मीलित तऽ सेगो मोती सेँ बढ़ जाइत। साँच हऽ, जे अपना काम मेँ ना आइल, से चूल्हा भण्डार मेँ जाए॥

दोसर बात।

कँगाल के पूछल आउर अतीत के जबाब दीहल।

एगो दुखिया केहू सिध महातमा सेँ आ के पुछलस के, हम भूखेँ मरौँ, आउर हमार परोसिया राज भोग सेँ दिन रात चैन करस; ओकरा मेँ कौन अइसन गुन बाटे, जे राम जी अतिना दिहलन आउर हमरा के दुखिया बनौलन। ई बात सुन के, बाबा जी बोलले, काहे बाबा, तूँ ई ना सुनले हऽ, राम जी ऊपर हो के सभका के देखत रहेलन; जेकर जइसन कमाई होला, तेकरा के तइसन देलन॥

तीसर बात ।

देस बिदेस फिरऽला के लाभ ।

केहू भल अदिमी कौनो बाबा जी सेँ पुछऽलेन के, महाराज जी, रवाँ देस देस गाँवे गाँव फिरऽला सेँ का मीलेला । एक ठाईं बइस के राम राम काहे नाँ करीं । कौनो मठिया मेँ बइस के परऽमेसर के गुन काहे ना गाईं । बाबा जी कहऽलन, बाबा, ई साँच हऽ, बाकि ई कहाउत तूँ नाँ सुनऽलऽ हऽ, बहत पानी साफ रहेला जमल पानी गमक जाला । साधु लोग के फिरऽले अइसन अच्छा हऽ, जे मेँ उन के दाग नाँ लागे ॥

चउठ बात ।

एक दीन जार का दीन मेँ केहू बड़ा* अदिमी का घर मेँ आगि लागल, उनऽकर सभ चीज बतुस जर के राख हो गइल । ऊ बहऽरा खड़ा हो के पछऽतावा करत रहस । एतऽना मेँ एगो गरीब अदिमी, जार का मारे, थर थर काँपत, घर सेँ निकस आइल, आउर हाथ के सेंके लागल । तब ऊ अमीर अदिमी बोलऽले; बाह जि बाह, केहू के घर जरे केहू तापे ॥

पचईं बात ।

बान्हल लऽकड़ी, आउर खुलल लकऽड़ी ।

एगो गिरऽहस्त के लड़िकन अपऽनन्ह मेँ लरत झगऽरत रहस; बात सेँ बहुत बुझाउलस बाकि ऊ सभ ना मनऽले । गिरऽहस्त अपऽना मन मेँ कहऽलस के, जब ले हम ई लोग के आँखि सेँ किछु ना देखाइब तब ले ना बुझिहेँ । ऊ एक दीन अपऽना बेटन के बोलउलस, आउर कहऽलस के, थोरे लकऽड़ी हमऽरा सामऽने ले आवऽ । गिरऽहस्त ऊ लकऽड़ी सभ के एक रसऽरी मेँ कस के बान्हऽलस । तब ऊ सभ सेँ कहऽलस के रसऽरी अन खोलऽ आउर लकऽड़ी सभ के टूड़ डालऽ । ऊ सभ बहुत जोर कइलन, बाकि किछुओ ना भइल । फिर गिरऽहस्त खोल के एक एक गो लकऽड़ी इन के देलस, ओकऽरा के ऊ लोग तुरन्ते तूर देले । तब उनऽकर बाप कहऽलस के, ए बेटा तूँ लोग बान्हल लकऽड़ी के नीयर अपऽनन्ह मेँ मीलल रहबऽ, तऽ सभ मुदइ के दबउले रहबऽ; आउर जब अलग अलग होइबऽ तऽ बूझऽ के बिगर गइलऽ । अलग अलग भइला सेँ बिगऽरल ।

* Obl. of बड़.

छठईं बात।

ऊँड़ाड़ आउर भैंड़ी के मेल।

एक दीन ऊँड़ाड़ भैंड़ी सँ कह भेजऽलस के, आवऽ, हम आउर तोहनीका अपऽन्ह मैं मेल करीं; काहे अपऽनन्ह मैं लरीं, आउर आपन अपऽना जान के गाहक रहीं। ईहे पाजी कुत्ता लराई के जड़ हवे सऽ। असऽन्हीं सब जगे भूक भूक हमनी के लरावत फिरेले सऽ, आउर हमऽरा तोहऽरा सँ झगऽरा करावेले सऽ। इनऽका के हमऽरा इहऽवाँ भेज दऽ। फिनु झगऽरा का बा। हमऽरा आउर तोहऽरा मैं सभ दीन सलाह आउर मेल रही। तऽ एको तोहर बार टेढ़ ना होई। गँवार भैंड़ी ऊ नटऽखट ऊँड़ाड़ के बात मान लेलस, आउर कुत्ता सभ के ऊँड़ाड़ का लगे भेज देलस। पहिले तऽ ऊँड़ाड़ कुत्ता सभ के खा गइल, फिनु भैंड़ी का पीछे हाथ धो के परल, आउर थोरऽही दीन मैं सभ भैंड़ी के खा गइल॥ साँच हऽ, दुसऽमन सभ दीन धोखा देला; ऊ बड़ गँवार हऽ जे दुसऽमन के साँच बुझेला॥

सतईं बात।

बाघ आउर ऊँड़ाड़ आउर चीता।

एक दीन बाघ आउर ऊँड़ाड़ आउर चीता अपऽनन मैं ई बात गोचर कइले के, हमनी का मील के सिकार करीं। फिनु अपऽनन्ह मैं बाँट लीं। ई बात ठहऽरा के बन मैं कूदे फाने लगऽन्ले, आउर एगो बड़ऽका एक हरीन करिया मारऽलन सऽ। तब बाघ बोलल के आवऽ, एकऽरा के बाँट लीं, आउर तुरन्तऽहीं ओकऽरा के तीन टूका कर दिहऽले सऽ, आउर गरज के बोलल के, पहिल टुकऽड़ा तऽ हम लेब, काहे के हम बन के राजा हईं, दोसऽरो हमऽहीं लेब, काहे के एकऽरा का मारे मैं बड़ि मेहऽनत कइलीं हँ; आउर तीसर टुकऽड़ा ईहे धइल बा, देखीं तऽ केकर टँगऽरी परेला के हमऽरा सामऽन्हे सँ उठा ले जाला। ई सुन के चीता आउर ऊँड़ाड़ पोंछ दबा के भगऽन्ले, आउर बाघ अकेले हरीन के खा गइल। ई कहाउत साँच हऽ, जेकर लाठी ओकऽरे भइँस॥

आठईं बात।

माटी आउर पीतर का घइला के बातऽचीत।

एक बेर कहिँ नदी बढ़ल रहे, ओह मैं एगो पीतर के घइला, आउर एगो माटी के घइल बहल जात रहे। पीतर के घइला माटी का घइला सँ कहऽलस के, हमऽरा साथ लागल

चलऽ, तऽ हम तोहन्रा के बचा लेब। माटी के घइला बोलल, ई बात अपन्ने बहुत अच्छा कहन्लौं, हम अपन्ना के भला मानब आउर सदा गुन गाइब; बाकि सच पूछौं, तऽ हमन्रा ई डर बा, कतन्हौं पानी का लहर का धक्का सेँ अपन्ने का पास ना आरहौं; काहे के अपन्ना फरक रहन्लौं, तो ऐसेही हिलत भूलत कतन्हूँ तीर पर आ पहुँचब; बाकि जौं अपन्ने सेँ भेँट भइल, आउर कतन्हूँ भूल सेँ ठोकर लग गइल, तो हमार पेट फाट जाई। सच बा, बड़न सेँ आस रक्खौं, बाकि लगे ना जाईं॥

नवईं बात।

एगो मुन्सी बजार मेँ बइसल चिट्ठी लीखत रहस। एगो परन्देसी अइले, आउर कहन्ले, मुनन्सी जी, का लीखत बानौं। मुनन्सी जी जवाब दिहन्ले के, भाई, चिट्ठी लीखन्तानौं। तब ऊ कहन्ले के, हमन्रो सलाम लीख दीहल जाईं। मुनन्सी जी कहन्ले के नाहीं जी, अरन्जी लीखत बानौं, तब ऊ कहन्ले के, हमन्रो सही कर दौं। मुनन्सी जी अगुता के कहन्ले के, तमस्सुक लीखन्तानौं, तब ऊ कहन्ले के, हमार गोवाही लीख दौं। मुनन्सी जी, बिचार कइलन, ई तऽ केहू अजब ढङ्ग के अदिमी देखाइ देत बाड़। पुछन्ले के, अपन्ने के नाम का हऽ। तब ऊ हँसन्ले, आउर कहन्ले के, हमार नाम ईहे हऽ, मान चाहे मत मान, हम तोहार मेहन्मान॥

दसईं बात।

एगो बड़ा अदिमी का घर मेँ रात के आगि लागल, ऊ तऽ आपन बाल बच्चा समेत निकस के भगन्ले, आउर नोकर के हुकुम देले, कि चीज बतुस निकासऽ। एहि मेँ आगि बहुत लहक गइल; सभ घर लहन्रे लागल। नोकर कहन्ले के, हम कौन कौन चीज निकासौं, तब ऊ बड़ अदिमी पछुता के कहन्ले, बाबा, मकान मेँ आगि लागल बा, जे निकन्से सेहौं लाभ॥

इगारन्हौं बात।

गँवार अहिरिन।

एगो गँवार अहिरिन माँथ पर दही के हँड़िया रखन्ले चल जात रहे। चलत चलत ओकन्रा मन मेँ ई उमङ्ग उठल के, ई दही के बेँचब, आउर ढेबुआ सेँ आम कीनब; किछु आम हमन्रा पास बा, सभ मिला के तीन से सेँ किछु बढ़ जाई। ए मेँ किछु सड़ जाई; बाकि तँ, अढ़ाई से तो बच जाई। आउर ओह मेँ सेँ जे बच जाई ओकर अच्छा दाम मीली, तऽ

छिपरी मेँ एगो हरिअर सारी कीनब। हँ, हँ, हरिअर सारी हमऽरा मुँह पर अच्छा सोभी आउर जब हम तऽ हरिअरे सारी लेब; आउर ओकऽरा के पहिन के मेला जाइब; आउर खूब अइँठ के अपऽना कपऽड़ा गहऽना के सोभा आउर मुँह के चमक दमक देखाइब; आउर बास मेँ से से गो ओढ़ आइब। अइसन सोच बिचार मेँ गँवार अहिरिन कुच्छो चमक के ठेढ़ चलल, के दही के हँड़िया ओकऽरा माँथ सेँ गिर के चूर चूर हो गइल, आउर सभ बर बनल बनावल बिगड़ गइल॥

बारऽहौँ बात।

चील्ह आउर कउआ।

एगो चील्ह का ठोर मेँ घोँघा रहे। कितऽनऊँ धरऽती पर पटकऽलस, बाकि टूटल नाँ। तऽ एगो कउआ ओकऽरा के कहऽलस के, एह घोँघा के ठोर मेँ ले के बड़ुत ऊँच उड़ जा, आउर उहऽवाँ सेँ गिरा दऽ तऽ घोँघा टूट जाई। चील्ह कहऽलस के, ई बड़ुत अच्छा कहत बा, आउर घोँघा के ले के उड़ गइल, आउर बड़ुत ऊँच जा के गिरा दिहऽलस। जइसे घोँघा धरऽती पर गिरल, के टुकऽड़ा टुकऽड़ा हो गइल, आउर कउआ ओकर गूदा खा गइल। थोरा देर मेँ चील्ह नीचे उतऽरल, तऽ खोइआ छाड़ के आउर किछुओ ना पउलस॥

तेरऽहौँ बात।

खट्टा अँगूर।

एगो खिखिर कौनो फुलऽवारी मेँ गइल; देखऽलस के अँगूर के अइसन घवद पाँकल टाठी पर लटऽकल बा, के जेह मेँ सेँ रस चूअत बा, आउर केहू रखऽवारो ना रहे। ई देख के ओकऽरा बड़ लालच भइल। ऊ बड़ुत कूदल फानल बाकि अँगूर का घवद के भीरे ना पहुँचल। जब कौनो तरह सेँ दाव ना लागल, तऽ अइसन बरऽबरात उहऽवाँ सेँ चलल. के खट्टा अँगूर के खाए जाव॥

चउदऽहौँ बात।

रसाइनी।

एगो रसाइनी केहू बड़ा अदिमी सेँ कहऽलस, जोँ तूँ किछु चाँदी हमऽरा इहऽवाँ ले आवऽ, तऽ हम एक अइसन जड़ी एह मेँ गाड़ौँ के तुरन्त ही ऊ चाँदी सोना हो जाए। ऊ लोभ अदिमी ओकऽरा दमऽपट्टी मेँ आ गइल, आउर कहीँ सेँ दुख सुख सह के दू से रुपैया के चाँदी ऊ रसाइनी के आन दिहऽले। रसाइनी ओही* रात के बिछउना उठा के कहीँ चल

* Emphatic for ओह.

दिहऽलस। तब ऊ बिधाता गरीब दुख मेँ पर के, ओह नटऽखट रधाइनी के खोज म दउरल फिरल, बन बन छान डलऽलस बाकि कतऽहीँ रखाइनी के पता ना लागल। एकऽरा के एह तरह सेँ घबऽड़ाइल देख के, एगो आदिमी कहऽलस के, तोहऽरा सेँ भूल भइल, के ओह नटऽखट अधीन के फन्दा मेँ परऽलऽ, आउर अब पछतावताड़ऽ। ओकऽरा खोज मेँ दउर धूप करला सेँ अब किछुओ नइऽखे होखत। एह बात पर एक बात तोहऽरा के कहत बानी, जेकऽरा के सभ दिना इआद करिहऽ॥

पन्द्रऽहीँ बात।

एगो चिरईँ केहू गिरऽहस्त का गाछी मेँ जा के कचा पाकल फल सभ के सभ काट के गिरा देत रहे, तऽ गिरऽहस्त सभ दिना ओकऽरा ताक मेँ रहे, एक दीन अँगूर का डाटी पर जाल लगा के ओकऽरा के धइलस, आउर मुआवे के चहऽलस। तऽ चिरईँ गिरऽहस्त सेँ कहऽलस के, जोँ तूँ हमऽरा के छाड़ दऽ, तऽ हम ई भलाई का बदऽला मेँ तोहऽरा के बहुत बात बता देब, जेह मेँ तोहऽरा बड़ लाभ होई॥ गिरऽहस्त कहऽलस के, पहिले बता दऽ तऽ तोहऽरा के छाड़ दीँ। चिरईँ तीन गो बात कहऽलस, एक तऽ ई बात जे, दुसऽमन अपऽना अखऽतियार मेँ आ जाए, तऽ छाड़े के ना चाही, दोसर जे बात अपऽना बुध मेँ ना आवे, तऽ ओकऽरा के ना माने के, तीसर बीतल बात के ना पछऽतावे के। आउर चउथ बात एगो आउर बा, के जब तूँ हमऽरा के छाड़ देबऽ तऽ कहब। गिरऽहस्त ई बात सुन के अइसन कहऽलस जइसऽने कहलस, आउर ऊ चिरईँ के छाड़ दिहऽलस। चिरईँ भीत पर बइस के कहऽलस के, हमऽरा पेट मेँ मुरगा का अण्डा सेँ ओ बड़ऽहन एगो मोती बा, जोँ तूँ हमऽरा के ना छाड़ितऽ, आउर मार दिहितऽ, तऽ ऊ मोती तोहऽरा हाथ लागित। गिरऽहस्त पछऽताए लागल। तऽ ऊ कहऽलस, ए गँवार, तेँ हमार तीनो बात अबऽहीँ भूल गइलस; काहे के हम तोहार दुसऽमन हईँ जब धइलऽ, तऽ छाड़े के नाँ चाहत रहे; आउर मुरगा का अण्डा के बराबर तऽ हमऽहीँ नइखीँ, फिर ऊ मुरगा का अण्डा सेँ बढ़ के हमऽरा पेट मेँ रहल, [illegible] बुध मेँ आ सकेला। बाकि तूँ एह बात पर भरोसा करऽलऽ, आउर जोँ अब तोहऽरा हाथ सेँ निकस गइलीँ, तऽ पछऽतउला सेँ का होला। एह सेँ ईहे फल निकऽसत बाटे, के पहिलहिँ सेँ सभ काम सोच बिचार के करे के चाही, आउर जेँ काम बिगर जाए, तऽ पछऽतावे के ना चाही॥

सोरःही बात।

केहू धनी के दूगो लरिका रहन्ले। जब उन कर बाप मर गइले, तठ दूनू भाई धन आपुस में बाँट लिहन्ले। बड़ भाई आपन रुपैया पइसा सुख चैन आउर खेल तमासा में उरावे लगन्ले, आउर छोट भाई जतन सँ बनिआई बेपार करे लगन्ले। एक दीन बड़ भाई छोटा भाई सँ ओरहन्ना दे के कहन्लस के, ए भाई, काहे दीन भर अनाज तउलत रहेलठ; हमन्रा साथ रहठ, खा पीअ, चैन करठ। बहुत दीन का बाद, जब छोट भाई लेन देन के बहुत रुपैया बिटोरन्ले, तठ उनन्कर बड़ भाई, जे राग रङ्ग खेल तमासा में आपन सभ धन उड़ा के भिखार हो गइले, उनन्का दुआर पर आ के कहे लगन्ले के, ए भाई, हम तोहन्रा के हन्सी में उड़ावत रहन्लीं। जों हमन्हूँ तोहन्रा लेखा बनिआई बेपार करन्तीं, आउर अनाज तउलन्तीं, तठ आज पाव भर अनाज एने ओने सँ माँग के ना खइतीं। साँच हठ; आसन्कत अइसन्ने कीड़ा हठ, के धन के धुर कर देला।

सतरःहीं बात।

लालची कुत्ता।

एक कुत्ता नदी का तीर पर हाड़ पउलस, आउर मुँह में ले लेलस। जइसीहीं परिछाहीं ओकर पानी में देखन्लस तइसेहीं समुझन्लस के दोसर हाड़ बाटे। मारे लालच के मुँह खोलन्लस, के ओकन्रो के पानी सँ निकास लीं। तठ ऊ हाड़ जे मुँह में रहे सेहू गिर गइल। साँच हठ, माँछी बइसल दूध पर, पाँख गइल लपटाए, हाथ मीँचे आउर माँथ पीटे, लालच बड़ि बलाए।

APPENDIX II.

BHOJPÚRÍ SONGS.

The following songs have been collected in the Sháhábád district with the help of Munshí Rádhá Lál, Deputy Inspector of Schools.

In reading them it must be remembered that (as in all poetry) there are no silent final consonants, as there are in prose. Thus सुभ is pronounced in poetry *subha*, while in prose it is *subh*.

In poetry, also, there is no neutral vowel. Thus, while in prose for 'you saw' we should say देख॰लस *dĕkh'las*, in poetry we should say देखलस *dekhalasa*.

Each line contains a certain number of instants, which is noted at the top of each song. A short syllable contains one instant, and a long syllable contains two. The rules for the quantity of syllables are nearly the same as in Latin. Sometimes a long syllable is read as a short one. Such cases I have marked with a perpendicular stroke over the long syllable. Thus सोँना in the first line of the first song. In this word both syllables are naturally long, but they are read as if they were short to suit the metre.

Many of the following songs contain words like रे, ना, हो राम, which are mere expletives, used to fill up the metre, and are not translated.

Several old oblique forms will be found noted in these songs, which are not given in the grammar.

The first three songs are specimens of those sung at marriages.

॥ १ ॥ मङ्गल ॥

(Metre : 6 + 4 + 4 + 2, + 4 + 4 + 4 = 28 instants.)

सुभ होऊ, सुभ होऊ, सुभ होऊ मङ्गल ।
सुभ होऊ सीता के बियाह हे ॥ ॥ १ ॥

सुभ होऊ, सुभ होऊ, सुभ होऊ परिछन ।
सुभ होऊ बर जनवास हे ॥ ॥ २ ॥

सुभ होऊ, सुभ होऊ, सुभ होऊ चुमवन ।
सुभ होऊ मण्डप आजु हे ॥ ॥ ३ ॥

सुभ होऊ, सुभ होऊ, सुभ होऊ बन्दन ।
सुभ होऊ बन्दनिहार हे ॥ ॥ ४ ॥

सुभ होऊ दुलहा ओ सुभ होऊ दुलहिन ।
सुभ होऊ धियां के सोहाग हे ॥ ॥ ५ ॥

सुभ होऊ समधि ओ सुभ होऊ समधिन ।
सुभ होऊ सकल समाज हे ॥ ॥ ६ ॥

सुभ होऊ ब्राह्मन ओ सुभ होऊ नउवा ।
सुभ होऊ नवकु तोहार हे ॥ ॥ ७ ॥

सुभ होऊ नैहर ओ सुभ होऊ सासुर ।
सुभ होऊ बर के बिलास हे ॥ ॥ ८ ॥

अम्बिका प्रसाद नित सुभहि मनावत ।
सुभ होऊ कन्या के सोहाग हे ॥ ॥ ९ ॥

A Blessing sung at Marriages.[1]

1. May the marriage of Sítá be thrice happy and auspicious.

2. Thrice happy be the *parichhan*,[2] and happy be the bridegroom and his party.[3]

---

[1] Marriage songs are generally written as if intended for recital at the marriage of Rám and Sítá or of Mahádeb and Gaurí. In the present one the bride is called Sítá.

[2] *Parichhan* is the ceremony performed when the bridegroom leaves his own house for the bride's, and also when he arrives at the latter.

[3] जनवास is the place set apart for lodging the bridegroom's companions.

3. Thrice happy be the scattering of rice,[1] and happy be the marriage canopy[2] to-day.

4. Thrice happy be the offering of garments,[3] and happy be the offerer.

5. Happy be the bridegroom, and happy be the bride, and happy be the married life of the damsel.[4]

6. Happy be the father-in-law,[5] and happy be the mother-in-law, and happy be the whole assembly.

7. Happy be the bráhman, and happy be the barber.[6] Happy be the ceremony of the cutting of thy nails.

8. Happy be the house of the bridegroom's father, and happy be that of the father of the bride. Happy be the bridegroom's honey-moon.

9. Ambiká Prasád[7] prays continually in the morning[8] that the married life of the damsel may be happy.

---

[1] चुमवन is a ceremony in which the bride and bridegroom are worshipped, while the female members of the household scatter rice over them.

[2] मण्डप is the thatch or canopy raised in the court-yard under which the marriage ceremony takes place.

[3] बन्दन is a ceremony in which the elder brother of the bridegroom offers ornaments and garments to the bride.

[4] धी means daughter: धिया is either the oblique form or the long form of the word.

[5] There is no word in English to express the relationship involved in the word समधी (*fem.* समधिन). When two persons are married, the father of one is *sam'dhí* to the father of the other.

[6] A barber cuts the nails of the bride and bridegroom just before the marriage. This ceremony is called *nah'chhu.*

[7] This is the name of the poet. Custom dictates that the last line of every poem, called the *bhanita*, should contain the name of the author.

[8] सुभहि is an old locative form. This old form in हि is common in poetry. Its use is not, however, confined to the locative.

॥ २ ॥ मङ्गल ॥

(Metre : 6 + 4 + 4 + 2, + 4 + 4 + 4 = 28 instants.)

पाँच सोहागिनि परिछन चलली ।
चौमुख दीयां संम्हारि हे ॥ ॥ १ ॥
पाँच सोहागिनि चुमवन चलली ।
गौरि गनेस मनाइ हे ॥ ॥ २ ॥
पाँच सोहागिनि खीर खियावत ।
गावत मङ्गल गान हे ॥ ॥ ३ ॥
पाँच सोहागिनि उबटन करहीँ ।
राम सिया बैठाइ हे ॥ ॥ ४ ॥
पाँच सोहांगिनि भुखन पहनावत ।
राम सरूप निहारि हे ॥ ॥ ५ ॥
पाँच सोहागिनि करत ठठोली ।
कहऊ पिता जि के नाम हे ॥ ॥ ६ ॥
सिढी बिहँसि कहत सखियन तेँ ।
कैसे कहस पितु नाम हे ॥ ॥ ७ ॥
शिंङ्गि रिखि आए खीर खियाए ।
तबहि भइलें चांरोँ भाइ हे ॥ ॥ ८ ॥
माता इंन्ह के बड़ि रंङ्ग रसिया ।
पिता कवन परमान हे ॥ ॥ ९ ॥
बहिनी इंन्ह के मुनि संङ्ग रसली ।
तेंहि से कहत लजात हे ॥ ॥ १० ॥
गाली सुनि सभ लखन बिहँसले ।
रौंरे ऐसन मोंरि माइ हे ॥ ॥ ११ ॥
बहिनि के लच्छन सभ रौंरां जांनेली ।
उन्ह कें ऐसन इ सुभाव हे ॥ ॥ १२ ॥
पिरिथवि से जे इहे सींतां जनमलि ।
पितां जन कैसे नाम हे ॥ ॥ १३ ॥

पिता हमार विदित सभ जानत ।
दसरथ हवें जें के नाम हे ॥ ॥ १७ ॥

अम्बिका कहत लखन सुनि लीजे ।
धन धन मातु तोहार हे ॥ ॥ १८ ॥

The Same.

1. Five matrons arranged the lamp with four wicks, and went to perform the *parichhan.*[1]

2. Five matrons invoked Gauri and Ganes and went to perform the *chumawan.*[1]

3. Five matrons fed the bridegroom with rice and milk as they sang auspicious songs.

4. Five matrons seat Rám and Sítá and apply odorous paste to their bodies.

5. Five matrons are apparelling him with ornaments while they gaze upon Rám's beauty.

6. Five matrons are jesting with him, saying "Tell[2] us the name of your father."

7. Siddhí[3] laughs and says to her comrades, "How can he tell the name of his father?

8. "Saint Sringi came and gave rice and milk (to the wives of Rám's father), and that is how the four brothers came to be born.

9. "His[4] mother was a great *rang rasiyá*[5]: what certainty is there as to his father?

---

[1] See notes[2], page 110, and [1], page 111.

[2] कहहु is an old form of कहहू.

[3] Siddhí was the wife of Sítá's brother.

[4] इन्ह के in this and the following verses is a dative of possession. See Grammar, § 34.

[5] A term for a woman of bad character.

10. "His sister went wrong with a saint, and consequently he is ashamed to mention her."[1]

11. When Lakhan[2] heard this abuse, he laughed, and said, "Yea, such was my mother,

12. "And you know the peculiarities of my sister; such indeed was her nature:

13. "But this Sítá here was born from the earth.[3] What name has her father got?

14. "Every one in the world knows my famous father: his name is Das'rath."

15. Ambiká says, "O Lakhan! pay attention:[4] blessed, blessed is your mother."

॥ २ ॥ कन्या निरिच्छन ॥

(Metre : 6 + 4 + 4 + 2, + 4 + 4 + 4 = 28 instants.)

धन घरि, धन दिन, धन ह्वे साइत !
ह्वे सींतां देइ के भाग है ॥ ॥ १ ॥

देव पितर रिखि किरिपां ऊँ कइले ,
बन्दन सींतां के लिलाट है ॥ ॥ २ ॥

दधि अच्छत लेइ सींतां के चढ़ावत ।
गौरि गनेस मनाइ है ॥ ॥ ३ ॥

---

[1] At marriages it is the privilege of the female relations of the bride to abuse the bridegroom. This is considered a great joke.

[2] Rám's brother. मोरि is a genitive feminine. See Grammar, § 22.

[3] Sítá was found in an egg which was ploughed up out of a field by king Janak.

[4] सुनि is an old form of सुन, the first verbal noun of √ सुन, 'hear.' लीजे is an old form of the precative imperative of √ ले, 'take.' The whole forms an intensive compound. (Grammar, § 113.)

भूषन बसन ओर सियां के पहिरावत ।
    सखि सभ गावत गान हे ॥ ॥ ४ ॥
बेद उचारत बंन्दिगन गावत ।
    सकल करहिँ असिर्बाद हे ॥ ॥ ५ ॥
अंम्बिका प्रसाद सियां राम बर पाए ।
    जुग जुग बाढ़े अहिवात हे ॥ ॥ ६ ॥

The Welcome[1] of the Bride.

1. Auspicious time, the day, the hour; auspicious is the lot of the lady Sítá.[2]

2. By the mercy of the gods, the heroes,[3] and the saints, we adore the brow of Sítá.

3. After adoring Gauri and Ganes we take curds and rice and apply them to Sítá's (forehead).

4. We also apparel her[4] in ornaments and garments, while all her bridesmaids sing marriage songs.

5. They are chaunting the Beds, while bards sing her praises and every one offers[5] her their benediction.

6. Ambiká Prasád (says) now that Sítá has obtained Rám for a husband, may her happiness increase through endless ages.

Next are a number of songs appropriate to certain seasons. The first two are poetic descriptions of the twelve months of the year—a class of poem very common throughout the whole of Northern India.

---

[1] निरिछन is the welcome of the bride at the husband's house by the women of the family throwing rice on her.

[2] See note [1] to first song.

[3] *Literally,* 'deified progenitors.'

[4] *Siyá* is another form of Sítá.

[5] करहिँ is an old Bihárí form for करत.

॥ ४॥ बारह मासा।

(Metre : 6 + 4 + 4, + 6 + 4 + 1, twice = 50 instants.)

चन्दन रगरौँ सोहासित हो, गूँथौँ फूल के हार।
    इङ्गुर मँगियाँ भरइतौँ हो, सुभ के मास असाढ़॥ ॥ १॥
साँवन अति दुख पावन हो, दुख सहलो नहिँ जाय।
    इहो दुख परेँ ओहि कुबरी हो, जिन कंन्त रखलेँ लोभाय॥ ॥ २॥
भादौँ रैनि भयावन हो, गरजे मेँह घहराय।
    बिजलि चमक जियरा ललचैँ हो, केकरा सरन उठ जाय॥ ॥ ३॥
कुँआर कुसल नहिँ पाओँ हो, ना केऊ आवेँ ना जाय।
    पतियाँ मेँ लिख लिख पठवौँ हो, दीहै कन्त का हाथ॥ ॥ ४॥
कातिक पूरन मासी हो, सभ सखि गङ्गा नहाय।
    गङ्गा नहाय लट भूखे हो. राधा मन पछताय॥ ॥ ५॥
अगहन ठाढ़ि अँगनवा हो, पहिरौँ आंगरा के चीर।
    इहो चीर भेँजैँ मोर बलमुआ हो, जीए लाख बरीस॥ ॥ ६॥
पूसहि पाला पर गैल हो, जाड़ा जोर बुझाय।
    नौ मन रुइया भरइतौँ हो, बिनु सैँयाँ जाड़ो नत जाय॥ ॥ ७॥
माघहि के शिव तेरस हो, शिव बर होएं तोहार।
    फिर फिर चितवौँ मँदिरवा हों, बिनु पिया भवन उदास॥ ॥ ८॥
फागुन पूरन मासी हो, सभ सखि खेलत फाग।
    राधा के हाथ पिचकारी हो, भर भर मारेलि गुलाल॥ ॥ ९॥
चैत फूलेँ बन टेसू हो. जब के हुण्ड हहराय।
    फूलत बेला गुलबवा हो. पिया बिनु मोहि नत सोहाय॥ ॥ १०॥
बैसाखहि बसवा कटइतौँ हो, रच के बँगला छँवाय।
    तांहि मेँ सोइते बलमुआ हो, करतौँ अचरनवेँ बाड़॥ ॥ ११॥
जेठ तबे मिरग हवा हो, बहे पवन हाहाय।
    भरथरि गावेँ बारह मासा हो, पूजे मन के आस॥ ॥ १२॥

A Song of the Twelve Months.

1. Gladly would I rub sandal paste upon my body and weave a garland of flowers. The parting of my hair would I have rubbed with vermilion in the happy month of *Asáṛh.*

2. The month of *Sáwan* is a fire of exceeding sorrow, which cannot even be borne. May this sorrow be the lot of *Kub'ri,*[1] who has captivated my love.

3. In *Bhádaũ* the nights are fearful; the clouds thunder and roar and the lightning flashes: so my heart yearns for him. To whom can I go for refuge?

4. In *Kũár* (*Ásin*) I get no good news: no one comes or goes. Writing, writing on a letter will I send it. Give it, I pray, into my love's hand.

5. At the full moon of *Kátik* all my comrades bathe in the Ganges. After the bath their hair[2] hangs down (to dry), while (I) Rádhá alone lament.

6. In *Ag'han* I put on a cloth of Agra and stand in my court-yard. This cloth was sent me by my husband. May he live ten thousand years.

7. In *Pús* snow has fallen, and the cold makes its power known. Even if I filled my quilt with nine *mans* of cotton, the cold will not depart in the absence of my lord.

8. The thirteenth of *Mágh* is the feast of Siw: may the blessing of Siw be upon thee. Whene'er I turn and gaze upon my dwelling (I see that) without my love my home is full of gloom.

9. On the full moon of *Phágun* all my comrades sport in the *holi,* and Rádhá is casting about red water from her syringe.[3]

---

[1] The speaker likens herself to Rádhá, the beloved of Syám (or Krishna), and is tortured by jealous fears. Kub'rí was a hunchback girl whom Krishna also loved and whom he made straight. She lived in Mathurá, while Rádhá lived in Brindában. A similar reference is made to Kub'rí in verse 3 of the next song.

[2] जट means the long hair of the head.

[3] At the holí festival it is customary to throw about red powder, and to squirt red liquids on passers by, as in the carnival in Europe.

10. In *Chait* the *palás*-trees[1] are flowering in the forest and the barley crop[2] is whispering (in the wind); the jasmine and the rose are blooming, but without my love they please me not.

11. In *Baisákh* I would have cut bamboos and adorned and roofed a bungalow. My husband would have slept in it, while I fanned him with the end of my body-cloth.

12. In *Jeṭh*, and specially in (the asterism of) Mirag, there is a wind which howls. The hope of her soul is fulfilled, and Bhar'thari sings this song of the twelve months.

॥ ५ ॥ बारह मासा ।

(*Metre:* 6 + 4 + 4 + 2, + 4 + 4 + 4. = 28 *instants.*)

चैत मास मोहि मदन सँतावे ।
बैसाख दैव दुख दाई ॥ ॥ १ ॥
जेठ मास तन तपत धूप में ।
कह त्रिकभान दुलारी ॥ ॥ २ ॥

(*Metre:* 6 + 4 + 4 + 2, + 6 + 4 + 4 + 2 = 32 *instants.*)

कौन उपाय करौं मोरि आली ॥
श्याम भैल कुबरी बस जाई ॥ ॥ ३ ॥
चढ़त असाढ़ घन घेरि ऐलैं बदरा ।
सावोन मास बहे पुरवाई ॥ ॥ ४ ॥
भादौँ अगम डगरियां नां सूझे ।
जल सँ भरि गैलैं ताल तलाई ॥ ॥ ५ ॥
आसिन मास सरद रितु आइल ।
कातिक मैं सखि सीन रचाई ॥ ॥ ६ ॥
अगहन अधिक कलेस श्याम बिनु ।
नैहर सँ हम सासुर आई ॥ ॥ ७ ॥
पूस मास सखि परत तुसारी ।
माघ पिया बिनु जाड़ो न जाई ॥ ॥ ८ ॥
फागुन का संङ्ग रंङ्ग सम खेलब ।
हर सियाम बिनाँ अकुराई ॥ ॥ ९ ॥

---

[1] टेसू is the red flower of the palás-tree (*Butea frondosa*).

[2] रूख is literally a tree or plant.

The Same.

1. "In the month of *Chait* love tortureth me, and will continue, O Heaven! to do so till the end of *Baisákh*.

2. "In *Jeṭh* my body is fevered in the sunshine," saith (Rádhá,) the beloved daughter of Brik'bhán.

3. "O my friend[1] what device shall I use, for Syám hath fallen under the influence of Kub'rí?[2]

4. "*Asáṛh* beginneth, the clouds thickly cover the sky, and the east wind bloweth in *Sáōn*.

5. "*Bhádáu* approacheth, and the paths are no longer seen: the lakes and ponds are filled with water.

6. "With the month of *Ásin* the autumn season came; in *Kátik*, O friend! I took to myself[3] a cotton coverlet.

7. "In *Ag'han*, without Syám great are my troubles: let me go to my father-in-law's house from my parents'.

8. "In *Pús*, O friend! the dew falleth, and in *Mágh*[4] without my beloved the cold leaveth me not.

9. "In *Phágun* with whom shall I sport (at the *holi*,) without Syám Jaduráí, O Sur Dás?"[5]

The following songs are sung in the month of Chait. Many of them refer to the well-known legends about Krishna's boyhood amongst the cowherds of the Doab, between the Ganges and the Jamuna. The first three are examples of this class of legendary songs.

---

[1] आली means 'a female companion;' it is a feminine word: hence मोरि is feminine.

[2] See note [1], page 117.

[3] लीन is Braj for लेनीं.

[4] According to all native opinion *Mágh* is the coldest month in the year, both in Bihár and in Bangál.

[5] The name of the poet.

॥ ६ ॥ चैतार (घाँटो)

(Metre : 6 + 4 + 2, + 6 + 4 + 1, twice = 46 instants.)

रामा एहि पारें गङ्गा, ओहि पारें जमुनां हो राम ।
तेहि रे बीचें किश्न खेलले, फूल गेंदवां हो राम ॥ ॥ १ ॥
रामा गेंदां जब गिरले, म्हाँ खरवा हो राम ।
तेहि रे बीचें क्रिश्न खिलले, रे पतालवां हो राम ॥ ॥ २ ॥
रामा लट धुनें केसिया, जसोमति मइयां हो राम ।
एही रे दहें मानिक, हमरों हेरांइल हो राम ॥ ॥ ३ ॥
रामा गोड़ तोहि लागों, केवट मंल्हवां हो राम ।
एही रे दहें डारऊ, रे महांजलवां हो राम ॥ ॥ ४ ॥
रामा एक जाल बिगले, दोसर बिगलें हो राम ।
बाझी गैल गैल घोंघवा, रे सेवरवां हो राम ॥ ॥ ५ ॥
रामा पैठि पताला, नाग नाथल हो राम ।
काली फन फन निरते, नाच कइलन हो राम ॥ ॥ ६ ॥
रामा दास बुधिया सम, घाँटो गांवल हो राम ।
गांइ रे गाई बिरहिन, सखि समुझांवल हो राम ॥ ॥ ७ ॥

A Song sung in the month of Chait.[1]

1. O Rám! On this side is the Ganges and on that the Jamuná, and between Krishn plays with a ball of flowers.

2. O Rám! When the ball fell into the midst of the river,[2] into it dived Krishn down to Hades.

3. O Rám! His mother Jasŏmati beats her locks and hair, (crying) "In this whirlpool my jewel has been lost."

---

[1] This song narrates how Krishna leaped into a whirlpool of the Jamuná and destroyed the snake Kálí by crushing its heads under his feet as he danced on its hoods. In this song several antepenultimate syllables, which should have been shortened under General Introduction, § 36, have been allowed to remain long for the sake of metre.

[2] खरवा is long form of खार, 'a deep hole full of water.'

4. "O Rám! I clasp thy feet. O Kewaṭ sailor! Cast thy largest net into the whirlpool."

5. O Rám! He cast one net and then another, and it caught nothing but snails and water-weeds.

6. O Rám! (But Krishn, who) had dived as low as Hades, bored the nose of the serpent Kálí and danced ceaselessly on his expanded hood.

7. O Rám! Your servant, according to his knowledge, sang this song, called a ghẫṭo, and as he did so consoled the damsels deserted by Krishn.

।७। चैतार।

(Metre: 6 + 4 + 4 + 2, + 6 + 4 + 4 + 4 = 34 instants.)

छोंटि मोंटि ग्वांलिनी चलि बड़ि नाजुक। हो रामा।
    चलि रे भैलि मथुरां नगर दहि बेंचन हो रामा॥ ॥ १ ॥
एहि पांर गङ्गा ओहि पांर जमुना। हो रामा।
    मांझे रे बीचें कांधां मोरां धरलां अँचरिया। हो रामा॥ ॥ २ ॥
छांड़ु छांड़ु कांधा हमरि अँचरिया। हो रामा।
    परी रे जइहैं दहियां के छिटकवा। हो रामा॥ ॥ ३ ॥
तोरां लेखें ग्वालिनि दहि के छिटकवा। हो रामा।
    मोरां रे लेखें चन्दन अतर गुलबवा। हो रामा॥ ॥ ४ ॥

The Same.

1. The young[2] milkmaid, so very delicate, started for Mathurá to sell curds.

2. On this side was the Ganges and on that the Jamuná, and between the two Krishn seizes hold of the border of my cloth.

3. "Let go, O Krishn! my cloth, or drops of curd will fall upon you."

4. "O milkmaid! You may consider them as drops of curds, but in my opinion they are spots of sandal, otto, and rose-water."

---

[1] This class of song is called indifferently a *chaitár* or a *ghẫṭo*.

[2] मोंटि is only a rhyming repetition of छोंटि.

॥ ८ ॥ चैतार ॥

(Metre irregular.)

ए री बाजेला बसुरिया, हो रामा ।
  ए री मधुबनवाँ ॥ ॥ १ ॥
ए री सखियाँ बिरह के माती ।
  तजि दिहलीं भवनवाँ, हो रामा ॥ २ ॥ ॥

The Same.

1. (O Rám!) (Krishn) plays his flute in Madhuban.

2. (O Rám!) The damsels that bear him company, maddened by the separation from him, have left their homes.

The following are other examples of songs sung in the month of Chait:—

॥ ९ ॥ चैतार ॥

(Metre: 6 + 4 + 4 + 2, + 4 + 4 + 3 = 27 instants.)
(Refrain: 3 + 6.)

REFRAIN.— मोरे रामा हो ॥

पियरी नाहीं पहनों रामा ।
  मोरे चैत के बहार ॥ ॥ १ ॥
झाझा पहनों रे मखमलवा । •
  चोलि पहनों बुटेदार ॥ ॥ २ ॥

The Same.

REFRAIN.—*O My Rám!*

1. I put not on, O Rám! my yellow (dress) in the happy month of Chait.

2. Muslin I put on, and velvet, and a variegated bodice.

॥ १० ॥ चैतार ॥

(Metre : 6 + 4 + 4 + 2, + 6 + 4 + 4 + 2 = 32 instants.)

(Refrain : 6 + 4 + 4 + 2.)

REFRAIN.—चैता मासे फुलली बेलिया ॥

फुलवा लोढ़ि लोढ़ि भरलौँ चँगेरिया । ॥ हो राम ॥
आइ गेल मलिया रखवरवा ॥ ॥ हो राम ॥ ॥ १ ॥
देबउ रे मलियां रे डाल भर सोनवाँ । ॥ हो राम ॥
सैयाँ आगे जनि लाइयो लरवउ ॥ ॥ हो राम ॥ ॥ २ ॥

The Same.

REFRAIN.—*The Jasmine flowers in the month of Chait.*

1. Gathering, gathering flowers I filled a basket, when up came the guardian *máli.*

2. I will give you, O *máli !* a full basket of gold, but do not lay a slander[1] (against me) before my husband.

॥ ११ ॥ चैतार ॥

(Metre irregular.)

REFRAIN.—ए री चलूं सखि सखि मलिया घन बगिया, हो रामा ।
ए री फुलवां में लोरही लोरही ।
भरलौँ चँगेरियां, हो रामा ॥ ॥ १ ॥
आइ गइलें हो बांवां के रखवरवा, हो रामा ॥ ॥ २ ॥
ए रे छुछ छुछ मलियां झोकरवा ।
डांरि मारि रें बरसवां, हो रामा ॥ ॥ ३ ॥
चरे अब घम अइबौँ सहुरवाँ ।
बरिया सपनवा, हो राम ॥ ॥ ४ ॥

---

[1] लरवा is long form of लाई, 'slander.'

The Same.

REFRAIN.—*O friends! let us come to the dense orchard*[1] *of the gardener.*

1. Plucking, plucking flowers, I filled my basket.

2. The watchman of my father came up.

3. 'O gardener's son! hear me. I am small[2] and of tender age.

4. 'When I go to my husband's house, this garden[3] will be like a dream to me.

॥ १२ ॥ चैतार ॥

(Metre: 6 + 4 + 4 + 2, + 6 + 4 + 4 + 2 = 32 instants, with refrain हो राम which sometimes forms part of the metre and sometimes not.)

मनहिं अँगनवां चनन गाछ बिरवा। हो राम।
तांहि चढ़ि बोलें बन कगवां, हो रामा॥ ॥ १ ॥
"देखउ रे कगवां रे दूध भात कउरवां। हो राम।
मोरां पियां के सुधि बताइ दें, हो रामा"॥ ॥ २ ॥
"पियां पियां जनि करहु पयां के सोहागिनि। हो राम।
तोरो पियां लुभुधल बारि तमोरिनि,॥ हो रामा" ॥ ३ ॥
"कैसन हइक रे देसवा मुलुकवा। हो राम।
कैसन हइक रे बारि तमोरिनि॥ हो राम"॥ ॥ ४ ॥
"अँगियां के पातर घरे मुख दुरकर। हो राम।
केसियन भौंरा गूँजरि गैल रामा"॥ ॥ ५ ॥
"घोरवौं मुड़रवा घरे बिख खाइब। हो राम।
मोरां आंगें उदरि के कैस बड़इया॥ हो राम"॥ ॥ ६ ॥
दास बुलाकि समैयां चौंठो गावल। हो राम।
(गाइ रे गाइ।)
बिरहिन सखि समुझांवल, हों रामा॥ ॥ ७ ॥

---

[1] बगिया the long form of बाग 'a garden,' usually means 'an orchard.'

[2] छारा means 'small' (of a person).

[3] बरिआ is long form of बारी, 'a garden.'

The Same.

REFRAIN.—*Ah Rám!*

1. In my sister-in-law's yard is there a sandal-tree,[1] and upon it sits and caws a forest crow.

2. "I will give thee, O crow! a morsel of milk and rice if thou wilt give me news about my love."

3. "Sweetheart of thy beloved! say not 'beloved, beloved,' for thy beloved also hath fallen captive to a young *tamorin*."[2]

4. "Alas! what is that country and that land like, and what the young *tamorin?*"

5. "Her body is delicate and her face is fair, and humble bees keep humming round her hair (so sweet is it)."

6. "Poison[3] will I pound, and venom will I eat, for he hath set that wanton before me."

7. Dás Buláki sang this ghắtô at a fit season, singing it, singing it, and her friends consoled the deserted one.

॥ १२ ॥ चैतार ॥

(*Metre*: 6 + 4 + 4 + 2, + 6 + 4 + 4 + 2, *with refrain* हो रामा.)

ननदि के अँगनां चनन घन गछिया। हो रामा।
तांहि चढ़ि बोलेला कगवा कुलच्छन॥ हो रामा॥ ॥ १ ॥
"देबउ रे कगवा, दूध भात दोनिया। ॥ हो रामा।
खबुरि नां ला दें बांलम परदेसिया"॥ हो रामा॥ ॥ २ ॥

---

[1] गाछ and बीरा (long form बिरवा) both mean 'tree.'

[2] A woman who sells betel-leaves.

[3] जहर is 'poison.' √घोर means 'pound.'

"पियां पी जनि कहु, पियां के सोहागिनि"। हो रामा।
"तोर पियां अवभल बारि बंङ्गालिनि"॥ हो रामा॥ ॥ ३

"तोहि पूंछौँ कागा अजगुत बतिया"। हो रामा।
"कौनां रूपेँ सुन्दरिं बारि बंङ्गालिनि"॥ हो रामा॥ ॥ ४

"डँड़वां के पातर अरे मुख दुरऊर"। हो रामा।
"केसियन मैँ भँवरवा गुँजारल"॥ हो रामा॥ ॥ ५ ॥

कांढ़ि रे कटरियां अपन जियां मांरितौँ। हो रामा।
उढ़रि के करेले अति सें बखनवा॥ हो रामा॥ ॥ ६ ॥

The Same.

REFRAIN.—*Ah Rám!*

1. In my sister-in-law's yard is there a thick sandal-tree and upon it sits and caws a crow with lucky marks.

2. "I will give thee, O crow! a leaf platter of milk and rice if thou wilt bring me news of my beloved in a foreign land."

3. "Sweetheart of thy beloved! say not 'beloved' or 'loved one:' thy beloved is entangled with a young Bangálin."

4. "I ask thee, O crow! a strange matter. In what feature is the young Bangálin beautiful?"

5. "Slender of loin is she, and beauteous is her face: bees hum about her hair."

6. "I would draw a dagger and take away my life, for thou dost praise exceedingly that wanton one."

The above two songs refer to a tradition about crows. Their "caw" is said by natives to be "ठाँय, ठाँय," meaning "place, place." Hence they are supposed to be able to answer any question as to the *place* where any person is, such as, "where (कोन ठाँय) is my beloved?"

॥ १४ ॥ चैतार, (बिरहागरा) ॥

(Metre irregular.)

मातल सैँयाँ रुसि गैलैँ बौरी ।
कोइली हो तोरि बोलियन ॥ ॥ १ ॥
ए री अधि रातं अगलि पहर रात पिछिलि ।
कोइली हो तोरि बोलियन ॥ ॥ २ ॥

The Same.

1. O cuckoo ![1] at thy notes my husband, who loved me, has gone mad and has become displeased with me.

At thy notes. O cuckoo ! when the first half of night had passed and the first quarter of the second half had commenced.

॥ १५ ॥ चैतार ॥

(Metre : 6 + 4 + 4 + 2, + 4 + 4 + 4 = 28 instants.)

(Refrain : 4 + 4 + 4 = 12 instants.)

REFRAIN.—ननदि सैँयाँ नहिँ आवे ॥

अँबवां मँजरि गैलें, लगलें टिकोरवा ।
डांल पतां झुकि मतवलवा ॥ ॥ १ ॥
चोलियां में जोबना बढ़ भैलि ननदि ।
कैसे करि के छिपावोँ ॥ ॥ २ ॥

The Same.

REFRAIN.—*O sister-in-law ! my lord comes not.*

1. The mango-trees are in blossom, and the young mangoes are forming : the branches and leaves hang down as if they were intoxicated.

2. (The fullness of) my youth cannot be contained within my bodice : how can I conceal it ?

---

[1] The note of the cuckoo is supposed generally to be a great incentive to love. Here the wife complains that it has had a contrary effect.

॥ १६ ॥ चैतार ॥

(Metre : 6 + 4 + 4 + 2, + 4 + 4 + 4 = 28 *instants.)*

भावे नाहीं मोहि[1] भवनवाँ ।
हो रामा, बिदेस गवनवाँ ॥ ॥ १ ॥
जौँ एहि मास निरास मिलन भए[2] ।
सुन्दर प्रान गवनवाँ ॥ ॥ २ ॥
केसो दास गावे निरगुनवाँ ।
ठाढ़ि गौरि करें गुनगनवाँ ॥ ॥ ३ ॥

The Same.

1. Ah Rám! on (my husband's) going abroad, my home did not please me.

2. If this month I become hopeless of meeting him again, my beautiful life will depart.

3. Keso Dás, the unworthy, says, "The fair one stands as she utters his praises."[3]

॥ १७ ॥ चैतार ॥

(Metre : 6 + 4 + 4 + 2 × 2 = 32 *instants.)*

भइ रैं नवेलि चलबेलि चौराही ।
उघकत उचकत चललि अँगनवाँ ॥ ॥ १ ॥
छन आँगन छन बाहर ठाढ़ि रे ।
जोहे लागे जोहे लागे सैंयाँ के अवनवाँ ॥ ॥ २ ॥
जिन्हि मोरां करें रामा सैंयाँ के अवनवाँ ।
ननदि हो तिन्हि देबौँ कंचन कँगनवाँ ॥ ॥ ३ ॥

---

[1] Lengthened from मोहि for sake of metre.

[2] Old form of होए.

[3] गुनगन is said to mean 'praises,' 'a telling of virtues.' It is a corruption of गनन, lit. 'a counting,' 'an appraisement.'

The Same.

1. A fresh, young, and coquettish maiden, yet mad with love, walking at random,[1] went into the court-yard.

2. Sometimes she stands in the court and sometimes outside, and begins to watch, to watch, for the coming of her lord.

3. "O sister-in-law! to him who tells me (Ah Rám!) of the coming of my lord, will I give a golden bracelet."

॥ १८ ॥ चैतार ॥

(*Metre*: 6 + 4 + 4 + 2 + 6 × 2 = 44 *instants*.)

देवरा चौरां रे लुटलऽ जोबनवा, हो रामा ॥
गरमि कां कसमांस सुतलौँ अँगनवा, हो रामा ॥ ॥ १ ॥

बाल्हौ से मैँ पोसलौँ देवरवा, हो रामा ।
दुधवां पियउलौँ से वो देवरवा, हो रामा ॥ ॥ २ ॥

लुलुसां कटइतौँ फँसियां दिअइतौँ, हो रामा ।
जोहूँ घरवां रे रहितै बलमुआ, हो रामा ॥ ॥ ३ ॥

The Same.

REFRAIN.—*Ah Rám!*

1. Thou thief, my husband's younger brother,[2] thou hast plundered my youth[3] (when) I slept in the court-yard on account of the excessive[4] heat.

2. O brother in law! From your childhood have I cherished you and given you milk to drink.

3. Had my husband been at home, I would have had you maimed and got you hanged.

---

[1] उधकल is literally 'to jump.'

[2] A wife may speak to, and joke with, her husband's younger brothers, but not to his elder ones.

[3] जोबना, literally 'youth,' commonly means the fulness of a young woman's bosom. Cf. song 15, line 2, and song 22, line 2.

[4] कसमास is literally 'tightness,' as of clothes: hence, when applied to heat, 'excess.'

The following is a specimen of the songs sung in the rainy season :—

॥ १९ ॥ बरसाती गीत ॥

(Metre irregular.)

मोरे टोपिवाला बारे भीँजत होइयोँ ।
ओहि गुलबदनि कां साथ ॥ ॥ १ ॥
आठहि काठ के हिंडोरवा छे रे लागि डोर ।
झुलति मैँ अपना रे बालम सङ्गे ।
अब दुख सहलो नऽ जाय ॥ ॥ २ ॥

A Song of the Rains.

(A wife expresses her fear that her husband, who has deserted her for another, is out in a rain-storm.)

1. My young husband[1] may even now be wet through and through with that rose-bodied one.

2. (Had he been here) I would have now been swinging in the company of my beloved, after affixing strings to a cradle of eight pieces of wood. Now my woes are not even endurable.

The following four songs are examples of those sung by women when sitting at the hand-mill. They are always sung to a very plaintive melody :—

॥ २० ॥ जतसार ॥

(Metre : 6 + 4 + 4 + 2, + 4 + 4 + 4 = 28 *instants.)*

(Refrain : 4 + 4 + 4 = 12 *instants. Chorus* : ओ रामा.*)*

REFRAIN.—ससुरा कैसे जाइब ॥ ओ रामा ॥

नइहरां मैँ कछु ढंङ्ग नहिँ सिखलोँ ।
पियवां के नइयाँ सुनाइल ॥ ओ रामा ॥ ॥ १ ॥
संङ्ग के सहेलिया सेहो भैले सुदर ।
अपने नां कछुवो बझाइल ॥ ओ रामा ॥ ॥ २ ॥

[1] *Literally* 'hat-wearer,' a term of affection.

बड़ जेठा के कहनां नां कइलौँ ।
　　जोबनां के मद बउराइल ॥ हो रामा ॥ ॥ ३ ॥
अंम्बिकां कहत गौरि चेत करहु अब ।
　　गवनां के दिन नियराइल ॥ हो रामा ॥ ॥ ४ ॥

A Song of the Hand-Mill.

(A pathetic song sung while women are grinding corn.)

REFRAIN.—*How can I go to my father-in-law's house?*

1. I learned no method in my father's[1] house. I forgot even thy name of husband. (Ah Rámá!)

2. Even the companion of my fellowship has become my enemy, and I myself was not understood.[2] (Ah Rámá!)

3. I acted not according to the advice of my elders, and I raved in the intoxication of my youth. (Ah Rámá!)

4. Ambiká saith, O fair one! take thought now. The day of thy departure (to thy husband's house) is at hand.

॥ २१ ॥ जतसार ॥

(Metre : 6 + 4 + 4 + 2, + 4 + 4 + 3, + 2 = 29 instants.)

REFRAIN.—बँरि बँरि जांलैँ सँयाँ पुरुबि बनिजियाँ । कैसे कटैं दिन रात हो ॥

गांड़ि जी चटकेलां चइत पवन मैँ ।
　　बेलां चटकैं गुँजरात हो ॥ ॥ १ ॥
ई दुनु नैन बनारस चटके ।
　　सैँयाँ जहानाबाद हो ॥ ॥ २ ॥
नलवां मैँ चमकेलां चंल्हवां मछरिया ।
　　रनवां चमकैं तरवार हो ॥ ॥ ३ ॥
सभवां मैँ चमकेलां सैँयाँ के पगरिया ।
　　सेजियां पैं टिकुलि हमार हो ॥ ॥ ४ ॥

---

[1] नइहरा is oblique of नइहर, 'the house of a bride's father.'

[2] Potential passive.

The Same.

REFRAIN.—*O my lord! often goest thou to the East to trade: how can the days and nights be passed?*

1. The cart gets stopped in the muddy plain, and the bullocks in Gujrát.

2. My two eyes (*i.e.* myself) stopped in Banaras, while my husband was in Jahánábád.

3. As the Chalh'wá fish shines in the lake, and as the sword shines in the battle,

4. So shines the turban of my lord in the assembly and the spangle (of my forehead) on the bed.

॥ २२ ॥ जतसार ॥

(*Metre*: $(6 + 4 + 2) \times 4, + 4 + 4 + 4 = 60$ *instants.*)

(*Refrain*: $6 + 4 + 4 + 2, + 4 + 4 + 4 = 28$ *instants.*)

REFRAIN.—पियाँ बटिया जोहत दिन गैलो[1] । तौंरि खबरियाँ नठ पाँईलो[1] ।।

केसियाँ अपने गुँधाँईला मँगिये सेँदुर भराँईला ।
पियाँ के सुरतियाँ लाँईला । जियरा हमर बँधेला[2] ।
नैनन निरयाँ ढर गैलो[1] ॥ ॥ १ ॥
बाँह्मन के बेँदाँ बोलाँईला । पोथियाँ खोंकर खोलाँईला ।
साँचेँ सगुन सुनाँवेला[2] । पीया नेखेँ आँईला ।
जोबन हमर बड़ भेलो[1] ॥ ॥ २ ॥
नौआँ के छौँड़ाँ बोलाँईला । पूरब देसाँ पठाँईला ।
उत्तर भे के आँवेला[2] । दखिन सुरत लगाँईला ।
पच्छिम घरेँ घरेँ ढुँढ़लोँ । ॥ ३ ॥
गुरू हुकुम मनाँईला । साजन घरवाँ आँईला ।
खुब खुब भोज बनाँईला । साजन के जेँवाँईला ।
राम मदारि गाँईला । लोगन के सुनाँईला[3] ।
दुसमन साँर जर गैलो[1] ॥ ॥ ४ ॥

---

[1] गैलो, पाईलो, and भैलो, are altered from गैल, पाईला, and भैल respectively for the sake of rhyme.

[2] In बधेला, सुनावेला, and आवेला the penultimate has been lengthened for the sake of metre.

[3] In सूनाईला the first syllable has been lengthened for the sake of metre.

The Same.

REFRAIN.—*My beloved, watching for thee,*[1] *the day has sped, nor I get news of thee.*

1. (Daily) do I tie up my hair and lay vermilion on its parting. I bring thee to my memory, but my soul is disappointed, and tears flowed from my eyes.

2. I call[2] a bráhman and make him open his books. He tells me some good (*lit.* true) omen, but my beloved comes not, while my youthful form[3] is growing.

3. I called the barber's son and sent him to the East country. He comes home by the north, while I seek through[4] the south and search in every house in the west.

4. I invoke Tukun, my preceptor. My good man comes home. Excellent food am I preparing that I may feed him withal. Rám Madári sang this, and told it to the people, while her enemy's soul is burnt up (with envy).

॥ २१ ॥ ॥ जतसार ॥

(Metre : founded on 6 + 4 + 4 + 2, + 6 + 4 + 4 + 2 = 32 *instants, but very irregular.)*

"सभ कें नगरिया (चुरिला)[5] बँसियां बजांवें रांम ।
"हमरां नगरिया कांहे नां बजावऊ (रे की)" ॥ ॥ १ ॥
"कैसें बजाईं (रानी) तौरि नगरियां रें ।
"कुकुरवां भूँकेला पहरू जांगेला (रे की)" ॥ ॥ २ ॥

---

[1] Literally, 'watching the way,' a common idiom. बटिया is long form of बाट (*fem.*), 'a road.'

[2] *Lit.* 'I call the holy books (Vedas) of the bráhman.'

[3] *Lit.*, 'youth.' The word is usually applied, as here, to a young girl becoming *apta viro.* Cf. song 18, line 1.

[4] *Lit.*, 'apply my memory.'

[5] Words enclosed thus, in brackets, do not form part of the metre.

“कुकुरां कें देवौं (चुरिला) दूध भात खोरियां रें ।
“पचरू कें मद में मतइवों रे की” ॥ ॥ ३ ॥

आधि रात बगिलि (ए रामां) पचर रात पिछलि रें ।
दुआरां पैं चुरिला रसिया ठाढ़े (रे की) ॥ ॥ ४ ॥

“खोलूं खोलूं खोलूं रांनीं संकुरि केवरियां रे ।
“आइ गैलें चुरिला रसिया रे की” ॥ ॥ ५ ॥

“कैसें मैं खोलौं रे (चुरिला) संकुरि केवरियां रें ।
“अँचरां पैं सूते राजा कूँवर (रे की)” ॥ ॥ ६ ॥

“तोचरां कें पांस रांनीं सुवरन छुरियां रें ।
“अँचरां कतपि चलि आवऊ रे की” ॥ ॥ ७ ॥

“अँचरा कतपत (चुरिला) बड़ निक लागें रांमां ।
“मुँहवाँ देखत छतिया फाटेला (रे की)” ॥ ॥ ८ ॥

“एक कोस चइलौँ (चुरिला) दुइ कोस आइलौँ रें ।
“चलत चलत पैरवाँ मोंर थाकल (रे की)” ॥ ॥ ९ ॥

“चलहू चलहू (हे रानी) थोंर कैत रतियां रें
“उचत कें लोके मोर धवरेंहर (रे की)” ॥ ॥ १० ॥

“सूरज कें उगले (चुरिला) मुख चटपटवां रें ।
“गोड़वां चलत चलबल्लर रे की ॥ ॥ ११ ॥

“बाढ बटोहियां रें तुऊँ मोंर भैयां बयठ ।
देखलठ कतऊँ तूँ चरिलां धवरेंहर (रें की) ” ॥ ॥ १२ ।

“नहिँ हम देखलौँ (हे बहिनि) कि नहिँ हम सुनलौँ हों ।
“कहवाँ तूँ सुनलू चुरिलां धवरेंहर (रे की) ॥ ॥ १३ ॥

“देखलौँ मैं देखलौँ (ए बहिनि) हाजीपुर डिहवां रें ।
“चुरिलां के मैया सुधरि चरांवेला (रे कीं)” ॥ ॥ १४ ॥

“जौँ हम जांनितौँ (चुरिला) जांत के दुसधवां रें ।
बांभां के नगरिया फँसियां दिअइतौं (रे की) ॥ ॥ १५ ॥

"छड पड पगिया (चुरिला) झाँमी झाँमी केथियां रें ।
गौरि सुरतिया हम भूलि गेलौं (रे की)" ॥ ॥ १९ ॥
"छांयवौं में खढ़लौं (चें रानी) छांयवौं में छुतलौं चौं ।
चन कैंचें जातियां तोर मेराइस (रे की)" ॥ ॥ १० ॥

The Same.

1. "O Churilá! You play the flute in all the towns: why do you not in ours?"

2. "How can I play, fair lady, in your town? for the dogs bark there and the watchman is vigilant."

3. "O Churilá! I will give the dogs a dish[1] of rice and milk, and the watchman will I make drunk with wine."

4. When the first half of the night had passed and the first quarter of the second half had commenced, my lover Churilá stood by the door.

5. "Open, open, fair lady, the narrow door: Churilá, thy gallant lover, has come."

6. "O Churilá! How can I open the narrow door? The prince (my husband) is sleeping on the border of my garment."

7. "Fair lady, you have a golden knife. Cut the cloth and come with me."

8. "O Churilá! As I cut the border it seems very pleasant to me, but when I look on (my husband's) face, my heart is bursting.

9. "O Churilá! We have come one kos,—we have come two: with continued walking my legs are weary."

10. "Fair lady, come on, come on; but little[2] of the night remains. My palace is but yonder."[3]

---

[1] खोरिया is a kind of small pot.

[2] *Lit.* 'how much:' hence, 'how little.'

[3] *Lit.* 'that which appears (झोके) there (चहृत) is my palace.'

11. "O Churilá! The sun is risen, and my mouth is dry and my legs fail[1] me through weariness.

12. "O wayfarer on the way! Thou art my brother. Have you seen anywhere Churilá's palace?"

13. "Sister, I have neither seen nor heard of it. Where did you hear of Churilá's palace?

14. "I have seen his sister in the village of Hájípúr, and Churilá's mother is a swineherd there."

15. "O Churilá! If I had known that you were a Dusádh by caste, I would have had you hung in my father's town.

16. "O Churilá! I forgot myself when I saw your swaggering turban your long, long hair, and your fair complexion."

17. "Fair lady, I have eaten and slept with you. How can I now restore[2] you to your caste?"

The following songs are known as jhúmars, which is a generic name for any song sung by women:—

॥ १४ ॥ झूमर ॥

(Metre: 6 + 4 + 4 + 2, + 6 + 4 + 4 = 30 instants. First line has two extra instants in second half.)

मारत बा गरियावत बा, देखऽ ।
    (हूबे) करिखहवा मोहि मारत बा ॥ ॥ १ ॥

आँगन कइलोँ पाँनि भरि लइलोँ ।
    ताड ऊपर लुलुआवत बा ॥ ॥ २ ॥

अस सौतिन के माने मारै ।
    चमरां बद्दर बनावत बा ॥ ॥ ३ ॥

ना हम चोरिनि ना हम चटनी ।
    झुठऊ अकरङ्क लगावत बा ॥ ॥ ४ ॥

लात गद्दां के मार मोहि मारे ।
    ऊपर अस घिसिआवत बा ॥ ॥ ५ ॥

---

[1] *Lit.* 'are heavy in going.' [2] मेराइब Hindi = मिलाऊँगा.

देखऊ रे मोर पार परोसिनि ।
    गाइ पर गदहा चढ़ावत बा ॥ ॥ ६ ॥

पियवा गँवार कहल नहिँ बूझत ।
    पनियाँ में आगि लगावत बा ॥ ॥ ७ ॥

हे अम्बिका तुम बूझ करहु अब ।
    अचरा उढ़ाइ गोहरावत बा ॥ ॥ ८ ॥

A Jhúmar.

(A kind of song sung by women.)

1. See how this black-faced one beats me, abuses me, beats me.

2. I cleaned up (*lit.* made) the court-yard and brought water, and still he chides me.

3. Thus does he regard, O mother! my co-wife, while he makes out evil (against) me.

4. I am not a thief nor a glutton, still he reproaches me falsely.

5. He beats me like seven donkeys, and drags me about as if I were a pig.

6. See, O my neighbours! how he abuses me for no fault.[1]

7. My stupid husband does not understand what I say, and keeps trying to set water on fire.

8. O Ambiká! understand that he is blaming me openly.[2]

॥ २५ ॥ झूमर ॥

(Metre : 6 + 4 + 4 + 2, + 6 + 4 + 4 + 2 = 32 instants.)

अपना पिया के मैं खोजे ला निकसौं ।
    पेन्हि लेलौं रंङ्गलाल चुनररया ॥ ॥ १ ॥

गोकुल खोजलौं बिन्द्राबन खोजलौं ।
    जौंनि ऐलौं हम कांसि नगररया ॥ ॥ २ ॥

---

[1] *Lit.* 'makes a donkey mount upon a cow,' a proverbial idiom.

[2] *Lit.* 'spreading out his garments.'

गोकुल खोजलीं बृन्दाबन खोजलीं ।

कतहिँ नऽ मिलले मोर पियवा के खबरिया ॥ ॥ ३ ॥

अंबिका पिया के घरहि में पाईं ।

मिलि गैलें रे मन मोहनि सुरतिया ॥ ॥ ४ ॥

The Same.

1. I put on a red cloth[1] and went to search for my husband.

2. I searched for him in Gokul, I searched for him in Brindában, and returned after searching for him in Kásí (Banáras).

3. I searched for him in the forest, I searched for him in the mountains, but nowhere could I find news of my husband.

4. O Ambiká! I found my husband even in my house, and I obtained soul-entrancing delights.

॥ २६ ॥ झूमर ॥

(Metre : 6 + 4 + 4 + 2, + 4 + 4 + 3 = 27 instants.)

कवना गुनहि ए चुकलीँ ए बालम ।

तोर नयनां रतनार ॥ ॥ १ ॥

सौति के बतियाँ करेजवा में साले ।

काँपत जियरा हमार ॥ ॥ २ ॥

अपना पियां लागि पेन्हलीँ चुँदरिया ।

ताकत देवरा हमार ॥ ॥ ३ ॥

अंबिका प्रसाद पियां हँसि हँसि बोलिहें ।

करबों मैं सोरहो सिंगार ॥ ॥ ४ ॥

---

1 चुनरइया is an irregular long form of चुँदरि or चुनरि, 'a woman's cloth,' usually with coloured border.

The Same.

1. In what fault have I been wrong, beloved, for thine eyes are red?

2. The words of my co-wife pierce me to my liver: my soul is trembling.

3. I put on a bordered cloth[1] for my husband, and my brother-in-law[2] is gazing at me.

4. O Ambiká Prasád! When my husband will speak smilingly, I will adorn myself with the sixteen graces.

॥ १७ ॥ झूमर ॥

(Metre very irregular, founded on 6 + 4 + 4 + 2, + 6 + 4 + 4 + 2 = 32 *instants.)*

भैलों भिनुसरवा बोलेलां कोयलिया ।
उठि साँवरि अँगनवां बुहारे । गे गोरियो ॥ ॥ १ ॥
अँगनवां बुहारते टुटलैं बढ़निया ।
बढ़नि कें बड़ दुख भइल गे गोरियो ॥ ॥ २ ॥
अँगनां छोरियें सांस गरिया पारे ।
बांझां छौंखि भैयां छौंखि पुतऊ बढ़ोरिया । गे गोरियो ॥ ॥ ३ ॥
बढ़नि कारनें उदवासलि गे गोरियो ।
बांट रे बटोहिया, तुहुँ मोर भैया ।
हमरो सनेसवां लेलें जाऊ गे गोरियो ॥ ॥ ४ ॥
तोहर भैयां कें चिन्हेलौं नां जानेलौं ।
कैसें कहब समुझाय गे गोरियो ॥ ॥ ५ ॥
हमरा भैयां कें लाँब लाँब केसिया ।
जैसें लागें मुगल पठानवां गे गोरियो ॥ ॥ ६ ॥
बांहु बांहु बांधेला बढ़नि बोझैवा ।
पांहु लांग बांधें बैठां भैयां गे गोरियो ॥ ॥ ७ ॥

---

[1] See last song.

[2] See note [2] to song 18.

The Same.

1. Morning dawned and the cuckoo sings; up rises the nut-brown maid and sweeps the court-yard. (O fair one!)

2. In the sweeping her broom broke, and for the broom great sorrow was there (in her heart). (O fair one!)

3. Her mother-in-law went about[1] the court-yard and abused her,[2]—"You daughter-in-law, wife of my son,[3] you eater of your father, eater of your brother." (O fair one!)

4. For the sake of the broom she became mournful (O fair one!) (and cried) "O wayfarer on the way! Thou art my brother: carry news of me (to my elder brother)." (O fair one!)

5. "Your brother I nor recognise nor know: how shall I tell him and explain." (O fair one!)

6. "My brother has long, long hair, as if he were a Mughal or a Paṭhán. (O fair one!)

7. Before him comes a carrier of a load of brooms, behind whom comes my elder brother." (O fair one!)

I conclude with a few songs of a miscellaneous character:—

॥ २८ ॥ समुझावनी ॥

(Metre: 6 + 4 + 4 + 2, + 4 + 4 + 4 = 28 *instants.)*

जांघि छिन ए पियां पिया भोर जगवथि ।
    तांघि छिन भइलौं उदास चे ॥ ॥ १ ॥
बेटां रविहत सेवा मोघि करिते ।
    बेठि पांक्षम छिन पार चे ॥ ॥ २ ॥

---

[1] घोरिअे poetical for घोरि = Hindí घूर कर के.

[2] गारी पारल is the ordinary phrase for 'to abuse.' It is literally 'to throw abuse.'

[3] पुतहू and बहोरी both mean 'a son's wife.'

अँचियां बैसांइ पियां दांन जब करिबो ।
तबइ जैहैं ससुरार घे ॥ ॥३॥
बेटी घेइ है दुलइ कहिहैं ।
सबघो पांहन धमार घे ॥ ॥४॥
पियां संङ्ग रचिहैं, पियां संङ्ग बसिहैं ।
पियां संङ्ग रचिहैं धमार घे ॥ ॥५॥
चार जना मिल डोलियां उठइहैं ।
पीछें सकल परिवार घे ॥ ॥ ॥६॥
अम्बिका कहता मांतां धर धीरज ।
• जग के इहै ब्योहार घे ॥ ॥७॥

A Song of Consolation.

1. My husband, on the day when my daughter was born I became sad.

2. Had it been a son, he would have served you (in your old age), but a daughter is but a four-days' guest.

3. When, love, you will give her in marriage,[1] she will go to live in her father-in-law's house.

4. This our daughter they will call[2] 'the bride' in her husband's house, but a guest in ours.

5. She will enjoy life and sit with her husband: with him she will sing songs.[3]

6. Four men will together lift her litter, and the wedding party will follow her.

7. Ambiká saith, "O mother! have patience: this is the way of the world."

---

[1] अँचिया or जांघा बैसावन refers to a marriage custom in which the daughter at the time of her marriage is made to sit on her father's thigh while he gives her hand to her husband.

[2] दुलहै is the name given to the bride by the women of her husband's house.

[3] धमार is a festival song, such as is sung at the holí. धमार रचब is used idiomatically to mean living happily.

॥ २९ ॥ भजन ॥

(*Metre* : 6 + 4 + 4 + 2, + 4 + 4 + 4 = 28 *instants.*)

(*Refrain* : 4 + 4 + 4 = 12 *instants.*)

REFRAIN.—रांम रस पी लें रे भाई ।

मीठ मीठ सभ कोउ पीए ।
    कड़ुआ पिअलो नठ भाई ॥ ॥ १ ॥
जेसन रोगी नीम पिअतु है ।
    आँखि मूँदि पिए जाई ॥ ॥ २ ॥
सुने सोँ गूँगा होई बैसे ।
    पीए से मरि जाई ॥ ॥ ३ ॥
एकतो पीए सन्त बिबेकी ।
    पिअत अमर होइ जाई ॥ ॥ ४ ॥
धूरव पीएं पहलाद पिअतु है ।
    पीं गरल मीरांबाई ॥ ॥ ५ ॥
दास कबीर जें अवर पिअतु है
    जगवां में रहलो नठ जाई ॥ ॥ ६ ॥

A Hymn.

REFRAIN.—*O brother ! drink the nectar of Rám.*

1. Every one drinketh sweet things, but that which is bitter no one drinketh.

2. As a sick man drinketh the bitter juice of the ním-tree, so closing thine eyes (at its astringency) dost thou drink it.

3. From hearing (its virtues common men) turn deaf, and those who drink it die.

4. Only the holy and discreet can drink it ; and when they do, they become immortal.

5. (Saints like) Dúrab, Pah'lad, drink it; yea, Mírábáí hath tasted it.

6. If Kabír Dás drink more of it, he shall have to leave this world.

NOTE.—This hymn contains many Hindí expressions. पिअतु is Braj for पीअत; अवर is Kanaují for और, 'and.'

॥ १० ॥

नागरी अक्षर कचहरियों में चलित होने के विषय में सरकार की प्रशंसा॥

(पूर्वी गीत।)

(Metre: 6 + 6, + 6 + 4 = 22 instants.)

धन्य धन्य गवरमिण्ट। परजा सुखदाई।
जामनी कें दूर करी। नागरी चलाई॥ ॥ १ ॥
भुवन देव करि पुकार। लाट ढिग्ग जाई।
परजा दुख दूर करहु। जामनी हटाई॥ ॥ २ ॥
नाना विधि जाल होत जामनी में राई।
परजा मन हरख होत। विद्या निज पाई॥ ॥ ३ ॥
धन बुद्धी धन विचार। धन मन्तर भाई॥
करि नेआव हिन्द बीच। हिन्दुई चलाई॥ ॥ ४ ॥
परजा नित सुजस गावत। अम्बिका मनाई।
जब लें चन्द सूर्ज रहे। राज रहे माई॥ ॥ ५ ॥

A song praising Government for doing away with the Persian and substituting the Nágarí character.

1. Thanks be to the Government, which bestoweth happiness on its subjects. It hath put away the Persian[1] character and introduced Nágarí.

2. Bhuvan Deb[2] went to the Lord, and called out, saying, "Remove the sorrows of your subjects by removing Persian.

---

[1] जामनी means the language and character of the Jabans or Mussalmáns. It is the ordinary Hindú name for Úrdú, or even for Hindí as distinct from Bihárí.

[2] *I.e.*, Bábú Bhú Dev Mukharjyá, C.I.E., Inspector of Schools.

3. "In the Persian characters, O king, many forgeries take place. Joy will be in the heart of your subjects if they obtain their own national knowledge."

4. Thanks to the wisdom, thanks to the discernment: thanks, O brother, to the counsel which has done justice in Hind by introducing Hinduí.[1]

5. O people! always sing the glory (of Government), while Ambiká prayeth that the reign of the mother (Victoria) may stand while the sun and moon endure.

॥ ११ ॥

(Metre : 6 + 4 + 4 + 2, + 6 + 4 + 4 + 2 = 32 instants.)

(Refrain : 6 + 4 + 2, + 6 + 4 + 2 = 24 instants.)

REFRAIN.—हुकुम भइल सरकारी। रे नर सीखऽ नगरिया॥

आमनि जी से देऊ दुराई।
    पढ़ि गुन काज करहु नरहरिया॥ ॥ १ ॥
जे पोथी नित पाठ करहु अब।
    आमनि ग्रन्थ देऊ पैसरिया॥ ॥ २ ॥
अब ले नागरि आवत नाहीं।
    कैथी अच्छर लिखऽ कचहरिया॥ ॥ ३ ॥
धन सन्नी परजा हितकारी।
    अंबिका मनावत राज बिक्टोरिया॥ ॥ ४ ॥

The Same.

REFRAIN.—*The Sarkár gave the order, 'O men, learn Nágarí.'*

1. Put away the Persian character from your heart, read and do a pious action (at the same time) pleasing to God (नरहरिया).

---

[1] हिन्दुई, *lit.* the language of the Hindús.

2. Take your books and now read them continually, but sell your Persian ones to the spice-seller.

3. Until Nágarí is thoroughly understood by you, write the Kaithi character in *kachahri*.

4. Thanks be to the counsellor, the friend of the subjects, while Ambiká prays 'May Victoria reign.'

॥ ३२ ॥

॥ झूमर पूर्बी राग ॥

(Metre : 6 + 4 + 4 + 2, + 4 + 4 + 3 = 27 instants.)

मचिया बैसि गौरि ओरेखि बटिया ।
　　कब ऐहैं तपसि हमार ।। हो राम । ।। १ ।
बरहठ बरिस पर एलें महादेवा ।
　　भेलें दुअरियां पैं ठाढ़ ।। हो राम । ।। २ ।।
" खलल बाड़ू कि आगल गौरी ।
　　कैलौं हम दोसरो बियाह ।।" हो राम । ।। ३ ।।
" ना हम महादेव चोरनि नां चटनी ।
　　नांहिं हम कोखियां बिहून ।। हो राम । ।। ४ ।।
" नांहिं महादेव सेवा से चुकलौं ।
　　कांहे कैलौं दोसरो बियाह ।।" हो राम । ।। ५ ।।
" नांहिं ए गौरि रौरां चोरनि नां चटनी ।
　　नांहिं रौरां कोखियां बिहून । हो राम । ।। ६ ।।
नांहिं ए गौरि रौरां सेवां से चुकलौं
　　भांभीं कैलें दोसरो बियाह ।। हो राम । । ७ ।।

1. Gaurí sits upon a stool and watches[1] for Siw, saying "When will my hermit[2] come?"

---

[1] See note [1], page 133.

[2] Siw was accustomed to devote himself to most arduous penances.

2. Mahádewá came after twelve years[1] and stood at the door.

3. "Are you sleeping or awake, O Gaurí? I have married another wife."

4. "I am not, O Mahádewá! a thief, nor gluttonous, nor am I a barren woman.

5. "Never have I failed in my devotion to you. Wherefore hast thou married another wife?"

6. "O Gaurí, thou art not a thief nor a glutton, nor art thou a barren woman.[2]

7. "Ne'er didst thou fail in thy devotion, but it was my fate that made the second marriage."

The following is a Bihárí version of the well-known nursery song '*hili mili paniyá*' (*Anglo-Indice* '*hilly milly punny ow*'):—

॥ ११ ॥

(*Metre* : 6 + 4 + 4 + 2, + 8 + 4 + 4 + 2 = 34 *instants.*)

ननदी भौजिया दुनु पनिहारिन। हो राम।
    मिलि रे जूंलि, सागर पनियां कें चललो। हो राम। ॥ १ ॥
घुठि भर पनियां घरिलवों नठ डूबे। हो राम।
    कैसें रे भरौँ नांजुक बँहियाँ लचकोरे। हो राम। ॥ २ ॥
घइला जें भरि भरि धरलौँ खररियां। हो राम।
    कवने रे रसियां रसिक दीठ लावल। हो राम। ॥ ३ ॥

1. The husband's sister and her sister-in-law, both carrying water-jars on their heads, went together to fetch water from the tank.

2. "The water is only up to our ankles, even the jar cannot sink in it: how am I to fill it? My delicate arms are weary.[3]

3. "I filled the pots and laid them on the bank. Who is the amorous lover who casts an evil glance upon them (so as to break them)?

---

[1] बरहठ is oblique of बारह, 'twelve,' a form which should be noted.

[2] *Lit* without (बिहून) progeny.

[3] *Lit.* 'elastic:' hence, 'bent backwards and forwards:' hence, 'weary.'

॥ ९४ ॥

॥ कुँवर सिङ्घ के गीत ॥

(Metre irregular.)

बाबू बनवाँ बनवाँ खेलेला सिकरवा ।
    रोवेली बनवाँ के हरनियाँ ॥ ॥ १ ॥
पहिल लड़इया बाबू हेतमपुर भेली ।
    रजवा बहेलिया दिहलें ना ॥ ॥ २ ॥
सतर से सतासी मौजे कछु नाहीं बुझले
    गढ़ लुटवाए दिहलें ना । ॥ ३ ॥

The Song of Kŭar Singh.

1. The Bábú (Kŭar Singh) is hunting in the forest, and the hinds of the forest are weeping.

2. The Bábú's first battle was at Hetampur, and the Rájá gave him no assistance.[1]

3. He thought not at all of his seventeen hundred and eighty-seven villages, and allowed his fortress to be plundered (by the English).

---

[1] *I.e.*, in the mutiny the Rájá of Ḍumráon refused to help him. बहेली is literally 'a hunter:' hence, 'a fighting-man.'

Reg. Nos. 11713 & 3922J.—430 8-1-84.